OVERCOMING EMOTIONAL CHAOS

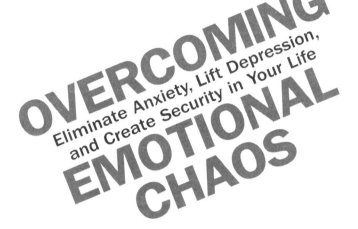

OVERCOMING

Eliminate Anxiety, Lift Depression, and Create Security in Your Life

EMOTIONAL CHAOS

Doc Childre
Deborah Rozman, Ph.D.

JODERE
GROUP

San Diego, California

JODERE GROUP, INC.
P.O. Box 910147
San Diego, CA 92191-0147
(800) 569-1002
www.jodere.com

Overcoming Emotional Chaos provides insight into new research on the heart, emotions and health that can be applied to daily life. There are a number of new or unusual words used in the book to describe the techniques and tools to help people understand the language of the feeling world. New word combinations are needed because nothing in the common vernacular adequately conveys the feeling experience the authors are trying to give the reader.

The authors of this book do not dispense medical advice or prescribe the use of any techniques as forms of treatment for physical or medical problems without the advice of a physician, either directly or indirectly. The intent of the authors is only to offer information of a general nature to help you in your quest for emotional and spiritual well-being. In the event you use any of the information in this book for yourself, which is your constitutional right, the authors and the publisher assume no responsibility for your actions.

Book design by Charles McStravick
Editorial supervision by Chad Edwards

CIP data available from the Library of Congress

ISBN 1-58872-033-0

04 03 02 01 4 3 2 1
First printing, September 2002

Printed in the United States of America

This book is dedicated to helping people
find the power of hope
in their own heart.

And they can.

From there,
individual and collective peace
can unfold.

CONTENTS

PREFACE

If we don't change our direction, we will end up where we are heading, reads an ancient Chinese maxim. Current wisdom offers a similar maxim, *If we keep doing what we've done, we'll continue to get what we've gotten*. Many think this is not a hopeful prospect.

There is an ongoing nervousness and underlying anxiety in the world today. We turn on the news to see and hear the latest on terrorism, biological and nuclear weapons, ethnic and religious conflict, new strains of infectious diseases—and the list goes on. With our advanced technology, it is a matter of fact that *every* crisis comes into our homes and impacts us deeply.

The next field of advancement in human evolution is the emotional frontier. It will take new intelligence—heart intelligence—to direct where the world is heading into beneficial outcomes. Heart intelligence starts with the power to manage one's emotions, and many doubt that human beings as a whole are capable of achieving this. The task is to learn *how* to intelligently resolve our emotions for our own and others' benefit, to enrich our experience of life. When change feels out of our control, stress happens—on personal and societal levels. Overcare, over-identity, and over-attachment become the results, and ultimately rule. Emotional management has been attempted through religions, moral codes, and laws throughout history. But since emotional management involves individual choice, it can never be totally legislated. When emotions are repressed, they don't just go away. They build historical accounts of wrongs done that seek release not in reconciliation, but in retribution. This won't work in a global society.

So what will motivate people to choose to manage their emotions? Survival? Understanding that if you don't manage feelings, then feelings will manage you? Improving quality of life? The answers to these questions have been part of the passion underlying my research over the past 30 years, and the reason for developing the Institute of HeartMath (IHM) in 1991.

The speed in which the world is moving is demanding accelerated decision-making. It is also speeding up emotional reactiveness. One of the upsides of this momentum of global change is that positive emotional changes can also happen more quickly. This energetic momentum is something to take advantage of *now*. If you've had a realization about something that your heart's told you to change but you haven't been able to pull it off, it's easier to finally do when so much is changing around you. Don't worry about getting it all done at once. Start with one thing that your heart is saying, then harness your emotional power to listen and follow your heart.

Emotions have rhythms and self-doubts rob you of your potential intelligence. Once you become attuned to your emotional rhythms, you can make emotional management fun. Sometimes an emotional chaotic wave can take you under, you get swamped by what I call *overcare* and succumb to despair. It's not the mistakes you make, it's fear projections, self-judgments, and blame that make it harder to get back on course. Instead of "hitting bottom," you can learn to hold to a bottom line of neutral. The tools we teach here help you go deeper in your heart and move back on track—the heart connection.

Throughout this book we'll provide proven techniques and tools for accessing heart intelligence, and present dozens of stories from people who've applied the tools we offer to address everyday stresses and periods of emotional chaos. In the final chapter, we offer a few new perspectives for creating security in your life, especially in these times of accelerated change.

Doc Childre
Founder, Institute of HeartMath

ACKNOWLEDGMENTS

Many people have contributed to the development of *Overcoming Emotional Chaos*, both in words and actions. We sincerely thank the staff members at HeartMath who have practiced, with dedication, the techniques and tools given in this book. You will find many of their personal stories in the chapters. We also thank the many individuals, from all walks of life, who contributed their stories for this book. The names of all contributors have been changed, to protect their anonymity.

We also want to acknowledge the pioneering scientific researchers of the exciting new fields of "neuro-cardiology," how the heart and brain interact to shape our experience of life, and "positive psychology," how positive emotions broaden our thinking and improve health and quality of life. Your work is making a valuable and much needed contribution to the world.

In addition, we extend our appreciation to all the dedicated business leaders, health care providers and educators who have brought HeartMath tools into their organizations to help people reduce stress, improve performance, and enhance creativity and innovation.

The following colleagues at HeartMath directly contributed to our writing and editing: Sara Paddison, President, Institute of HeartMath; Dr. Rollin McCraty, Director of Research, Institute of HeartMath; Bruce Cryer, President and CEO, HeartMath LLC; Howard Martin, Executive

Vice President, HeartMath LLC; Sibyl Cryer, HeartMath LLC; Wendy Rickert, Institute of HeartMath; Tom Beckman, HeartMath LLC; and Dana Tomasino, Institute of HeartMath. Much appreciation for your care and contributions that helped make this book possible, with special thanks to Wendy, Tom, and Dana.

We also sincerely thank Priscilla Stuckey for her wonderful initial editing of the entire work; Bernadette Doran for her last minute editorial creativity; our publisher Debbie Luican of the Jodere Group for her ongoing excitement and encouragement; Chad Edwards, editor for the Jodere Group, for his patience with our rewrites; and Brian Hilliard and Arielle Ford for their assistance and support.

Our deepest thanks to all these contributors, and the many others too numerous to name, whose love and dedication have made this book what it is today.

INTRODUCTION

Overcoming *Emotional Chaos* is the first HeartMath book that completely explains the seduction of emotional stress and chaos in individuals and society. The techniques and tools the book offers are not presented as a cure-all or fix-all. But as people practice them, they'll increase their capacity to live their values while reducing their stress. It's by learning how to listen to and follow the core feelings of the heart, that life shows us new opportunities for reward and fulfillment.

When Doc Childre asked me to assist him in writing this book a few years ago, he said, "There's a planet in need. Stress is increasing and people need a deeper understanding of emotions." I was honored. I knew this book was going to be a treatise on emotions, along with tools to help people reduce their emotional stress. As both a business executive and psychologist, I have dealt with a lot of people's stress over the past 30 years.

Years ago, I studied attitude change theory because I felt that changing attitude was key to psychological well-being. Yet the focus I found was on the mind and mental illness with little about the ordinary person's emotional experience. I continued my studies hoping to find some answers. At the same time, I began to practice meditation and yoga, and studied Eastern and Western spirituality. I was disappointed that the courses available focused mainly on past history, with little emphasis on the future or where we were going. I found a ray of hope in working with children, so I completed my masters and doctorate on awareness development in children, wrote books and started a private school. After awhile, still searching, I became a business executive for a company with an altruistic mission. Our products and the people I worked with were wonderful. Yet I was swept up in the business stress grind and wearing myself out. I knew that the only way to deal with the pressures would be to make a change *inside* first. But I didn't know what change to make.

When I met Doc Childre through a friend, I was intrigued by his care for people and by his intelligence. Through his years of research, Doc had uncovered something remarkable, and remarkably simple. That the heart has an intelligence that can be accessed, an intelligence that comes to us *through love* as heart feeling and intuition, and is available once we learn and practice a few simple steps. Doc showed me a technique to go deeper into my heart, in order to distinguish the difference between my mind, emotions and real heart. I started to listen to my heart more honestly and make needed changes. It wasn't until I made that one simple discovery of *how* to shift to the heart and see life *through* the heart to access the intelligence it provides, that I was able to significantly reduce my own stress and find greater personal fulfillment.

I accepted the position of Executive Director of the Institute participating in the research along with others and helping Doc with his work. Now I am Executive Vice President of Quantum Intech, Doc's pioneering Intui-Technology company. I honor Doc's focus on putting "first things first." All of his techniques, tools, and concepts (what he calls the "math") are an expression of his love and care (the "heart"). We all need tools we can use in the midst of the action to get back in balance when we feel overreactive or anxious. We *can* learn how to live our values versus living mechanically just to get by.

As you read through this book, I invite you to take pause at the questions and personal evaluations proposed throughout the chapters, and contemplate how they might relate to you. After you have finished, you will find that we have created a group of exercises and worksheets offered in the Appendix if you desire to go deeper with your process.

Deborah Rozman, Ph.D.

Chapter 1

EMOTIONS:
THE NEXT FRONTIER

*If each of us sweeps in front of our own steps,
the whole world would be clean.*

— GOETHE

For the vast majority of us, living *is* feeling. Imagine spending time with a loved one, experiencing a beautiful spot in nature listening to your favorite piece of music, or viewing an exciting sports game without any connection whatsoever to the emotional experience. Feelings allow us to experience the *textures* of life. They are such a natural part of our existence that often we take them for granted; but life without feeling is a terribly empty place. In fact, when our feelings are numb or shut down, we're just mechanically surviving. We shut down feelings as a defense when we can't manage or handle the discomfort they bring us. *Not feeling* often seems the least painful alternative.

When we don't understand the purpose of feelings or know how to interpret them, we can get anxious, angry and overreact. Feelings can complicate our life and lead us to heartache and heartbreak. Not that this is always bad. We often learn from heartache, but just as often we end up trapped for years in judgment, blame, and resentment.

Unmanaged feelings and unresolved anguish lead to a lot of misunderstanding and hate.

The next frontier of human advancement is the emotional frontier. The task is to learn *how* to intelligently resolve our emotions for our own and others' benefit, to enrich our experience of life. While this sounds wonderful, many would think it idealistic for society, let alone for themselves. Hard as they might try, they just can't control their anger, lift their depression, or move beyond fears and insecurities—their emotional chaos.

The world is faster and busier than ever. People have more pressures than they can handle and are more uncertain about the future. Emotional stress is not going to go away. We need to raise our emotional *set point*—our threshold of emotional overreaction—and we can, once we understand how.

Overcare, over-identity, and over-attachment are an emotional virus in our society. They are the unsolved mysteries behind much of our vulnerability to overreaction, anxiety, anger, hurt, overwhelm, depression, or fatigue. Yet we are unaware of how this *virus* functions in us and spreads to others.

Let's look at a description of overcare, over-identity, and over-attachment, followed by a situation that illustrates how each one "played out," and conclude with the emotional outcome it had on the people involved. Although overcare, over-identity, and over-attachment *intertwine* very intimately, the intention of these three extreme examples is to illustrate how each can become the dominant factor in a situation.

OVERCARE

When the basic human need *to care* is out of balance, we move into overcare or not enough care. We all know what not enough care feels like, but we may not be aware of how *overcare* affects us. Overcare about people, issues, and things can pervade our feeling worlds and shape our thoughts and actions.

Illustration:

Celeste believed that she wasn't a loving mother to her children unless she was constantly worrying about them. Even though they were 35 and 42, she worried when they had a cold, worried when they went on vacation that something might happen, and when they visited, she worried whether they were dressed warmly enough when they went outdoors, just as she had always done since they were little. After all, she was a mother and this is what mothers do. To Celeste, her worry (which translates as overcare) expressed her love for them. To the kids, who were now adults, Celeste's overcare made them want to avoid her. As a result, they rarely called or visited.

Outcome:

Celeste has developed health problems that are stress-related, according to her doctor, but is unaware (in denial) of the stress in her life. For Celeste, worrying about her children is love and she sees it as an endearing quality. What she has been unable to recognize is that her overcare is more about her remaining in the role she has played all her life. The role is familiar and is what has defined her sense of who she is and her personal value. She doesn't realize that everything could improve across the board if she would give herself permission to move into a more balanced type of care with her children.

OVER-IDENTITY

When one's own identity is overly invested in a person, place, issue, or thing, then we have *over-identity*. Over-identity with ideas, beliefs, and others' values spawns anger, judgment, and blame, ultimately placing us in the *victim* mode.

Illustration:

Don was so over-identified with his projects and performance at work that it took a toll on his people skills. Whenever Don's boss would call and leave him a voicemail, Don would anxiously redial his boss every two minutes and wouldn't talk to anyone else until he could reach him. Don lost clients and his co-workers felt put off. He was overly concerned with his projects and performance and what his boss might think, because to him, his work was his identity. Therefore nothing could ever be perfect enough.

Outcome:

Don was never able to see that his over-identity led to a blind perfectionism that cost him his job. Angry and depressed after he was fired, he became fanatical about his religion and politics, and alienated all his friends. Don's story illustrates clearly that when we don't take the time to find out *who* we are (create our own value), we will continue to allow other people, places, issues, and things to define us. This can only lead to blame and resentment.

OVER-ATTACHMENT

When our self-worth is low or lacking in some area, we overly attach ourselves to someone, some place, some issue, or some thing that would send a message back that we were valued or 'of value.' *Over-attachment* represses those we love and suffocates our inner peace and security.

Illustration:

Joan and Brad had been married four years. Brad felt he couldn't do anything without being under the ever-present *watchful eye* of Joan. As for Joan, she just wanted him to know she was *there* for him. When they went to parties, Joan would spend the whole evening trying to make sure that Brad was having a good time. She would constantly ask him if he wanted another drink or let him know who was coming into the room in case he wanted to talk with them. Brad felt so suffocated by Joan's over-attachment that he insisted on going to a marriage counselor.

Outcome:

Because Joan felt so insecure about her own value and identity, she felt the need to create a *reason* (attachment) for Brad to keep her around and not "stray." Brad was feeling stifled and choked by the obsessive attention. Brad and Joan eventually divorced, leaving Joan feeling rejected, betrayed and not understanding why.

In each of the above examples, overcare, over-identity, or over-attachment was an unconscious emotional habit. When our feelings cause us suffering, we often end up in overwhelm, anxiety, or depression. Most of us don't understand why and we haven't a clue as to how to release our feeling world from the clutches of habit. We suffer silently, or we reach for solace from friends, religion, therapy, or self-help, movies, and stimulants. We often feel alone, yet we share the same feeling world with countless others today and throughout the ages. The outcomes are the same—repression, happiness interspersed with suffering, unbridled emotional expression, and endless conflict. If we take an honest look, humanity's emotional advancement can seem no farther along than it was during the caveman days, even though mental advancement has soared far ahead. This isn't wrong or some evolutionary mistake. It's just that it is time now for our developed intellects to understand the most sensitive of human qualities—*feelings*.

Just as those airplanes ripped open the World Trade Center, so they ripped open our hearts. We were forced to feel things we never acknowledged before, and discovered a level of emotional connectedness with everyone in the world that we never dreamed we had. We also became more aware of our own emotional stress.

Even before those world-unhinging terrorist attacks, people were experiencing an unprecedented degree of stress that had become widespread. Numerous studies have consistently shown emotional stress is highest among the impoverished and repressed. It is also extremely high among executives, professionals, and full time working mothers, where nearly one out of five men and one out of two women feel high stress. In the United States, almost one out of five school-age children have behavorial problems as a result of emotional distress, more than double the number in 1980.[1]

Depression, eating disorders, adjustment difficulties, hyperactivitu, and other "psychosocial" problems are increasing in children as well as adults, and are a disturbing reflecvtion of the emotional stress of modern life. The questions we need to pause and ask ourselves, personally and collectively, include: How long can we keep up with the accelerating speed of life and uncertainty? What will be the ongoing emotional and health consequences? And the social consequences?

Nathanael West once said, "Man spends a great deal of time making order out of chaos, yet insists that the emotions be disordered." Nevertheless it's emotions that often control our lives, perpetuate our stress, and portend our future. Most of us do spend a lot of time keeping our house clean, our bills paid and our workplace in order. We have relatively happy lives, but we also have one or two scenarios that are a constant, nagging source of stress and emotional drain. Celeste's unnecessary worry about her adult children, Don's blinding perfectionism and Joan's suffocating watchfulness were isolated situations that created all sorts of problems in their lives.

If you've been aware of nagging areas of stress in your life, odds are you've tried to deal with it. You may have told yourself to eat differently, to rest more, to see what you could change or to just get over it. You may have tried affirmations, prayer, and positive thinking, talked to friends or visited a doctor. But if out of control emotions and emotional drain are still going on, you have probably never recognized overcare, over-identity, or over-attachment at the root of it. These are difficult to spot because they are so closely connected to basic human needs—to care, to have identity, and to feel secure. Because these needs relate to feelings, attempts at rational control alone won't work. Answering these needs requires a power beyond the intellect. The answer lies in the power of the human heart.

It's no coincidence that ancient cultures from Greece to China looked to the heart as a primary source of feeling, virtue, and intelligence. They felt that only through the heart could greed be replaced by charity, selfishness by compassion, and fear by love. Religions all over the world talk about the heart as the seat of the soul and doorway to spirit or higher self. The ancient Chinese considered the heart as the primary organ capable of influencing and directing our emotions, our morality, our decision-making ability, and the attainment of inner balance. It's interesting that the Chinese characters for "thinking, "thought," "intent," "listen," "virtue," as well as "love," all include the symbol for "heart."

Neither is it a coincidence that western languages also refer to heart both as a physical organ and as a metaphor for feeling, intuition, and the center of our total personality or being. After all, it's in the area of the heart that we experience the physical feeling of many emotions, like joy, love, hurt, and sadness. We talk of "losing heart," "having heart," "being heartfelt," "playing with a lot of heart," "going deep in your heart to find an answer," and so forth. It was only in the 1990s that science discovered there is in fact a link between the physical and feeling heart—therein lies the secret to emotional management and freedom. This discovery may prove to be one of the most profound for us as individuals, and provide hope for humanity.

The process of *feeling* a feeling or *experiencing* an emotion is both biochemical and neurological. It involves the heart, brain, nervous and hormonal systems, and sensory organs. We use the words feeling and emotion interchangeably in society (and throughout this book) because the process is so complex. A combination of feeling sensations, associated mental thoughts and biochemical reactions shape human beliefs and emotional experience, in gradations from very pleasant to very painful. Emotions like worry, anxiety, hurt, anger, guilt, fear, sadness, or depression are usually experienced as uncomfortable or distressing; whereas emotions like love, joy, forgiveness, compassion, appreciation, or bliss generally uplift, release and energize us.

The world is more ready today than ever to learn about the ability and power of the heart to manage the emotions. With our very survival at stake, more people are looking deeper into their hearts for solutions. We see a more heartfelt quest for spirit everywhere. We are coming to understand that the heart is where we go when the mind has no answers. Now, science is verifying the heart's role in feeling and intuition, at the same time as the global need increases for more people to engage their hearts. Being able to understand the language of the heart, the language of our feeling world is our next step. It's heart time on the planet. As we learn how to manage our emotions with the heart, new intelligence and understanding can emerge.

The heart's intelligence and power are seated in love, and the world is more ready than ever before to learn about love. Most of us feel that the meaning of life has something to do with love. That's really why we're all here—to learn how to love more and love better, and it's becoming an obvious imperative. Everyone wants to love, but few of us have been taught how to love or be loved.

This lack of understanding of love is at the heart of overcare, over-identity, over-attachment, and emotional chaos. If we multiply our own overcare, over-identity, and over-attachment by six billion people who share the same feelings in different disguises, we can understand why the world is like it is.

Understanding brings hope. If we can learn to understand *the language of the feeling world* at the root of our beliefs and actions, we can better understand how to love and embrace hope for new solutions. The hope of the new millennium and this decade is that we will recognize that emotions are the next frontier to be understood and managed for personal, social, and global peace, and quality of life.

PERSONAL EVALUATION

- Where in your own life do you feel you are not doing enough? Being enough? Giving enough? Or doing too much? Being too much? Giving too much?

- Where do you feel you *compromise* yourself?

- How do you feel about that? Any judgments, resentments, or blame?

- On a scale of 1–5, with 1 as very low and 5 as very high, estimate your emotional *set-point*, your threshold of overreaction to things that trigger irritation, frustration, or anxiety in you.

Chapter 2

OVERCARE, OVER-IDENTITY, AND OVER-ATTACHMENT:
HOW TO OVERCOME THE DRAINING CYCLE

That the birds of worry and care fly over your head,
this you cannot change,
but that they build nests in your hair,
this you can prevent.

— ANCIENT CHINESE PROVERB

Nature seems to have programmed care into our very DNA. Watch a mother lovingly attend her newborn, or a father tenderly bandage his child's skinned knee, and you'll see that nurturing is a natural response. When we love, we care, and when we care, we nurture. Philosopher Martin Heidegger put it well: "The essence of love is caring."

We all want to feel cared for and to have our care appreciated. Care generates a sense of security and connection, a life-affirming bond. Yet, surprisingly, if you look up "care" in most dictionaries, the first definition refers to "a troubled or burdened state of mind; worry; concern." It takes several lines before our *Webster's* gets around to defining *care* as "to feel love for, to look after, provide for, attend to." Language is a reflection of human perception, and for many in society, care has become what we call *overcare*—more a source of burden, worry, anxiety, even manipulation, than a nurturing experience.

We've heard the phrase "too much of a good thing," and everyone has experienced that. Have you ever had a great dessert, perhaps a slice of rich, creamy cheesecake that's so irresistible you practically gobble it down? It's so delicious that you just can't help having another piece.

While it was good going down, when that cheesecake hits your stomach you feel over-full and bloated, maybe even nauseous. If someone offers you another piece, you push it away.

The same thing can happen with care. You might be thinking, but caring means love. Can there really be such a thing as too much love, too much nurturing, or too much care? Yes, when we get *over-identified* or *over-attached* to what we care about. Then it stops being *care* and becomes *overcare*. It gets us worried or anxious and causes guilt or even anger. What's more, our care can make someone feel just as sick as having too much cheesecake. When we over-care about others, they feel overwhelmed and smothered, and push us away.

We've probably all known mothers, like the one described in Chapter 1, who don't feel like they are caring unless they are worrying and anxious about their children. Years ago when Doc was looking at his own life, he recognized that this was also true for him. "The more I cared for family, friends, work, or issues, the more worry and anxiety I had about them. What I cared most about kept giving me the most stress. 'Why?' I kept asking myself. 'Well, because I care,' I told myself. And I saw that this was true for most people. Suddenly a lightbulb went on inside and many types of stress began to make sense."

"Most of the time when people get anxious, angry, over-reactive, or manipulative, they are caring about something, but in a draining and usually ineffective way," says Doc. "I saw that most of my own and other people's problems started with care. But then the mind would take that care and turn it into worry and stress."

So Doc coined the term *overcare* to describe the kind of care that creates stress. Overload, overwhelm, going overboard—all these terms mean *too much to the point of undoing or downfall*. So does overcare. Although the term may be new, overcare is as old as history and causes endless misery. It affects men as well as women. Overcare occurs when the mind turns our genuinely caring intentions into a mental and emotional drain.

The draining cycle begins as we *over-identify* with a situation, an issue, or a person we care about—in other words, we identify too much. We begin to overcare and want to see things go a certain way. We get *over-attached* to how we want things to turn out, and are unable to see other options. We're less able to let go of that issue, that situation, or that person. When we over-attach, we become obsessive. And, ironically, just the opposite of what we want usually happens as a result—we get fired instead of promoted, or a person we want to bring closer avoids us. And we're astonished. After all, we cared so much!

This self-destructive cycle is insidious. Over-identity, overcare, and over-attachment spill into and feed each other. They can quickly spread to others and infect an entire family or workplace like an emotional virus. Here's an example of how the virus typically spreads. See if you can find similar examples in your life.

Someone storms into your office all upset because of what *he* said. "Can you believe that?" she hisses. "No way!" you exclaim. You feel your anger rising. You're identifying. She goes on, laying out what she heard in the lunchroom. As she's talking, your mind is going a mile a minute, recalling similar incidences that have happened to you. Your anger grows stronger. Now both of you are judging and blaming him. You are totally over-identified. Blood pressure rising, you start worrying about what will happen. Will that bozo tell the boss? Will she get stonewalled? What will you do? Will you be asked to take sides? Anxiety creeps in. You're now in overcare. You'd better protect your turf. You're already creating your strategy. Hold onto the report you're working on and don't let him see it. Your mind is manipulating next steps. Who else should you tell? Your anxiety has turned to fear. You're over-attached to this whole situation.

The next day you find out that *he* never said that. It was a rumor she heard from someone else at lunch. This kind of thing happens, every day, anywhere, for many of us and it's energy spent and wasted. Even if it were true, if *he* had said that, if you over-identify you become the victim. You're the victim of your own and others' emotional chaos.

When we look at the world situation through the eyes of over-identity and overcare, we quickly take sides based on partial information. This is the cause of emotional chaos. This is what's behind the growing epidemic of anxiety, depression, hypertension, and stress. This is what's behind most divorce, conflicts, riots, and war. Whole countries build their belief systems on over-identities, overcares, and over-attachments. The result is a blind refusal to understand another's point of view, leading to non-negotiation, suicide bombings, and terrorism. Without being willing to let go of our over-identities and be open to a bigger picture, there is no possible resolution. The strongest will dominate by manipulation or force but won't resolve the underlying misunderstandings.

If we want to help those we care about or the world, we need to start with ourselves. When we don't manage over-identity, overcare, or over-attachment, they become a habit. This leads to overreaction or to lack of care and burnout. We wear out from trying. Our emotional stamina is drained, and that leads to a lackluster quality in day-to-day experiences. When emotional quality is low, we mechanically operate at half-mast; our peace, fun and power to adapt are significantly reduced. We stay so stressed that we end up feeling ineffective, or that we've cared too much and can't care anymore.

So often we think that overcare will somehow make things better. That all the energy we put into worrying will give us the answers we need or achieve the outcomes we want. We think that worry and anxiety somehow motivate productive action. They don't. It's when we finally let the worry go, decide to sleep on it or talk to a friend who helps us to release the worry, that answers come to us.

Energized emotional involvement and passion toward a goal is different from worry. It opens the mind to creative possibilities. But over-identity and emotionalism close the mind and can delay accomplishment of a goal or spoil its celebration.

Overcare in one area usually results in a lack of care in another area. It's like squeezing a balloon at one end so that it pops out at the other end. This lack of balance in care is causing much of the increased stress and burnout we see in individuals and society today.

The *Mitchum Report on Stress in the '90s* shows that work, money, and family are constant sources of overcare and stress for most people in the U.S. More than half worry most about work or money, and a quarter say conflict between work and family is their greatest source of tension and stress. Small incidents—like being late for an appointment, waiting in traffic, or standing in line at a store—also cause worries and stress. In fact, it's often the smallest things that cause the biggest stress. The problem is that these little things can stack up until "one last straw breaks the camel's back" and we have a mental or emotional crash or health crisis.

A television producer quoted Winston Churchill saying, "It's the broken shoelaces that destroy men's lives." She added that she finds his words coming to mind often. "I can control my anger and my bigger emotions. It's not the big things that get to me anymore; the little things are what get me all day long and worry me." A friend describes it this way. "Stress is death from 1,000 paper cuts. You never know how many you can handle before it's too much."

If this feels like you, realize you're not alone. But you can do something about it by recognizing and releasing overcare. When you look at your life through the lens of overcare, you can see that a lot of your stress and strain is based on real care that somehow slipped into overcare. Recognizing this is, in itself, a relief. The tools, techniques, and examples in this book will show you how to recognize and release your overcares. This will give you the inner security and strength you need to understand and let go of the over-identity behind the overcare.

For most of us, the root motive *is* to care. We care that we look good, do a good job, get a promotion, are thought well of, or have enough money to raise our children. We care if we're slowed down from what we want to do next when we have to wait in line at a store. There's nothing wrong with that. But when we don't manage our cares and they turn into overcare, often without our realizing it, we end up frustrated, drained, and exhausted. The rest of this chapter will focus on different ways that overcare shows up in our lives. All the examples are common to millions. They're normal responses to stress, but it's time we learn more effective responses.

Jon and Sandi spent their lives rushing—rushing to get breakfast; rushing to get the kids to school; rushing themselves to work; rushing the kids to after school lessons (soccer, swim team, theatre); rushing to get dinner, get the house cleaned and bills paid; then dropping exhausted in bed only to have to rise early the next day to do it all again. Their schedule was frustrating and stressful to both of them and to the kids. They felt bad that they didn't have much family time together but couldn't see any way out. They wanted their children to have the best.

Families need to bond together for real care to flourish. When care about children's activities turns to over-identity and overcare, it drains the entire family and fuels out of control emotions. Balanced care helps children, but parental overcare leads to frustration, overload, and then, too often, to a lack of care. Habits of overcare and lack of care get handed down from generation to generation.

Jim's father wanted him to become a doctor or lawyer so badly that he pushed Jim hard. Jim became a lawyer but wasn't happy. In turn, Jim pushed his own son hard to get higher grades and learn computer programming, though his son wanted to spend time in drama and film-making. His son felt that Jim was always on his case and that they couldn't communicate. He dropped out of school and ran away from home. Jim cared enough to find him, and they went to family counseling. Jim saw how he had treated his son the same way his father had treated him.

Overcare is most apparent in relationships. Children tend to shut out parents who are always overcaring about their grades, their activities, their appearance, or their friends. Just as children recoil from overcaring parents, most adults also turn off from overcaring lovers, friends, bosses, and co-workers. When someone you overcare about doesn't respond to you in the way you'd hoped, the mind goes right to worry and fret, "Did I do something wrong?"

or "Doesn't he like me anymore?" This, of course, results in even more overcare.

Overcaring about self-worth in relationships is what sustains our long-standing hurt, guilt, and blame. Whenever we blame others, we drain our energy and feel like a victim. Whenever we blame ourselves, we feel guilty and drain more energy. Outgoing blame creates incoming drain. Blame and guilt tend to work like a dripping faucet that leaks our emotional power away, even when we're not thinking about it. They sap our power to make constructive changes.

In the workplace overcare runs rampant, creating office politics. Millions exhaust themselves daily with overcare about how they are treated, how they come across, or how they compare to others. They set themselves up for hurt, disappointment, and feeling like they have no control. This finally results in a defeated attitude: "I don't care any more. I'll just do the minimum I have to and *they* can do what they want." *They* get the blame, but who gets the drain? No wonder so many wake up in the morning tired, overwhelmed, and irritable.

We don't realize how overcare has become a highly contagious emotional virus in most workplaces. It has become so common, most everyone catches it. In fact, in some companies, if you're not stressed from overcaring, you're not considered a good worker. Some executives don't see workplace stress as a problem because it masquerades as care for the company. Yet, workplace overcare reduces productivity, leads to absenteeism, and negatively impacts the bottom line.

Millions, today, overcare about society. With terrorism, economic uncertainty, and global warming, it's hard not to overcare about what might happen. We tell ourselves, "How can I not overcare about that!" but overcare either leads to overreaction, inaction, or mere token attempts to help. Why? Because, overcare squelches clarity, incapacitates, creates panic, and dilutes creative thinking. Just watching the news can lead people to rail at the president, cry over the abused, fear, uncertainty, and violence, and go to bed emotionally drained.

While all these human emotional reactions are understandable and there's nothing wrong with them, our heart intelligence will tell us they still need to be managed. We need to come back into balance, to our deeper heart values. Heart intelligence is the harmonization of feelings and thoughts that give us emotional balance and intuitive common sense (which is often uncommon these days). If we use our feelings to open our hearts and find heart balance, we can take overcare or undercare back to balanced and productive care.

It's critical that all of us learn how to manage our mental and emotional energies and not drain them, so that we can adapt to the unpredictable, whether in social or natural disasters, relationships, work, or parenting. *We eventually have to adapt anyhow*. Overcare only lengthens the adaptation time and impedes clear thinking. Adapting through balanced care saves energy and shortens the time it takes to find new possibilities. Understanding the purpose of adaptability and how it's sustained is extremely important in this era of rapid and unpredictable change.

Genuine, balanced care is regenerative to our bodies and minds and can help us adapt and see what common sense things we can do. Genuine heart care can motivate us to help a religious, political, or social cause with heart intelligent attitudes and contributions, whereas, over-identity about a cause easily turns care into overcare reactions. Overcare never results in any real solutions to a problem; it can't. It siphons off our original caring intentions and passion, and then decreases our ability to find solutions. In fact, people overcaring about the same issue often get into conflict with one another about what to do, thus reducing or even destroying the effectiveness of their efforts.

It's through managing overcare that we come back to center and find balanced care, which is what gives us clarity on how to help. Balanced care is not some placid state that lacks drive and passion. Balance is a dynamic place in the heart that allows us to flex through stress and stay resilient under pressure. It builds emotional stamina and opens our minds to more options. When overcares stack up, our capacity to handle challenges diminishes. By releasing our overcares, we prevent stress from building and we increase our creative capacities. Then we can enjoy the fruits of *wholeness* care.

> When Bonnie first heard the word overcare, she knew what it meant immediately. She could see overcare in herself and in her friends so clearly. Bonnie had been a passionate advocate for social causes and was worn out from overcares. She suffered panic attacks and was on anti-depressants like so many other people she knew. She'd withdrawn from her friends because they were all going through trying times and it depressed her more to be around them. Yet, this also made Bonnie sad.

When we are trapped in overcare, life loses its luster and meaning, just as it does when we don't care at all. This is because stress-motivated action has become a habit. It's through our genuine care that we find value and positive meaning in life. Studies show that for most of us, experiences of positive meaning come in a few basic and simple ways, all of which involve genuine care. These include feeling warmly connected with others and cared about; having an opportunity to be distracted from everyday problems; feeling a sense of achievement, pride, or self-esteem; feeling hope or optimism; and receiving affirmation or facilitation from others. It's through these experiences that all people broaden their views about life. Daily experiences of positive meaning are what predict long-term psychological well-being.

Learning to identify your overcares and over-identities will not only start to free you from stress, it will give you new direction on how to enhance your life and unfold who you really are. As you cut through overcare, you'll bring yourself back into balance and connect with your heart intelligence to express true care. It will create an inner security that adds to your energy and turns your care into passionate living.

There is often a very fine line between balanced care and overcare, but you learn to distinguish them by *how they make you feel*. It's important to learn the language of your feeling world. To start with, ask yourself, "Is what I care about stress *producing* or stress *reducing*?" If it's stress *producing*, then you know there's overcare involved and it's draining your energy. If it's stress *reducing*, that's where your care is in balance, regenerative, and adding to your energy.

Think back to a time when you cared about something, and cared so much that eventually you found yourself frustrated. Then think back to a time when you cared about something and it felt great. That's the difference you're looking for in your feeling world. If you recognize the feelings or emotions that follow your attempts to care, you'll start to understand when your care is stress producing, rather than a regenerative experience. You can make a list in your mind or on paper of who and what you care about to see where you are draining or adding to your power.

Cutting through overcares is like separating the wheat of one's real care from the chaff of one's stress and insecurities. To do this, we need to look at four common disguises that overcare can wear—attitudes that mask care and sink us into worry, frustration, anxiety, and stress. Then we can look at how to use the power and intelligence of the heart to cut through those attitudes and distressing feelings to gain inner peace and security.

Sentiment, attachment, expectation, and *sympathy* are symptoms of overcare that can often masquerade as care. These attitudes and emotions dilute the effectiveness of our intended care and pull us into emotional chaos. How this dilution occurs may not be obvious at first. After all, these *masks* seem like heartfelt expressions of care. They are the stuff *Hallmark* cards are made of. Yet, if you look deeper, you can see how they are behind much suffering and heartache.

SENTIMENT

Sentiment starts with a sincere loving or caring feeling that becomes colored by emotional memories, resulting in worry or sadness. When a tender feeling turns sentimental, like missing someone with whom you shared good times, the sense of loss can sink your heart into deep sorrow. This isn't bad, as people often grow from these deeply felt experiences. But you will accelerate your recovery and your growth if you shift back to a balanced heart to gain some intuitive understanding. If you stay in sentiment, it will cause what's called a *bleeding heart.* The mind over-identifies, imagining what could have been, which ignites sorrow and hurt, ultimately cascading into anxiety and guilt and even depression. One sentimental emotion quickly attracts more, until before you know it you're down in the dumps.

Managing sentiment isn't about cutting off the feeling or repressing it. By learning to recognize it as a sentimental pull, you can bring the energy back into your heart and shift to balance. Then the deeper values of the heart can be expressed. You honor your memories of other people by lifting sentiment back to real love and care.

> Sally's only child went off to college and the house was empty. She was terribly lonely and didn't know what to do with herself. She would look at photos of her child growing up and cry. Her minister suggested that she look at each picture and pause to really appreciate the happy times they had together. Sally found that this lifted her spirits. Whenever she found herself lonely and unsure of what to do, she would look at a picture and appreciate her daughter.

Appreciation is a quick access code to finding more of your real spirit. As you focus on feeling appreciation, your intuition can *clarify* more. Your thoughts and perspective change. Heart intuition—not mind sentiment—is what will guide you to a new secure attitude that feels better to your spirit. Often intuition comes as calming *whisper thoughts* that show you the direction to take. Even if you don't intuit an immediate direction, you'll rebuild your energy and sense of security.

Watch out for feelings of sentiment toward yourself. If you are overweight and dwell on memories of when you could fit into smaller size clothes, that sentiment can turn to despair. It's not the memory itself but the over-attachment to what once was and sense of failure that bring heartache and drain away your power. Dwelling on failure brings up more memories of past failures or parts of your life that are not working now. Lingering there won't bring you any clarity.

As soon as you recognize sentimental thoughts taking over, find a feeling of appreciation for something in your life now and enjoy that appreciative feeling for a few moments. This will bring you back to the present moment and start to restore your emotional power. It can also provide you with new perceptions on how to move forward.

ATTACHMENT

Being over-attached will sap your spirit and block the expression of your deeper values. It binds you to people, things, or ideas to the extent that you lose clear perspectives. A mother has a natural feeling of attachment and love for her child. However, if she frets every time she's apart from her child, or fusses over and spoils her child when they are together, she reinforces an insecurity in both of them, and misses out on the richness of a deeper love. This isn't what she really wants, but it's what she gets. Over-attachment seriously reduces the quality of love and leads to a lot of unhappiness.

It's our insecurities that feed our attachments. We can build over-attachments even to our habits and feel insecure if we must change them. Some feel they must drive the same route to work no matter what the traffic is like, or put household items on the shelf in a certain order, or hang on to their beliefs regardless of evidence to the contrary. They become set in their ways and are no longer open to possibly more effective options. Similarly, many get over-attached to their desires, whether for a perfect home or a perfect relationship. Over-attachment to desires occurs when we fear we won't get what we want or need. Yet, our real heart may need something other than what we think we ought to have. It is easy to mistake mental and emotional desire as true heart's desire. Over-attachment to desires, habits, and addictive behaviors that arise from them, narrows our perspective and takes away our emotional freedom.

When Diane was in college, she was fraught with over-attachment to her desire of finding a fun, romantic relationship. She compensated by overeating, swelling to 50 pounds above her normal weight in six months, and became bulimic before it was fashionable. Becoming overweight added to her worries, because now she felt unattractive. She drowned her worries in more food, and watched many of her friends drown theirs in alcohol or drugs. Over-attachment can act as a continuous drug in our system that is self-prescribed through repetitive thoughts and attitudes, but the unseen source is insecurity.

Once an emotional desire gets programmed in your neural circuits through repetition, it takes on its own emotional momentum. You know those emotional pulls that make you say and do things you later wished you hadn't. Unmanaged emotional pulls usually lead to unsatisfactory outcomes. Managing desires with heart intelligence will help keep you from being blindsided by insecurities that may be propelling you. It will also give you the strength to delay gratification until you are clear that you are following your real heart and not just an emotional pull. Attachment to a particular outcome actually blocks the fulfillment you are hoping for. Fulfilling experiences find you, as you replace insecurity with balance and self-security.

EXPECTATION

All of us have some expectations. We expect the sun to come up in the morning; we expect our family and friends to be pretty much the same tomorrow as they were yesterday. Most of us expect those we care about to behave in certain ways. But the more we care about them, the more disillusioned we tend to become if they don't act according to our expectations. This is because we have an emotional investment in a particular outcome—in things going the way *we* think they should.

Expectations of colleagues, wives, husbands, children, or events are the source of most feelings of hurt, anger, and despair. Hope is lost as disappointment drains our emotional reserves. By understanding and managing our expectations with heart intelligence, we can love and care without becoming devastated when our expectations aren't met.

> Karen, like so many women she knew, had given up finding a mate because none of the men she'd dated could live up to her expectations. She preferred to immerse herself in her career and not date anymore rather than go through another devastating round of expectation and disappointment.

Managing expectations is often what distinguishes the optimist who will keep trying from the pessimist who gives up. Balanced optimism comes from not setting yourself up for constant disappointment. Pessimists tend to have negative emotional expectations. Optimists learn to distinguish between balanced expectancies and emotionally invested expectations. You can have a fun expectancy that you will enjoy an upcoming vacation sunning yourself by the ocean and be flexible enough to enjoy yourself if it rains the whole time. But if you have too much emotion invested in the expectation that it be sunny, then your disappointment at the rain could ruin what might have been a fun, spontaneous change of plans. The pessimist would say, "I told you so," and not see any options. Not everyone is a born optimist. Intelligent optimism, not false idealism, can be learned.

Using the power of the heart allows you to see new options quickly when your expectations aren't met.

Let's say you completed a creative marketing project and are about to prepare a report on it. Holding an expectation that your boss or team be as excited as you are could set you up for feeling devastated if they aren't. Approaching the report with a fun yet balanced expectancy—rather than an attached or emotional expectation—will give you a lot more flexibility; you can deliver the report with dynamic sincerity, be receptive to any feedback, and maintain the self-security you need to improve. Whether the feedback is positive or negative, you will be able to appreciate yourself for your effort and move forward without loss of energy.

Usually we place the heaviest expectations on ourselves. Perfectionism and performance anxieties perpetuate stress and undermine happiness. We expect ourselves to live up to an image and ideal, and then we overcare and feel guilty when we don't. A friend of ours valiantly set out to take care of his health. He planned a low fat diet and bought an expensive rowing machine. Five days later he still hadn't used the machine and had blown his diet with a chocolate mousse he couldn't refuse. His self-care turned to guilt from not achieving his own expectations. Idealistic expectations from the mind will undermine your efforts, while fun expectancies from the heart give you creative ideas that encourage you. Heart intelligence releases perfectionism so you can enjoy following through with your plans or recognize when you need to create more realistic ones.

If expectations continually cause you disappointment, try the following. Several times throughout the day, ask yourself if there is anything you are looking forward to with high expectations, where you find yourself attached to a particular outcome. Then ask yourself if you aren't on a sure-fire course for disappointment if things don't turn out the way you'd like. Ask your heart to help you replace the expectation of a specific outcome with balanced hope and anticipation for the best outcome for all concerned. Recognize that life's gifts can arrive in unexpected packages.

SYMPATHY

The fourth mask of care is sympathy or sharing in another's sadness. Sympathy is tricky because it looks like deep care. However, sympathetic feelings actually diminish your ability to care. When you sympathize, your mind commiserates with another person's stress and often projects more misery into it than is there. The same can be true of empathy if you don't stay balanced. Before you know it, you are consumed with overcare, and now there are two pitiful people instead of one.

Compassion is the core heart feeling that lifts you out of draining sympathy. It is deep care with understanding. Compassion helps you feel what it's like to walk in someone else's shoes but to know when to stop so you don't walk off a cliff with them. A buddy once described sympathy like this: "If a friend's bucket has a hole in it and all its water is leaking out, it doesn't help to punch a hole in your own bucket." Sympathy bleeds energy; compassion accumulates energy and provides productive insight and action.

Notice when you are slipping from compassion to sympathy. You can feel it as a pull on your heartstrings or a heavy feeling in the pit of your stomach. Lifting your energy from the stomach to the heart, and away from mind worries and fears that underlie sympathy, will help you regain balance.

SELF-PITY

In addition to unmasking the four common disguises of care—sentiment, attachment, expectation, and sympathy—we also need to cut through the logical consequence of all of them: *self-pity*. Feeling sorry for yourself is where you bottom out in each of the four most common overcare habits. In self-pity, overcare turns on itself, and before you know it you've caught the fast train to despair.

For instance, if you are feeling sentimental, missing the good times from days gone by, your sadness can drag you down until pretty soon you're counting all the ways in which you're missing out on life. You've hit bottom—a full-blown pity party for your own miserable life. Or you get attached to a person or a habit or a way of looking at the world, and when circumstances change, as they inevitably do, you're flung into chaos and confusion. Look at the dirty hand life dealt you! Self-pity has definitely come to call. Expectations that aren't met can be another sure-fire route to self-pity. You bear a disappointment, only to find yourself wallowing in something deeper: the feeling that life's a bear, and you got screwed. Sympathy, too, can bottom out into self-pity, for if you get over-identified with another's sadness, you can start feeling that all life is sorrowful—including your own.

Overcaring to the point of self-pity saps your power and leaves you feeling flatter than a pancake. Self-pity bleeds so much energy that after indulging in it, you can feel drained for a full day or more. Sometimes even a good night's sleep doesn't dispel the mood, and it can be days before you feel a spring in your step again.

Self-pity is the opposite of true compassion for yourself. You can notice the difference between compassion and self-pity in your body. Compassion feels soothing and relaxing to the heart, while self-pity creates an ache in the heart or pit of the stomach. When you give yourself compassion, you hold yourself gently in the heart in a humble, open attitude of not knowing what's best or why things happened the way they did. This opens your mind to new possibilities. When you give yourself pity, you send your mind racing to post blame and find justifications for why you're feeling so badly. Compassion is absolutely essential to the process of releasing and cutting through your overcare.

Left unchecked, self-pity turns into a chronic case of the "poor me's." It happens most often when you feel that someone, or life in general, hasn't been fair or shown you the attention you deserve. You then drain your energy for days, weeks, or months by feeling sorry for yourself. Pretty soon you're feeling so sorry for yourself that all of life is tinted with despair. When the "poor me's" occupy the mind, new solutions simply can't get in. You're unable to take effective action.

The inner expression of self-pity is "pout." We've all seen young children turn out their lower lips and scowl when disappointed. Most of the time a child's pout doesn't last long. Children have more plasticity and flexibility than adults, so they don't tend to brood for days or weeks. They just pout until life offers a new opportunity, and then they move on—usually in a matter of minutes.

As adults, when we don't manage our perceptions that things are unfair, our minds turn inward and we pout for a longer time. We can stay distressed or angry for weeks or even months about the way life dealt the cards, and we brood about our problems.

Self-pity can become an ingrained pattern that distorts reality. The mind justifies holding onto hurt, resentment, or blame because of the principle of the matter. It feels entitled to hold onto those feelings, and views life through that filter. When the mind habitually pouts, it can't see straight and misinterprets the communications and feelings of others. We program and reprogram hurt and resentment over and over into our neural circuitry, skewing our hormonal balance, depressing our immune system, and aging before our time. Leaving the pouts unchecked, or dramatizing them to prove a point, often leads to depression, other emotional or physical disorders, or even violence.

Most of us recover from pouts over time. We eventually re-accumulate the lost emotional energy as new events distract us from the issue. That's why we say that time heals. We let the self-pity go and move on, but it can remain stored in our cellular structures, resurfacing with the appropriate triggers. We tend to keep reprocessing major pouts until our ego feels vindicated or until we gain a freeing intuitive insight about what happened and why. But that insight often comes after months or years of being pitiful and operating with less energy than we could have.

Although seemingly sweet and sincere, sentiment, attachment, expectation, and sympathy can lead you down a road paved with good intentions to misery. The goal is not to throw them out, but to use your heart intelligence to bring them back into balance so your care turns into an asset instead of a drain.

Without heart intelligence, the untamed mind and emotionalism will keep you duped into believing that your vitality is being squandered by external circumstances beyond your control. It's from heart intelligence that you gain the intuitive insight and power to make the attitudinal changes you need to minimize emotional stress. The techniques and tools provided in later chapters will show you how to manage your emotions and bring in this intelligence. There is a physiological state of heart balance, which brings your entire system—heart, brain, mind, emotions, and nervous system—into a dynamic state of internal coherence and flow. It's in this coherent state that *heart intelligence* becomes more available to you. Heart intelligence empowers you to *adapt* to life's challenges and save the emotional energy required to get your life back together. Heart intelligence opens pathways from the heart to the brain that give you access to the information you need to free yourself. Once your mind has new understanding there's no longer any need to pout.

So many people believe that life has to be painful, and that where there is no pain there is no gain. Religions have taught that the soul matures through trial by fire—self-doubt, heartache, and despair. By learning to use the power of your heart to connect with your deeper heart intelligence, you realize that you don't have to keep learning that way. You have compassion for your struggles but see how to face yourself off and rise up to new heights of awareness. You let go of your guilt, connect with wholeness care and move on from there. To linger in guilt is to stay out of sync and drain more, which stops you from knowing your next step.

With heart intelligence, learning, and growing are seen in the light of energy economy. You invite in more of your spirit and you see with new eyes. The passion and depth of discovery isn't missed—it's that your downtime and recovery happens a whole lot faster. You unravel the mysteries of life with far less effort and time waste. Managing your overcares with heart and using the power tools offered creates a *time shift* in learning. You make more efficient and effective choices within a time span. You learn where to save energy for increased fun and quality in life. The result is that life has enhanced value and positive meaning for you. Hope appears on the horizon again. You unfold potentials hidden within your heart that you didn't know were there. You become more of who you really are. You become your own hope generator.

We've seen that it's not our love, compassion, appreciation, or care that squelch hope, but the tendency to allow these core heart feelings to become compromised by overcare and its disguises of sentiment, attachment, expectation, sympathy, and self-pity. You'll find that relinquishing overcare in even one area will often unravel overcares in many other areas at the same time. Experiencing this brings in a tremendous sense of freedom and hope. And with hope comes a renewal of energy and passion for life.

PERSONAL EVALUATION

Listen to and watch your feeling world as you consider these questions. Notice any changes in your feelings as you answer them.

- In what areas is care adding to your energy and reducing your stress? Why?

- In what areas is care draining your energy and giving you stress? What do you overcare about in the situation? Is there over-identity with someone or some issue? Do you have over-attachment to a particular outcome?

- Which of the masks of care: sentiment, attachment, expectation, or sympathy, best describes your type of overcare?

Chapter 3

UNDERSTANDING EMOTIONAL VANITY

If a person is to get the meaning of life
he must learn to like the facts about himself—
ugly as they may seem to his sentimental vanity—
before he can learn the truth behind the facts.
And the truth is never ugly.

— EUGENE O'NEILL

Our true identity or *core self* is who we really are and what we really want to be. With all the stressors of life, most people don't have enough energy or time to find out who they really are. They are caught up in everyday overwhelm, anxiety, and fatigue. This can seem pretty heavy or intense, but we can't get out of the stress grind unless we look at why we're in it. For many of us, it's because of our emotional vanity or what some call ego.

Ego is a word that's been bandied around a lot, but few people really understand it. The ego is the "I" or self that experiences and responds to both our inner world and to the outside world. The ego is actually made up of different layers. In addition to our core self, the ego has identities based on our beliefs about ourselves that others have developed over the years. They may come from our own experience, or they may be what parents, friends, or society told us: hand-me-down beliefs. When we over-identify with these beliefs and act from them rather than our core self, we create false identities. They are not who we really are, but who we think we are or have to be for one reason or another.

Learning to be your true self means learning how to free yourself from the false identities that have formed around your core self. These shells are what hide your core self, and they are held in place by what we call *emotional vanity*. Not vanity in the sense you may be most used to hearing it, which means being excessively boastful or vain, like the man or woman who primps endlessly in front of a mirror. But vanity in the sense of over-identity with how worthy we think we are, that plays out in various ways. *Emotional vanity* is a distortion of the true self, created through insecurities and emotional investment in *who* we believe we are, or *should* be.

For most people, a lot of energy is locked up in ego or emotional vanities. Everyone has vanities. It's important to understand that having them doesn't make you bad and releasing them is not about correcting wrongs. As you are able to "tag" or become aware of your emotional vanities, you simply become more conscious of where your positive energy is being drained so you can reclaim it. To increase your vitality, you need to learn to take back the energy that's locked up in vanities. It's important to try and find some humor in them, so you can observe yourself with detachment as you begin to reclaim your energy. This way you increase your capacity to be creative and have much more power to deal with the standard stressors that go with day-to-day life.

A familiar story can provide more understanding of emotional vanity.

> Remember the evil queen in Snow White? She was vain in the traditional sense, because she continually sat before her mirror, asking, *Mirror, mirror on the wall, who is the fairest one of all?*

But underneath was her emotional vanity. She emotionally over-identified with just one aspect of herself—her physical appearance—so much that it ruled her life. She obsessively overcared about her looks, fearful of never being beautiful enough (otherwise why would she keep asking?). She was over-attached to what other people thought, always seeking confirmation, and insanely jealous of anyone who might be considered more beautiful.

Few of us are so driven by vanity that we would set out to kill someone we are jealous of, like the evil queen. Yet, we all have vanity insecurities, and they drive us to do and feel things our heart—our core self—wouldn't and doesn't want to do or feel.

Have you ever felt preoccupied with how you'll come out in situations? Have you worried about whether people think poorly of you or think you're great? Everyone does this to some extent and it's okay to have a certain amount of concern. But when overcare starts to preoccupy your thoughts and emotions, that's when it turns into an emotional vanity. You're over-identified to the point that your very sense of who you are is affected. You make emotional decisions based on vanity, not on your deeper heart.

Emotional and ego vanities stem from underlying insecurities that block the mind from acting on what the heart really knows. That's why we often hear religious and self-help philosophies talk about getting rid of the ego. In our view, the ego isn't bad. Our ego can become a creative expression of our personality, but it needs to be managed from the heart. Accessing our heart intelligence can help release emotional vanities and balance the ego so that it can express our true self.

Emotional or ego vanity plays out in various ways. It can be inflating to our own image at another's expense, or it can be inverted, causing us to put ourselves down and feel we are less important, or even worthless. Either way, a vanity is going on, which runs a continuous energy drain in our emotional nature.

Since understanding the emotional nature is the next level of advancement for humanity, we have to look at vanities. They can snuff out the spontaneity and pleasure of life as well as our potential for joy and real love. Emotional vanities cause self-centeredness, which shuts a part of our heart off to others and to ourselves as well. When aspects of our heart and care are shut off, we stifle a needed nurturing from our own spirit. This results in diminished textures of appreciation, joy, and fulfillment as we move through life.

Emotional vanities are spin-offs of basic insecurities. Jealousy is a vanity of insecurity. Envy is a vanity of insecurity. We've all seen people act out envy by jockeying for position, or "pooh-poohing" what others have, or using self-effacing flattery to get what they want. These are standard human reactions. We're not bad for having vanities, but it's effective and empowering to mature through them. In the same way, it's not bad for a teenager to show off while growing up, but it sticks out more when it's time for him to mature.

Social pressures encourage us all to build emotional vanities. Have you ever felt swayed politically or socially by others' opinions? Have you ever cared so much about what others thought of you that you did something you really didn't want to do—or *didn't* do something you really did want to do—as a result?

Social, religious, and political vanities are easy to be drafted into. The reason is because they're handed down from generation to generation. We get swept into them because we don't want to be different—or because we want to be different. When your vanity insecurities dissipate, then your opinions and beliefs are more inspired from your true self.

Social vanities cloak you in judgments of others or of yourself. They make it seem so natural. After all, everyone else is doing it. Or they allow you to judge and not call it a judgment because it's "just the way things are." Here's an example:

Back when Doc was growing up in North Carolina, white people were or would be irate if black people sat in the front of the bus. That's a racist, social vanity. Many white people, in their hearts, may truly not have cared if blacks sat up front. But as long as they were caught in the vanities of having society decide good or bad, right or wrong, they would fall into the same handed down judgment if the black person didn't sit in the back of the bus.

Social vanities, whether in a family, school, workplace, or country, give people license for mechanical judgments that create racism, sexism, ostracism, and abuse. But no matter how much we go along with others socially, in our deepest self, we know when something doesn't feel right in our heart.

Realize that everyone has personal and social vanities to deal with. Find out what's more agreeable to your heart now. Then it's easier to create the security you need and trade vanities for empowerment.

As you replace insecurity with security, you will no longer need a particular vanity. You'll transform the locked-up energy into inner strength and self-approval. No one is going to take out all emotional vanity overnight. The important thing is to be onto it. If you judge it as wrong, you'll inhibit your willingness to look. If you beat yourself up for "doing it wrong again" or for "not having learned the lesson," it's simply vanity on top of vanity. When you approach vanities with compassion and understanding, you loosen their stranglehold on you. You are inviting yourself to become your true self.

Releasing the shells of vanity identity is one of the last hurdles before love can be expressed through people unhindered. We increasingly bring in more spirit and find more love in our hearts as we peel off each layer of false identity we've built to navigate our way through life.

If we look back at our lives, most of us can remember situations, relationships, issues that felt so right—at first. We were so sure of what we wanted and of the choices we made. Later, however, we realized that fear, ambition or glamour had motivated us, and we ended up disillusioned. We either matured from that experience and made new heart intelligent choices that moved us forward, or we kept repeating the same old mind choices and stayed stuck in the same game.

Emotional vanity is often hard to see because we are looking through our own self-image. Yet we can uncover what our true self wants to show us if we take it step by step. With each step we take, we free up energy that can go toward the fulfillment of our deeper heart's desires.

Many of us have passive-aggressive emotional vanities. We are humble in one area, but when we don't get our way and our ego is threatened, we become aggressive. Passive-aggressive emotional vanity hides a deep insecurity, creating a gap, which blinds us to our ego's motives.

Most emotional vanities appear in one of three categories. These are:

- Approval vanity
- Communication vanity
- Desire vanity

Our true self can get trapped by all of them. We'll provide some examples and commentary for each category. See if you recognize yourself in any of them. As you do you can start to reclaim your freedom.

APPROVAL VANITY

- *They'll like me better if I say this.*

- *What will they think of me if I choose this over that?*

- *If I do this you might be mad at me.*

Approval vanities are all those ways the ego tries to feel okay by winning approval from others. The vanity concern is about our "being good enough." When we depend on approval from the outside, we compromise our power inside. There's nothing wrong with external approval. It feels good and can motivate us to continue on the track we're on. But if we crave external approval to validate who we are, we give our power away. We feel powerless if our approval craving isn't fed. If someone criticizes us, we let it prick our vanity and drain our emotional energy. While some constantly seek and need approval or recognition from others, some go the other direction, holding a self-righteous attitude about how they don't need approval from anyone. If you hear someone saying, "I'm my own person and I don't care what anyone thinks about me," recognize that as inverted insecurity and vanity. There's a balance between these extremes, a secure place of not needing but enjoying and sincerely appreciating others' approval.

Approval and love are not necessarily the same thing, although we can think they are. For example, in raising children, it takes heart skill to know the balance between encouraging children through approval and reinforcing their budding emotional vanity to the point they become addicted to approval. Children can suffer handicaps later in life because they were given too much or too little approval while growing up. When we constantly give them approval or rewards for every little thing, eventually the gifts have less meaning. That's what the word *spoiled* implies. Children get so used to getting, that they can't find peace within themselves when life doesn't go their way. They've learned to rely on outside approval for their sense of self-worth.

In reality, only the heart can ultimately give you the approval you need. The heart sends messages of approval throughout the body, through different glands, hormones, neurotransmitters, and other messenger molecules confirming your choices. But often, before they can do their work, those messages can become clouded by emotional vanity. Here's a picture:

> You feel slighted by a friend and stay upset for hours. You go to your heart for direction and get an intuitive understanding about what to do and a feeling of approval to go do it. But before you act, an emotional vanity fear that the friend won't approve and will slight you again, overrides what your heart has told you and reshapes the problem back to your previous viewpoint. Pretty soon you're ignoring what your heart had said.

The heart also gives us signals when we're going a different direction than our heart intelligence would want, but we have to know how to listen to the heart's signals. Sometimes they come as a stress feeling, an inner voice of conscience that says "no," or in other ways that we can learn to recognize as we decipher the language of our feeling world. All of these signals from our heart's intelligence are intended to align us with our core love, that which would be the highest good for ourselves and the whole, whether we understand it or not. As we learn to sense and follow the heart's intuitive direction, we come to trust how it plays out in life. Often we can't see the bigger picture until we go down the road. Through practice and experience, we mature in stages from insecurity-based questioning of our heart's signals to secure knowing. (Is that really my heart intuition? How can I be sure? What if I just made it up?)

Most approval vanities develop from overcare about ourselves. This is standard fare as we mature from insecurity to security. For example, overcare about self is a common thread running through preoccupations about performance—whether we did something right or not, whether we will get approval or not. Acting from performance over-identity, we may quietly bolster ourselves, glorify our talents, or feel more important than others. Or we put ourselves down in comparison to others and feel less worthy. Either way, overcare about self creates comparisons that cut us off from our heart's signals and the hearts of others. We end up thinking that our problems are so unique and different that no one else could possibly understand.

Underneath this belief we fear not being special (because if we're not special we're not loveable), and we fear being less than we hoped. This fear keeps us bottled up inside. It keeps background thoughts and feelings of wanting attention rising in our mind. It bleeds power from our real self and prevents us from living solidly in the heart. Overcare about self comes about because we are identified with the mind and all its insecurity antics; we have slipped out of true self-care. This can lead to all sorts of compensations to try to assuage our feelings of insecurity.

Sue's inner dialogue was a running tape of perform-ance approval concerns. "When I stopped to look at my background thoughts—the ones that always seem to be there—the themes went like this. Am I a good enough mother? Shouldn't I be doing more for my son? Am I a good enough lover to my husband? Will he find someone else more spontaneous and attractive than me? It went on and on and all I wanted to do was go to the fridge and eat whatever sweets I could find to ease the feeling and take care of myself."

Another potentially devastating approval vanity is wor-rying about whether we'll get enough recognition, whether we'll have our moment in the sun. This overcare usually leads to disappointment and suffering because we are pre-occupied with wanting it. Then any recognition is never enough.

Vanity defines success by how the outside world sees us. The heart defines success as an expression of our real self; then life becomes a reflection of an ever-deepening connection with our real self and with others. External recognition, if it comes, is an add-on, not something we depend on for a false sense of security or satisfaction.

Comparisons are probably the most common approval vanity trap. Judging ourselves in relation to others is a debilitating vanity that runs rampant through university faculties and most workplaces where people are vying for prestige and position. Thoughts akin to "Everyone else is dumb, but I'm so smart" are emotional vanity. So are thoughts of, "Everyone else is smart, but I'm so dumb." We feel we have less worth than others, so in our thoughts and feelings we put us down in comparison.

In many cases, people consciously involved in spiritual growth or personal development, get tricked by comparisons.

When they start searching deeper inside for self-improvement, they get knocked off the path by comparing themselves with someone else they think is doing better. Then self-pity sets in. Or their progress gets slowed by self-righteousness because they feel they have become better than others. Here's an example:

In the 1960s and 1970s, thousands started meditating or trying alternative healing or vegetarian diets to improve themselves. Yet a powerful ego vanity accompanied that movement. Many felt self-important about their new discoveries and inner work. If the phone rang or someone knocked on the door while they were meditating, they felt annoyed; their vanity went crazy at the interruption. And because it was righteous vanity, they didn't think twice about it. Many who decided to stop eating meat held self-righteous attitudes toward those who didn't. There were also vanity clashes between the New Agers who judged the fundamentalists and fundamentalists who judged the New Age. Vanity clashes are just as common today in the endless conflict between religious fundamentalists and moderates, and they thwart tolerance or understanding.

People and groups often resort to righteous vanity in order to protect their sense of identity and importance. Fred, commenting on this tendency in himself, describes how righteousness built up inside.

"I spent 20 years meditating, searching, fasting, exercising, breathing, stretching, and detoxifying myself into a pretty good place. I felt happy, energetic, and smart to what I needed in life—well on my way to enlightenment." But Fred now admits that he was stuck and didn't even know it. "Because I felt that I had accomplished my goals,

I didn't look deeper. Yet something was missing. I heard about spiritual vanity, so I decided to look deeper and see if the shoe fit. One thing I discovered was that I unconsciously judged people who ate greasy foods and were fat. I also saw that I was spacey, ungrounded, and too much in the clouds from all the meditation I did. Meditation is wonderful, but I needed to integrate my energies more in my day-to-day work."

Sincere self-approval for doing what your heart tells you or self-appreciation for accomplishing your goals or coming up with a creative idea is a healthy expression of self-worth. It's when your mind over-identifies with the good you've done, that self-importance vanity seeps in, causing a low-grade righteousness to flow through your psyche. It creates separation from others and from your deeper self. Then you can wonder why people aren't as approving of you as you'd like them to be.

Appreciating ourselves, but with a negative slant, is another inverted emotional vanity. It shows itself in thoughts like, "I'm trying, but poor me, I'm not there yet." Or, "Things seem to be a little harder for me than for others, but don't get me wrong, I appreciate the work I've done." Or, "I appreciate myself and all I have; however, I really don't deserve it." A lot of people seesaw up and down between vanity extremes of self-importance, pride, and false humility.

A healthy, balanced ego expression is what gives you a truer picture of yourself. A balanced ego expression would mean appreciating yourself not just when things are going well, but especially at those times when you slip backward. Appreciate yourself for whatever progress you've made, and then use that energy of appreciation to move forward. Recognize that to dwell in "poor me" attitudes or pitiful feelings is a convenient hiding place, but it's still a vanity.

Much of people's social upbringing has involved shame-based learning. The praise/scold process starts when we are babies and continues through schools and jobs. We internalize the process from an early age and learn to praise and scold our own feelings, thoughts, and behaviors. This shapes our values and self-worth. When praise/scold is based on the heart's intelligence, there is a balance in our values and appreciation for learning. When praise/scold is based on extremes (usually heavily weighed to the scold side), we tend to become judgmental in our pursuit of perfection and approval. This sets us up for ongoing guilt and shame. A friend wrote:

> *I have become more aware of how regret and guilt have prevented me from appreciating myself and my life's unfolding. For example, it's common for me to feel that I'm not growing fast enough, can't seem to get out of old patterns or honor my heart enough. I can see that behind this is a lot of perfectionism and insecurity. Going deeper in the heart, I've realized I could more deeply acknowledge how much I have learned about myself and about loving deeper. When these issues come up now, I try to go to a deeper compassion for myself and appreciate my unfolding.*

We come to appreciate everything as simply part of the process of learning and growing in life, as we peel off the layers of false beliefs. Studies show that aging gracefully and healthfully has a lot to do with how much we can appreciate or forgive whatever has happened in our lives.[1] We are not better or worse, good or bad, right or wrong for learning a harder way. We just come to realize that there are more effective ways to mature as we learn to listen to the heart.

COMMUNICATION VANITY

- *If I let him know he hurt me, he might see it as a weakness to take advantage of me.*

- *If I truly express my needs, I might be rejected.*

- *If I just talk over her I might get my point across and get what I want.*

The second major category is communication vanity. It often gets intertwined with approval or desire vanities.

Emotional vanity about communications with other people can eat away at us with anxiety or resentment. This can age us faster than most anything. Much of the time our resentments continue because of overcare about not having spoken from our heart to another person. We may have unloaded on them, which goes nowhere, or *wimped* out, fearful of their reaction. It's vanity that keeps us quiet because we just don't want somebody to get upset. It's also vanity when we chicken out of saying something we need to say, excusing ourselves by thinking, oh, I have that same fault, and so I shouldn't say a thing.

All the things people *don't* communicate in relationships make up the biggest obstacle to openhearted relating. Something happens between co-workers or friends that bothers one or both people. After talking awhile, one of them says, "I'm all right, are you all right?" They agree they're fine, and one or both go off and seethe.

People may not remember exactly what you did or what you said, but they remember how you made them feel. Heart vulnerability is the prescription for releasing communication vanity blocks. This means speaking and listening openly from the heart as sincerely as you can. Learn to practice being heart vulnerable in communications and face off your fears. It won't happen all at once, but put on a solid business heart and say what your heart tells you to say, without worrying about being walked all over.

So often people say, "I really want to be in the heart. But I've been walked on so many times, I just had to put up a shield." Authentic heart vulnerability is not an invitation to be used as a doormat. You are open and sincere from the heart, but you can draw the line if you need to and express firmness or "mean business" from the heart at the same time. It takes courage and practice, but it's well worth the effort to gain your empowerment.

Needing to be understood or worrying about how we came off during an interaction is another communication vanity trap. We can drain ourselves emotionally and physically by investing so much in wanting to be understood. We rehearse what to say, or replay and rehash what we wished we'd said, mentally churning, "All I meant was . . ." over and over. Very often the need to be understood masks a deeper need to "be right" or to control.

> Phyllis says, "In my relationship with my boyfriend, John, I kept feeling frustrated because it seemed like as soon as we started arguing a little bit, he no longer listened to me. Phyllis sighs, "I can't tell you how many arguments we spent late into the night with my repeating, 'What I'm trying to say is . . .' All to no avail. He never saw it my way. He never 'got' what I was trying to say. He'd just turn into this brick wall."

The pattern of their arguments wearied them both. The life was draining out of their relationship, and after months of these disagreements, Phyllis was feeling deeply hurt and misunderstood. Then she realized that an attitude she held was contributing to the trouble.

"I looked deeper at this need to be understood and saw that what I really wanted was to teach John something. I thought I was seeing 'how things really are,' and I was wanting John to agree with me."

A wise friend counseled Phyllis to let go of her need to teach John anything. In effect, he told her to go to neutral—to let John be John, and see if he saw things differently. This advice paid big dividends.

"From then on I began to notice that deep, insistent feeling that he get what I was trying to say. I noticed when I was getting terribly invested in having him hear me. So I began to back off, to stop myself in the moment, to let go of the need to be understood—which was really the need to teach him something. As soon as I stopped trying to get my point across, it seemed to free John to work out things for himself. He no longer put up that brick wall, we stopped fighting, and he went ahead and made some changes in himself that smoothed our relationship."

To free ourselves from the trap of needing to be understood, we have to go to neutral, find that deeper place inside where our own views, as well as those of others, can be right. When you notice, as Phyllis did, "that deep, insistent" need to be understood, don't let it take over. Hold to neutral and take the energy out of it. But do it with a light touch. When you make it fun, more often than not your heart intuition can come in and show you a truer picture of what is going on or what to do next.

"Needing to understand" can also be a vanity. If you hear yourself saying, "Well I don't mind adjusting to the situation as long as I can just understand," it may just be your control vanity, thinking it needs to have things make sense in a linear and logical way. On some things, we will never achieve a linear understanding. More often than not, when we "just want to understand" something, we are already feeling that something was not fair or not right and we're looking for reasons to justify that judgment. Neutral is the place that leaves the door open for the higher, intuitive logic of the heart to enter and give you new insight.

Ego vanity, by its very nature, will tend to resist neutral because it's trying to hold onto its identity. But if you keep going back to the heart you'll start to see the insecurities behind your need to understand. It takes commitment to keep releasing them to the heart and not buckle. You'll build heart power while opening a door for receiving new clarity, especially about what to do next. Often the heart's insight is to just let it go for now. Understanding will come later when you're not so attached to what the mind wants.

Sometimes we can have what feels like a hole in the heart after we've lost a relationship or an opportunity that we dearly valued, through death, divorce, or another significant life change. When we can't reverse what happened and feel like we hadn't completed our communication with the person, we can easily fall into an inverted vanity of regret, blame, and self-pity. Feeling pitiful is like a sinking boat. We can heal the heart by using the power of the heart to release the ego's grasp. Often we discover a more enlightened interpretation of the situation that we couldn't see before. We free ourselves from perceptions that were convincing but did not accurately reflect reality.

DESIRE VANITY

- *I'll choose this because I'm sure I can get it.*

- *I won't choose that because it might not happen.*

- *If I don't get what I want I can never be happy.*

This type of vanity can also get entwined with approval or communication vanity. Desire is wonderful. It's what motivates us and keeps us moving. But we'd like our desires to bring us reward and satisfaction, not pain and suffering. When we uncover the vanity motive behind certain desires, we can begin to direct our choices toward more fulfilling outcomes.

In a society obsessed with consumerism, millions are building their ego identities upon money and possessions, thinking these will bring prestige and happiness. They may bring temporary reward, but we will not find fulfillment in them. The problem is, we've always "got to have" more. This can lead to selfishness and the vanity of entitlement, feeling you should have or are owed more. Then when you are inconvenienced by circumstances or can't get what you want, your entitlement vanity triggers self-justified unfair, anger, and blame reactions.

You can never be happy if you're trying to live up to someone else's or society's ideal, or even your own projected ideal of what you should be or have. When you really want something badly, you can think, surely, this desire is from your heart, and not see the vanity motive mixed in. To balance your desires, you need to take the mental and emotional energy out of the "want" and release it to the heart. That allows your heart intuition to show you the deeper heart's want, which may not be the ego's desire. Then you can put your passion and commitment behind your true heart's want. Trying too hard or wanting something too much from the ego creates static so you can't *tune-in* to the deeper heart's want.

Another desire vanity trap is in wanting to "be somebody" or worrying that your talents are not being used. Its inversion is thinking you don't have any talents and therefore can never be anybody important. Frequently people who live together or work together feel jealous of one another's capabilities. These jealousies usually lurk in a secret stored feeling world, while everyone pretends to get along or work together for the good of the whole.

Increased heart intelligence will reveal to you that effectiveness at loving and living has nothing to do with talents. It's not ability or position that brings happiness, which is why people who are highly talented often have no more peace than people who aren't. Talents or the lack of them are not what decide quality of life. One of the most potent abilities that anyone can develop is the ability to be happy with *who* you are. Effectiveness at being yourself is what brings fulfillment. Then if someone else is more skilled at speaking, writing, or golf than you, you're secure and happy that they're talented in their own way.

There's nothing wrong with striving to reach your highest potential. Learning how to live in the heart, balancing and managing yourself from the heart, leads you to fulfilling your greatest potentials. It will open doors that you can't even see as long as you're living from your desire vanity. Fulfillment happens faster as you learn to love more effectively and be more fully in the now. Without intuitive heart guidance, mind ambition can lead you to make choices that either keep you stuck on an emotional treadmill or take you in unrewarding directions. Through living in the heart of each moment, and balancing and managing your emotions and mind to make choices in alignment with your heart, all things that add real quality to your life will find their way to you. Passion and commitment, focused from the heart, have real power to create satisfaction in your life. You start by committing yourself to waking up your heart. Then you follow your heart to direct the unfolding of your talents and skills.

Another common desire vanity is, "I can't get what I want—love, success, enlightenment—until I'm perfect." For some, perfect means being perfect in a role—the perfect daughter, father, wife, mother, husband, student, employee, or friend. For others, the need to be perfect can become an obsession about looks—the perfect body, hair, or clothes. When you are obsessed with being perfect, you strive for an ideal you can never reach. Desire vanity wants to manipulate the situation to get it all right and not make a mistake. This drains energy and rarely has rewarding outcomes.

> Sue worked out in the gym to have the perfect abs and thighs. She ate very little as she was afraid of gaining any weight. At the same time, she was high strung and irritable with friends and went through a string of unsatisfactory relationships with men. Yet she was trying to have the perfect body, feeling that would bring her the relationship she wanted.

In reality, there is no such thing as perfect. We are always doing things more or less effectively until we learn to do them better. We can't become our real self until we can be honest about what we judge as imperfect in ourselves. Self-admittance brings in common sense intelligence and heart power to improve and become, not perfect, but whole.

Many of us have vanity traps related to the desire to "be good" or "do good." Our good intentions and good works are motivated at first by care. But after a while, good intentions get mixed with ego vanity. Have you ever redone a project several times trying to make it perfect in the name of "doing good"? Out of over-identity you kept soldiering on with your effort, then ended up in overcare, overwhelm and energy drain. We call this "good getting in the way." This is not a criticism of *being good* or *doing good*. It's about understanding good from the intelligent heart.

Good getting in the way is what some of us get most upset about in ourselves. We try to *do good*, and then we feel unappreciated for our efforts or frustrated when our efforts are not working. We are doing the best we know. Good getting in the way typically causes a feeling of victimization or blame toward others. It can lead to the lament, "But I did all this for you."

Good getting in the way is a common problem in workplaces and organizational efforts dealing with good causes. A lot of us take on extra work at our jobs or "for a cause" when it's really time to do something else. Yet we strain to keep going because "we're good." Our heart keeps signaling us it's time to make a change, but our ego is so identified with the good we're doing that it overrides the courage to do what's best. This *do-gooding* vanity underlies a lot of overcare in families and workplaces.

For example, parents develop routines with their children that work well up to a certain age. When it comes time to change the routine for the well-being of the child, and the child doesn't want to change, many parents keep the routine going in the name of good.

A friend, Bob, was still cutting up his son's food into bite-sized pieces when the boy was nine years old and easily could do it himself. Bob admitted it was time to make a change but didn't because he wanted to be good to his son. He created an unhealthy dependency in his child as a result.

The solution is not to give up the desire to *do good*, but to consider how to turn good into effectiveness. Otherwise, *doing good* will be the storefront for a lot of stress. When children continue wanting things beyond the time when those things are good for them, it really can be hard for loving parents to turn them down. A combination of openness and business heart gives parents the power to say no, with love, to the emotional pull. We can learn to parent our own desires in the same way.

It may seem strange to look at hurt as an ego vanity. But in many situations where we get hurt, it's our desire vanity that is hurt—our desire for respect and confirmation of our worth. Ego hurt usually requires a long time to heal because it feels like our value or integrity was totally disrespected. It takes even longer when a sensitive emotional investment is involved. We've all heard someone say, "I gave my heart, and he hurt me." This implies that a sensitive emotional connection was hurt. When that occurs, it's often hard for those who hurt you to do anything to make it up. The hurt feels so deep and so justified that there's not much they can say or do to make it better.

It's up to you to do something yourself to heal the hurt: forgive, let go, or understand that it was the other person's lack of awareness that caused your hurt. Usually deep forgiveness is the easier way out because in most cases, when our sense of worth has been deeply hurt, the other's remorse doesn't give us the release we want. We have to go deeper inside to understand that it's never our real love that has been hurt or betrayed, but our desires and expectations. When we feel pain in our heart, it's the emotional stress generated by strong disappointment that hurts. Forgiveness is a deep core heart feeling that helps to release and heal the hurt so we can move on.

Desire vanity that places our fulfillment in the hands of someone else can be the most deluding and ego crushing of all vanities. When our ego gets crushed, we often feel that we were entitled to better, or our broken desires turn into guilt for having not done enough and we can feel that we deserved the hurt we got. Either way, when our vanity receives a nasty blow, we can end up locked in pitiful resignation. Regret and guilt can open the heart so we become open to change, but if we let guilt consume us, it traps us into feeling hopeless. Too much regret and guilt is inverted vanity that gets justified in the name of shame and self-blame. Many believe that guilt will cause us to rethink our behavior so as not to repeat it again. But it depends on whether we take our emotional fragility to a deeper heart opening and find new insight.

Too often, regret and guilt create a hiding place where we don't have to care anymore. We linger in "would've, could've, should've" mind tapes. That keeps us locked in self-blame and drains the energy we need to create a better future. We can't change the past, yet guilt can tie us down with strings, often causing us to repeat the very behaviors we need to free ourselves from blocking us from seeing new opportunities. The emotional vanity of resignation and ongoing guilt cuts off the heart, and no new ray of sunshine can get through. Freeing our energy from this prison of guilt requires connecting with a deeper heart's desire to perceive new options and make heart choices.

CUTTING THROUGH OUR EMOTIONAL VANITIES

Recognizing vanity behind our motives, feelings, or thoughts doesn't come easily. Uncovering ego vanity to get to our root insecurities usually means uncoiling layers of emotionally invested over-identities and beliefs. The answer lies in going from *muddling* through to *cutting* through. This process can feel threatening to our self-image and *modus operandi*. What we see can seem ugly and awful to us at first. We may have developed a quick-reacting defensiveness so as not to have to look or to protect our ego sensitivity. All of us have something that pushes our buttons. It's only human. As we embrace our humanness with love and compassion, and release our vanity resistances, the beauty of our real self emerges behind the facade of defensiveness.

Ego identities peel off in layers as we replace emotional vanities with new security. The ego can feel threatened by even the thought of this. We can wonder who we will be without the comfort zone of all the shells we've built around our self through the years. It takes the power of love to cut through the layers. That's what love is designed to do—to make us whole. Through love and love alone, a new identity with our real self emerges. Your real self feels like, well, your real self—like who you really are and want to be. The more vanity we unmask, the more real self can come forth. We balance the expression of our emerging real self by managing our mind and emotions with the heart. We release the layers of false self as we release overcare, over-identity, and over-attachment. Our spirit and humanness merge into an enlightened personality that uses the balanced ego, free from vanity insecurities, to fulfill our real heart's desires.

Remembering that our standard trigger reactions are forged from over-identities, we can be on the lookout for them. When you notice an emotional vanity flare up, take that energy back to the solvent of the heart. Keep filtering resistance and emotional defensiveness through the heart, and it will ease out. Have compassion for yourself. The heart will guide you and reassure you that everything really is all right. Releasing vanity is not about trying to be perfect. Remember that perfection is just another vanity trap. Realize that everyone has emotional vanities. Learn to measure your progress in ratios, like three steps forward and two back, then try to improve your ratio. That way you build in latitude, and you can make the process of identifying vanities more fun. As you free yourself from vanity, you will feel your spirit come rushing in to free your cares.

Whenever we experience breakthroughs on issues related to emotional vanity, we have to walk steadily in the new realization for a while so we don't backtrack. Walk as if there is a book on your head. Most ego patterns have been so ingrained that you can't simply check them off after the first breakthrough and a couple days of feeling great. Each new insight is a gift to pay attention to, or else it can fade. This requires walking steadily in the light of the new. Do it from a sincere heart, with heart poise, not out of fear that you'll regress.

Toward the end of his life, Albert Einstein eloquently expressed his seasoned understanding of ego: "A human being is a part of the whole, called by us the 'universe,' a part limited in time and space. He experiences himself, his thoughts and feelings as something separated from the rest—a kind of optical delusion of his consciousness. This delusion is a kind of prison for us, restricting us to our personal desires and to affection for a few persons nearest to us. Our task must be to free ourselves from this prison by widening our circle of compassion to embrace all living creatures and the whole of nature in its beauty. Nobody is able to achieve this completely, but the striving for such achievement is in itself a part of the liberation and a foundation for inner security."[2]

Our true identity or *core self* is love. Our higher potential finds us when we set our course in that direction. The power of love, appreciation, and compassion are what transform insecurity and vanity. Surrendering to our heart's love releases us, step by step, from false identities and beliefs so that we uncover our real self, free of the shells of old, limiting patterns—free to passionately love and live without fear.

PERSONAL EVALUATION

- Take a moment to think about the emotional vanities and examples that you recognized in yourself, or write them on a piece of paper or in a journal so you can see them clearly. You might find that some are intertwined. Identifying and admitting them to yourself is the first step to freeing yourself from them.

- When have you experienced inverted emotional vanity? How much did it drain your energy?

- What social vanities have you taken on from society, friends, or your upbringing?

Chapter 4

THE HEART OF THE MATTER

When man is serene,
the pulse of the heart flows and connects,
just as pearls are joined together
or like a string of red jade,
then one can talk about a healthy heart.

— THE YELLOW EMPEROR'S CANON OF INTERNAL MEDICINE,
2500 B.C.E.

The expression "cut through" means "get to the heart of the matter." If you're working on a project, and the details, opinions, and options are multiplying in the face of an impending deadline, someone is likely to suggest that you had better cut through and make a decision. The implication is that the project has lost focus and needs a solution now, one that is efficient and intelligent.

The same is true in human psychology. We simply don't have time to go through all the mental complexities and details of our past to decipher an efficient and intelligent solution to an emotional stress or problem. We need to cut through. For ease and flow, Doc has shortened it to "Cut-Thru."

According to ancient Greek texts, Gordius, king of Phrygia, tied a knot so entwined that no one could see the beginning or end of it. An ancient prophecy foretold that anyone who succeeded in untying the knot would become ruler of all of Asia. Alexander the Great was struggling to figure out the intricacies of how the knot was formed, when in a flash of insight, he realized, "It makes no difference how it's untied!" and *cut thru* the knot with his sword. In keeping with the prophecy, Alexander the Great went on to become the ruler of Asia.

The Cut-Thru Technique shows people how to *cut thru* the Gordian knot of their overcares, over-identities, over-attachments—their emotional stress—and become the ruler of their own self. If you already are emotionally managed, secure, and energetic, Cut-Thru can take you to new levels of emotional empowerment and increase your healing and creative capacities. Bringing your emotions into balance and alignment with your real heart and spirit generates a shift in personal effectiveness. This is preventive maintenance at the emotional level—preventing overcare, overreactivity, unnecessary dips in energy, loss of time, and having to recoup.

You may be working out or dieting and taking care of your body, but physical self-care is only half of the picture. We need emotional self-care, too, yet many of us don't know where to start. We're taught in school to manage emotional outbursts, but lacking effective ways of caring for our inner stress, we spend our emotional energy carelessly. Once emotional energy drains away, nervous energy takes over. We lose access to enriching feelings, as we run on adrenaline and half a tank of nervous energy. Learning to use our intelligence to stop emotional energy drains can restore emotional buoyancy and vitality to our feeling world. Emotional self-care means not having to repeat the same old stresses again and again.

Some people feel guilty caring for themselves, confusing it with selfishness. How many times have you heard people say, "Well, I don't care about myself, I just care about my family (job, friends, church, social cause)?" Caring for others is important, but it can't be as effective when it's at the expense of your own emotional balance. Emotional self-care is like putting money in the bank. If your account is full, you have more to share with others. If it's empty, there's less to go around, so you can't respond to other people's needs adequately.

Emotional self-care requires having the power to Cut-Thru stressful feelings *on demand.* When you feel distress while standing in line, dealing with work pressures, or handling family problems, you can't always go jogging or escape to meditate. But you can use the Cut-Thru Technique.

When emotions are repressed, they don't just go away. They get stuffed back inside, waiting to be unleashed. To manage your emotions is not to drug or suppress them, but to know how to deftly direct your emotional energy and intentions for productive outcomes. There is no question that wonder drugs have helped many to better cope with life, but rarely do they cure the underlying causes of emotional stress. Drugs can be like disarming a fire alarm without addressing the fire.

Today, we have a world where our very survival can be threatened by the lack of emotional stability of a few. No magic pill will fix that. It's time for human beings to mature into emotionally managed citizens. Yet, emotional management can seem unappealing to those who want to be free to do what they wish regardless of who it affects, including one's self. So what will motivate people to want to manage their emotions?

Breakthrough research at the Institute of HeartMath and other institutions is providing new hope. It is bringing to light powerful, yet simple techniques we can use to quickly improve how we feel, think, and perceive life. Techniques that increase heart intelligence and clarity, help us self-regulate our brain chemicals and hormones, give us natural highs, the real fountain of youth we've been searching for, and enable us to drink from elixirs locked within our cells, just waiting for us to discover them. With just a little education and practice, you can move into a new experience of life so rewarding that you will be motivated to keep on managing your emotional nature in order to sustain the good feelings. The payoff is delicious in terms of improved quality of life.

Emotional management imparts the ability to know one's own feelings and to recognize feelings in others, to have a positive outlook on life, and to exhibit good interpersonal relationship skills. To use the Cut-Thru Technique for emotional management, it's helpful to know a little bit about the science behind it.

Scientists used to believe that rational thinking alone could direct feelings in ways that are beneficial for oneself and for the whole. This has not proven true. Despite attempts at rational control, individuals remain in chaos from out of control emotions. Scientists also used to think that emotions are produced only in the brain. However, sophisticated instruments now show that emotions are the product of dialogue between the body and the brain. Here's an example of how it works. Hormones are chemical messengers that regulate most of the body's functions, profoundly impact our emotions, and affect the way our brain processes information. Hormones are found in the brain, heart, and throughout the body. The repeated triggering of stressful emotions often leads to a chronic elevation of the stress hormone, cortisol, along with a reduction in DHEA (dehydroepiandrosterone), the vitality or anti-aging hormone. The cortisol/DHEA ratio is often used as a biological marker of stress and aging.

Cortisol levels rise when we feel stress, especially emotional stress such as irritation, anger, anxiety, and guilt. Cortisol levels go down when we feel positive emotions such as love, joy, compassion, and kindness. While cortisol is essential for metabolism, too much cortisol impairs immune function, triggers excessive fat build-up especially around the waist and hips, decreases bone and muscle mass, impairs memory and learning, and destroys brain cells.[1, 2] This is especially true when accompanied by low levels of DHEA.

DHEA is the most prolific hormone in the human body and the precursor of other hormones, including testosterone and estrogen. Scientists have linked reduced levels of DHEA with a multitude of disorders, including exhaustion, depression, immune disorders, fertility, and menstrual problems, Alzheimer's, heart disease, obesity, and diabetes. Higher levels of DHEA can produce increased feelings of general well-being and enhanced vitality.[3]

Research at the Institute of HeartMath has shown that managing our emotions with heart intelligence activates positive feelings and attitudes and healthier hormonal responses. In one study, participants using the Cut-Thru Technique reduced their cortisol levels by an average of 23 percent and increased their DHEA levels by over 100 percent in just 30 days of practice.[4]

Researchers are also finding that emotional stress is one of the strongest risk factors for heart disease and sudden cardiac arrest, as much or more so than smoking or sedentary life style.[5, 6] Negative stressful emotions, like fear or sadness, aren't wrong. We need them to warn us of impending danger or when something needs our attention. It's when we let them become a habit that they become negative, producing many emotional and biochemical problems, such as anxiety disorders, aggression and violence, depression, eating disorders, heart problems, and many other stress related physical disorders.

We can easily tell the difference between positive and negative emotions in our body. Anxiety and judgment can tighten our necks and shoulders; fear can be a churning in the stomach. By contrast, love, appreciation, compassion, and kindness relax us, allowing our body's communication systems to flow with greater harmony and efficiency.

Bill describes how the difference feels to him, "I easily fall into impatience and get over demanding with my eight-year-old daughter. My body becomes rigid; my breath is shallow; my muscles tighten." Bill learned, through using Cut-Thru, that he has a choice about which emotional road to go down. "I can stay impatient, or I can immediately go to my heart for greater calmness. The question for me then becomes one of choice; as to what kind of a person I want to be. Would I rather be righteous and rigid, or would I rather be happy, centered, grounded, and joyful?"

A new field of research called "positive psychology" is finding that positive emotions are far more important to mental health and physical well-being than scientists had ever realized.[7] University of Michigan researcher Barbara Fredrickson says, "Positive emotions can have effects beyond making people 'feel good' or improving their subjective experiences of life. They also have the potential to broaden people's habitual modes of thinking and build their physical, intellectual, and social resources. In addition, these resources last longer than the transient positive emotional states that led to their acquisition and can be drawn upon in future moments, when people are in different emotional states, to help them overcome current stresses faster and make them more resilient to future adversities."[8]

According to researchers, when you're experiencing a negative emotion, the thoughts available to your mind are limited, yielding fixated and more predictable thinking and action. When you're experiencing a positive emotion, a broader thought-action potential is called forth. Positive emotions produce patterns of thought that are notably unusual, flexible and inclusive, creative, and receptive, and lead to more creative action. [9, 10]

Positive emotions also have an "undoing effect" on negative emotions. They loosen the hold that negative emotions gain on your brain and body. Positive and negative emotions are fundamentally incompatible because you can't be thinking in a redundant mode simultaneously. This incompatibility accounts for why positive emotions seem to serve as effective antidotes for the lingering effects of negative emotions. [9] A purpose of the Cut-Thru Technique and other HeartMath tools is to help you cultivate more positive emotional experiences and more creative thinking. Cut-Thru teaches you how to shift out of a negative emotional state into a positive one (psychologically and physiologically) right in the midst of stress in order to gain a more intelligent perspective.

Fredrickson concludes, ". . . Through experiences of positive emotions people transform themselves, becoming more creative, knowledgeable, resilient, socially integrated, and healthy individuals. . . . Intervention strategies that cultivate positive emotions are particularly suited for preventing and treating problems rooted in negative emotions, such as anxiety, depression, aggression, and stress-related health problems." [9]

HeartMath research on the relationship between the physical heart and emotional states, and the science behind HeartMath Techniques and tools, is explained in depth in several of our other books. [11–13]

THE ROLE OF THE HEART
IN CUTTING-THRU EMOTIONAL CHAOS

The 1980s saw the birth of a new scientific discipline called neurocardiology, which combines the study of the nervous system and brain with the study of the heart. Cutting edge research in this new field revealed that the heart is an *information processing system.*

Beyond pumping blood and nutrients to every part of the body, the heart has its own nervous system, a "brain in the heart" containing around 40,000 neurons. This brain in your heart can sense, feel, learn, and remember. The heart-brain senses hormonal, heart rate, and blood pressure information; translates them into neurological impulses; and processes this information internally. With every beat of your heart, it relays complex bursts of neural activity to the brain in your head through nerves in the spinal column and the vagus nerve.[14]

These neural messages from the heart affect your cortex, that part of your brain that governs higher thought and reasoning capacities.[15] In addition, the heart's input to the brain affects neural activity in the amygdala, an important emotional memory center.[16] Any change in the rhythmic beating patterns of your heart alters the pattern of neural messages that your brain receives and affects the way your brain processes information. This is important in how the Cut-Thru Technique works. Depending on the nature of your heart's input, it either inhibits or facilitates your cognitive processes.[17]

The heart's neurons also have the ability to sense and feel like any other sensory neurons found in our skin, eyes, or mouth. That's why sensations can be felt in the area around the heart. Learning to use the Cut-Thru Technique trains you in how to tune into this area of the heart and change the information being sent from your heart to your brain and the rest of your body.

In 1983, the heart was reclassified as part of the hormonal system because a new hormone, produced and secreted by the heart was discovered.[18] Nicknamed the "balance hormone," atrial natriuretic peptide carries information throughout the body and has receptors in the brain where it helps to regulate stress. Since then, a number of other hormones have been found that are produced in the heart, including, in large quantities, oxytocin (called the "love hormone" because it is secreted more during satisfying sex, in social bonding and by mothers at childbirth).[19]

The heart is also the most powerful rhythmic electromagnetic generator in the body. Each heartbeat produces 40 to 60 times more electrical amp than the brain and broadcasts an electrical signal that permeates every cell in the body. The strength of the heart's magnetic field is 5,000 times greater than the field generated by the brain and can be measured several feet away from the body in all directions.

Your brain, respiratory, digestive, and autonomic nervous systems also generate rhythms. In scientific terminology, when the rhythms of two or more systems synchronize and lock-in to the same frequency, it's called *entrainment*. Systems that *entrain* operate with increased harmony and efficiency. You can see examples of entrainment when flocks of birds or schools of fish move together in synchronized harmony. It's an example of Newton's law of conservation of energy. Another example is a room with several pendulum clocks, each ticking to its own rhythm. After some time has passed, all the pendulums will swing in concert provided they are the same length. The pendulum that weighs the most is the dominant one and the other pendulums all entrain to it.

In the physical body, the "dominant pendulum" is the heart. One's respiratory and digestive systems and higher cortical functions dance to the beat of the heart's rhythmic pattern. When your heart's rhythms are harmonious, they create an ordered, coherent pattern and your whole body comes into increased harmony and coherence. When you experience emotional stress, the heart's rhythms become disordered and chaotic, and your whole body falls into stress. [20]

Scientific studies show that positive emotions long associated with the heart, like love, care, and appreciation, quickly bring heart rhythms into coherence.[20, 21] Coherent heart rhythms also bring your feelings and thoughts into coherence. This gives you access to heart intelligence, the organizational aspect of love streaming into the individual consciousness and physical system. Heart intelligence underlies nature's process of cellular organization, guiding and evolving an organism towards increased order, awareness and systemic coherence. Heart intelligence manifests as a flow of intuitive awareness and insight that you can experience once your mind and emotions are synchronized through self-initiated effort. It's the balance and coherence of your entire system that results in increased mental, emotional, and physical health and extra energy.

The more loving and relaxed your emotions, the more coherent your heart rhythm patterns will be, while heart rhythms that are stressed create irregular and incoherent heart rhythm patterns. Research shows that positive changes in brain function occur when we are in a state of heart coherence. One study using the Cut-Thru Technique found that when heart rhythms were most coherent, cognitive performance was significantly improved. There was a significant change in the frontal lobe activity that was related to increased heart rhythm coherence and the heart's input to the brain.[17]

EMOTIONS AND HEART RHYTHM PATTERNS

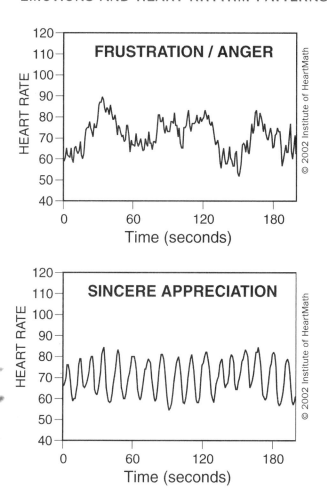

These graphs compare heart rhythm patterns typically produced during the experience of negative versus positive emotions. Negative emotions, such as anger and frustration, produce a jagged, disordered (incoherent) heart rhythm pattern, which reflects disharmony in the nervous system and body. In contrast, sincere positive emotions, such as appreciation and love, lead to a smooth, harmonious, ordered (coherent) heart rhythm pattern, reflecting harmony, synchronization, and efficiency in the functioning of the body's systems.

As society transitions through uncertainty and change, it's going to become more essential to bring the heart and brain together into decision-making processes.

It's through heart intelligence that we harmoniously integrate all other aspects of intelligence. We anticipate that research will eventually prove that the physical heart is the central distribution station for one's true spirit and the intuitive regulation of one's mental, emotional, and physical systems. And, that managing our emotions allows us to access and follow our heart perceptions and intelligence with consistency.

To access this heart intelligence, we need to become conscious of the signals and information encoded in feelings and emotions. Now, here's a physiological key to the whole process: understanding the feelings we experience often determine whether our heart rhythms—and therefore our whole body—will be harmonious and balanced or dissonant and chaotic.

In other words, love and related positive emotional states, measured by heart rhythm coherence, are beneficial for mind, emotions, and body. Sustaining positive emotions during daily living activities, programs our heart rhythms into more efficient coherent patterns, and this brings more intuitive perception, mental clarity, and better health to the whole body.

Feelings of love, care, compassion, or appreciation are *core heart feelings* or "higher heart feelings" because they come from the core values of your heart. They are uplifting and feel good to the entire body. Activating the memory of a higher heart feeling can give you a powerful reference point of coherence from which you can build your heart power to shift perception and cut through areas of stress and incoherence in your life. When you consciously evoke core heart feelings, you get in sync and nourish yourself at every level—mental, emotional, and cellular.

There is also a brain in the gut that responds to certain emotions. Dr. Michael Gershon, professor of anatomy and cell biology at Columbia-Presbyterian Medical Center in New York says, "When the central brain encounters a frightening situation, it releases stress hormones that prepare the body to fight or flee. The stomach contains many sensory nerves that are stimulated by this chemical surge—hence the butterflies."[22] That's why we feel nervous or get a knot in our stomachs when we're anxious or upset.

Many people confuse gut feelings with intuition, but in fact the gut brain is more instinctual than intuitive. When our central brain perceives fear and signals the gut, we can experience a gut feeling that warns us of danger. If we become used to this gut stress response, we can have chronic abdominal upsets and anxieties even when there's nothing to fear. The gut brain and heart brain affect each other, as do all bodily systems, but it's the heart that provides us with more sensitive intuition that brings understanding. To increase coherence within our body's systems, we can learn to bring our heart, gut, and head brains into sync with one another, and this is the purpose of the Cut-Thru Technique.

For decades it was thought all information from the senses went first to the neocortex, where it was understood, and only then to the amygdala, where an emotional response was added. But it doesn't always work that way. New research shows that the amygdala can initiate an emotional response even before our brain has a chance to consider the situation. That's why we so often feel and act before we think.[23]

For instance, we might try to avoid anything having to do with math, even a math puzzle in a magazine, without consciously understanding why. The clue we need is the memory of being criticized or told that we were stupid when we learned arithmetic as a child. If a dog snarled at us when we were two years old and it caused a strong feeling of fear, the amygdala will send out danger messages when we encounter a dog later in life. Outdated emotional reactions can take command in our relationships. If we opened our heart to someone in the past, and after an initial period of warmth and intimacy, we ended up feeling hurt and rejected, our automatic response to initial feelings of intimacy now might be to fear and close off our heart.

To further complicate matters, the neural connections going from the emotional centers in our brain to the cognitive or thinking centers are stronger and more plentiful than the wiring going the other direction.[23] That's why we often get confused by our emotions or tempted to believe that we have no control over our emotional reactions. While this can sound like the cards are stacked against us, that's not the case. The truly hopeful news is that brain circuits are flexible and continue to be shaped by experiences throughout life. It's never too late to learn or to change. However, since emotional processes can work faster than the mind, it takes a power stronger than the mind to bend perception, override negative emotional circuitry, and provide us with intuitive feeling instead. It takes the power of the heart.

As our heartbeat changes, so does the electrical activity in the cells of the amygdala. In fact, the cells in the amygdala have been shown to synchronize to the heartbeat.[16] Thus, familiar emotional patterns, like fear or anxiety, can be Cut-Thru and reprogrammed by utilizing the power of our heart. Our theory is that cognitive therapies or emotional healing techniques work best when they disrupt the electrical patterns stored in the brain and introduce coherent rhythmic patterns from the heart. That's when people connect with their heart and experience emotional release or "ah-ha" insights.

In our experience, the heart is our principle point of connection with our real spirit. There is biological evidence to support this. In the fetus, the heart is the first organ to develop, even before the brain stem. The heart starts beating on its own without any known physical stimulus. The source of the heartbeat is within the heart itself and is not controlled by the brain or any other organ in the body. From our research, we see that coherence appears in the heart's rhythmic beating patterns before we see it appear in the brain or other systems of the body. Intuitive feelings and perceptions arise once heart rhythms are in coherence. Throughout the ages, in all the major world religions, the qualities of spirit are said to include love, compassion, care, appreciation, and kindness. It's no coincidence that these feeling qualities generate coherent heart rhythm patterns. From this evidence, we look at heart coherence as a state where more spirit can come into and merge with humanness.

Fortunately, we don't have to wait for science to develop the instruments to prove the existence of spirit before we start to connect with the organizing intelligence in our heart. The more we experience the state of heart coherence, the more easily our brain's neural circuits may be retrained to healthier levels of functioning. When our body experiences a particular emotional state repeatedly, the neural circuits for that state become reinforced and become traits. Positive emotional memories are also reinforced by the amygdala.

Through practicing the Cut-Thru Technique, you can allow the positive, health-promoting, coherent power of love to build new memory patterns that will nourish and sustain you to the end of your life.

The Cut-Thru Technique and other HeartMath power tools given in the next few chapters aren't the only way to increase heart coherence to transform emotional stress. But they are a way that works. They will show you how to harness the power of your heart to create balance and coherence.

With practice, you will be able to shift from incoherence into coherence at will. Tests also show that people who have regularly practiced HeartMath tools for a while exhibit spontaneous periods of coherence in their heart rhythm patterns throughout a day, even without any intentional focus to generate that state. They find themselves moving in a state of intuitive flow more consistently. That's what the tools are for. With a little practice, you'll be able to manage your emotions and perceptions with heart and regenerate yourself throughout your day-to-day activities.

The power of coherence cannot be underestimated. For example, the light from a laser beam is far more coherent and powerful than light from an ordinary light bulb because the photons are all in alignment. Stanford University professor emeritus Dr. William Tiller points out, "The shift from incoherence to coherence can bring such dramatic effects that if the light waves from a 60-watt light bulb could be made as coherent as a laser, it would become equivalent to a million or more watt bulb with an energy density 1,000 to 1,000,000 times the surface of the sun." Dr. Tiller goes on to say, "By the same principle, heart rhythms that are coherent can more powerfully impact mind and body than heart rhythms that are incoherent and chaotic. This understanding that we can harness the power of the heart brings great hope to humanity."

Harnessing the power of the heart will bring security to the world in which we spend all of our waking hours—the world of our feelings and thoughts. This is where we ultimately create our happiness or misery, individually and collectively. When we learn how to discern with the heart and begin to take responsibility for our feelings, our lives can return to balance.

Through practicing the Cut-Thru Technique, you will be able to shift control to the heart and become the architect of new hope and power within yourself. You'll live your core values rather than just wish you did. The process will become increasingly automatic as you practice, so that without consciously using a tool you can stay centered in a flow of heart intelligence throughout the day and night. Practice will then become a process of fine-tuning yourself. Life will still be life, but you'll have the flexibility and know-how to go back to the heart when a stressor gets to you. And, you'll have the power to Cut-Thru.

As you use the Cut-Thru Technique, you will unravel many unsolved mysteries about your past. You'll discover that some emotional attitudes can be shifted very quickly, while others laden with history will take more time. The poet Rainer Maria Rilke once said, "Be patient toward all that is unsolved in your heart. And try to love the questions themselves." Developing your heart intelligence provides solutions to the "why" questions. By repeating the Cut-Thru steps, you can stop going around the same old circuits, and your physiology will respond accordingly.

Chapter 5

THE CUT-THRU TECHNIQUE

*The part can never be well
unless the whole is well.*

— PLATO

Since the Cut-Thru Technique deals with a complex process—transforming incoherence into coherence—the wording of each step has been very carefully chosen to help you achieve the emotional shifts needed. Notice that some words are italicized for emphasis. These are key words for each step.

Read the explanations of the steps and observe how they are used in Tracy's examples. Contemplate the attitude and emotional shifts intended with them. The easiest way to learn the Cut-Thru steps is to practice on an issue as you read through the steps. Try not to pick your biggest or most emotionally charged issue first. Pick a minor issue to start.

After a few practices, you'll see how the six steps flow together naturally to help connect you with your heart intelligence. Once you find the flow, the steps will seem simpler and be easy to memorize so you can use them any-where, anytime. Soon you'll be able to use just the key words as memory triggers, or create your own simple buzzwords for each step.

THE STEPS OF CUT-THRU
AND HOW TO USE THEM

STEP 1:
Be aware of how you feel
about the issue at hand.

When any issue comes up, learn to observe your feelings about it more closely, and honestly acknowledge what they are. This is the first step in emotional awareness. Many times, how we feel is clear. We acknowledge that we feel angry, anxious, or overwhelmed. Or we say that we feel fine or happy. Yet often we have undercurrents of feeling that we aren't conscious of unless we stop and check in with our heart more deeply.

Tracy, a customer service manager, describes her experience with *Step 1*.

> Right now I have to give one of my employees an evaluation. I usually enjoy this process. However, when the evaluation I have to give is "performance improvement needed," I want to find a hole to crawl into. I begin to feel really anxious. This is how I'd been feeling. For days I'd been conjuring up all types of pictures of how it might go. Maybe I should have been a movie producer instead! So I decided to use Cut-Thru. Using Step 1, I easily recognized the feeling of anxiety and worry; no Sherlock Holmes needed on this one!

Like Tracy, you may easily recognize how you are feeling about your issue. But if you're like most people, on some issues you've probably "numbed out" your feeling signals. We're busy people, and we don't want to become self-absorbed. The problem is that while we're trying to ignore disturbing emotions or pretend they're not there, our subconscious thought and feeling currents stay absorbed in them. We shove aside their signals, but we're still draining away our energy.

Your body still monitors and responds to your feeling world as its truth, even if your mind isn't paying attention or doesn't like what you are feeling. It's like you're operating on a split screen; your intellect is saying one thing, and your underlying feelings another. This is why "positive thinking" doesn't often work. Learning how to track your deeper feelings will bring a fuller picture to your mental screen and give you more energy to navigate life day-to-day.

Your brain is always monitoring your feeling world (like a barometer monitors the weather), then signaling your neurochemistry to respond.[1] Feeling blocked, numb or nothing at all are still feeling states; they create their own signature in your neural circuits and hormonal patterns just as stronger emotions like anger or love do. So, *Step 1* is to become more aware of your feelings so that you can gain more information.

Most of us notice how thoughts are constantly flitting through our minds. But we may not be aware that feelings, too, are skimming along inside. We have more trouble noticing this because shifts in feeling often occur faster than thought and faster than our mind's ability to intercept or explain them. We can feel helpless, since we know that thinking, by itself, isn't powerful enough to change our feeling state. This is why we often choose simply to shove feelings aside. In *Step 1*, we learn to sense what we are feeling even at a subconscious level, so that we can engage the power of our heart to bring more coherence into the feeling world.

Until we develop the power to shift our feeling state, even the idea of acknowledging feelings can make us feel vulnerable. But we can't choose or direct our emotions until we become open to what we are feeling and how our body is responding. By admitting, then naming a stress feeling—whether it's tension, resistance, anger, hurt, anxiety, numbness, or even a vague emotional disturbance you can't put your finger on—you slow down the emotional energy running through your system. Labeling your feelings in this way helps you regulate the energy in the feeling. Here's an example of what frequently happens when we don't admit and regulate our feelings.

> You call your wife from work and have an angry reaction to something she said. You go back to a meeting with your project team, but the disturbed feeling lingers. You can't focus and can hardly hear what's being said. You keep up with the meeting agenda, yet, inside, your thoughts keep surging back over the things that bother you about her. You try to fight them and quell the disturbance so you can be present for the meeting but these angry feelings are dominating your internal world. Soon you feel dull and drained inside. That one conversation created an emotional imbalance that you dragged around the rest of the day. When you get home that night, your wife is happy to see you, as if nothing had happened. Not wanting to cause an argument, you plop down in front of the TV to try to forget the whole thing. You go to bed exhausted, still bothered inside but unable to talk or even think about what is troubling you.

Your day could have gone completely differently if you had taken just five minutes to go through the Cut-Thru steps right after you'd gotten off the phone. You might have gone to your desk and sat quietly alone, or you might have gone through the steps while you were in the meeting. Admitting what you were feeling and moving through the steps to shift your mood would have allowed you to capture your emotional energy to work for you instead of draining your entire day.

Whether we're dealing with big issues or small ones, we can find ourselves turning things over mentally or emotionally. This is called "processing." Plenty of worry or blame can be sprinkled in the mix, and the processing may be so subtle that it runs unnoticed in the background of our thoughts and feelings. Yet the drain of energy goes on and on. This can cause sleep disorders, hormonal imbalances, disease, and premature aging.

When a problematic issue comes up, about the past, present, or future, learn to be aware of your feelings. Use *Step 1* to admit and name the feeling, and you will start to slow the energy drain and clear your internal screen on the spot. Then you can use *Steps 2–6* to harness and direct your emotional power where it will be most productive.

STEP 2:

Focus in the heart and solar plexus:
Breathe love and appreciation through
this area for 30 seconds or more
to help anchor your attention there.

Step 2 begins to bring the solar plexus into sync with the heart. Feeling love and appreciation as you breathe helps create the heart rhythm coherence needed to shift your feelings toward a calmer state. When you feel stress or negative emotions, your brain detects a "mismatch"; something doesn't feel right.[1] *Step 2* helps you make an adjustment by shifting your feelings to create a "match," resulting in more peace and often new perceptions about the issue.

Breathing in through the area of the heart and out through the solar plexus (located about four inches below the heart, just below the sternum) helps keep your emotional energies grounded. Remember that the solar plexus also has its own little gut brain with neurons, neurotransmitters and oscillating rhythms. Strong instincts affect this brain, giving us *gut feelings* that tell us to take or avoid action. We often feel sensations of anxiety or fear in the solar plexus area. At times this sensation can be a helpful warning signal, but frequently it's an instinctual stop-go reaction that's not based in current reality.

Since the heart is the strongest rhythmic oscillator in the body, it can pull the body's other rhythms into entrainment with its own. *Step 2* is designed to create this harmonizing effect. By focusing on your heart and solar plexus as you breathe love and appreciation, you synchronize the brain in the gut with the brain in the heart. The heart will automatically harmonize the energy between them, increasing internal coherence and clarity.

Simply focus in the area of your heart and solar plexus while breathing in a feeling of love and appreciation through that area of your body for 30 seconds or longer. Imagine love and appreciation flowing in and out with your breath, right through your chest, downward to your stomach. Don't stress about whether you are doing it right. Just practice this gently and sincerely. After 30 seconds, you may find your feelings shifting toward a more pleasant state. Strong emotional reactions will need longer. Don't hesitate to practice *Step 2* for as long as you'd like.

Here's what happened when Tracy practiced *Step 2* on her issue:

> *Breathing love and appreciation for myself and my employee, through the heart and solar plexus, immediately calmed me and created more of a solid feeling inside.*

Martial artists and professional singers learn to breathe through the solar plexus to anchor physical and emotional power. Anchoring in the heart and solar plexus together adds heart power while anchoring emotional energy. When we put more heart into what we do, it brings in coherence to powerfully clear our mental and emotional screen of static and uncertainty. That's why we tell people to sing or play with all their heart.

Practicing *Step 2* will help you get back in sync with yourself. If you can't feel any love or appreciation, just breathe the *attitude* of love or appreciation for something in your life to get back in sync. It's worth the time. You will set up a new reference feeling of synchronization that gets easier to get back to at any time throughout your day.

STEP 3:
Assume objectivity
about the feeling or issue,
as if it were someone else's problem.

When we become ensnared in a feeling, whether overly positive or negative, we can no longer see clearly. Since the feeling part of the brain operates at a higher speed than the thinking part, it is hard to be objective. We evaluate everything through our emotions. According to Dr. Jonathan Bargh, a psychologist at New York University, "It is emotion that decides for the brain and body the value of information being processed."[2]

Step 3 involves finding the maturity to disengage from an issue for a few moments, to let the emotions disengage and come back to balance. You can pretend you are watching another person dealing with your issue. It's like looking at yourself from a distance or from the point of view of your higher self. This helps give you a more dispassionate and objective view. You might imagine yourself as another person sitting a few feet away or standing below you, as if you are watching this person from a helicopter or from a bird's-eye view. One of the first things you may notice is how much more compassionate and understanding you are toward this other person than you have been toward yourself. Compassion is a core heart feeling that also helps increase heart rhythm coherence and synchronization between heart and brain.

Most of the time when our emotions get hung up over an issue, it's because we are overcaring, over-identifying, or over-attached to the issue. We get tangled up in it because at some level we believe that our identity or our fulfillment is at stake. We need to learn how to step back from the issue, to say, "I'm not the same as this problem," so that we can keep a more open mind about what is really happening. Marriage counselors and mediators spend about 80 percent of their time trying to get their clients to step back and see things more objectively. The same is needed when mediating a dispute within your own self. You'll never get anywhere if your mind is made up and your emotions are rigid.

Whatever you perceive in *Step 3*, keep your attention and energy focused in the heart throughout the step to stay in coherence. Without objectivity from heart intelligence, you can wallow in an issue for hours, days, months, or years. The mind tries and tries to figure things out and find release but simply can't, as long as reactivity keeps it stuck in the little picture. Have compassion for yourself. Know that your root motive to care about the issue is right but that you're getting caught in the emotions surrounding the issue. Knowing this is loving yourself! *Step 3* allows you to step outside the maelstrom of emotions so that your common sense—your heart intelligence—can intuitively guide this other person, you, to appropriate action.

When Tracy applied *Step 3* to her issue on giving a less-than-stellar review to her employee, she found her perception begin to shift:

> *By looking at the situation as if it were someone else's problem or situation, some clarity emerged. I needed to keep in mind how I would want to be communicated with if I were the one getting the review. I know in my heart that I would want to be told if I needed to make a change that would benefit my team, colleagues, or me. I bet my employee feels that way deep down, too. This was promising!*

STEP 4:

Rest in neutral:
in your rational, mature heart.

By trying to find more objectivity, you enter into a state of neutral and can rest in a more peaceful heart. Being neutral doesn't mean you feel release or that you have to buy into anything. It just means surrendering your thoughts and feelings to your heart.

Ease them into the heart. This allows the heart to transform incoherent emotional energy. It provides an opportunity for more peace and new possibilities to emerge. In neutral you ask yourself, "What if there are other motives than the ones my mind has been focusing on?" "What if there's something I don't know?" The attitude of "I don't know" helps the mind become humble and surrender, so that heart intelligence can surface.

The "rational mature heart" is the place inside that is more balanced in its attitudes. The balance provided by heart intelligence will allow your intuition to present you with common sense strategies that are best for you and the whole situation.

Here's what happened to Tracy when she used *Step 4*:

> *Resting in neutral, I found a peace here, but every few seconds I felt some of the old thoughts and feelings resurface, so I went back to breathing through the heart and solar plexus to anchor myself back in the mature heart—a place where I could remain calm and objective.*

Like Tracy, you may find that you are not able at first to remain in neutral. Don't worry. This is natural, especially if the issue you are working on is upsetting. Just do as Tracy did, and go back to *Step 2* for a few moments, breathing through your heart and solar plexus so you become more grounded. Then move again to *Step 4*, resting in this neutral, mature heart that is willing to say, "What if I don't know?"

From this place, you are ready to see what needs to change and why you need to make a change. Your rational, mature heart intelligence can offer direction and help retrain your mind to let go of inflexible ideas. Your emotions can then flow in a new direction and open the way to new insight.

Steps 1 through *4* have prepared you for the last steps of the technique, which will help you to clear out residues of feeling and expand your perspective.

STEP 5:

Soak and relax any disturbed or perplexing
feelings in the compassion of the heart.
Dissolve the significance a little at a time.
Remember it's not the problem that causes
energy drain as much as the significance
you assign to the problem.

When you feel disturbed about something, it's not the issue itself that's bothering you or causing discomfort. It's the emotional importance or "significance" that you have invested in the issue. You feel disturbed because of the way your mind and emotions have interpreted the facts of the issue and assigned it personal meaning. This is a very subjective process.

Now in *Step 5*, you use the coherent power of the heart to take out the emotional investment and significance (or meaning) that you've attached to the issue. Remember, feeding the issue is what has kept you locked into your old pattern. Taking out the emotional investment will bring you back to balanced care. By doing *Steps 1* through *4* you got in sync with your heart, which increased your coherence. That coherence now gives you the extra power needed to change your patterns at the electrical and biochemical levels. In the coherence of the heart, you can clear out the old residues and lay in a new pattern.

Tracy wrote the following after practicing this step:

> *I began to relax more and was able to remove some of the significance that I had placed on the situation with my employee. It was now getting clear that my emotions were being fueled by not wanting to hurt another person's feelings. I did not want her to think I was bad or unhappy with her as a person. This was my own vanity reaction and a common pattern in many areas of my life. That insight gave me some release. I felt calmer and more objective about the issue, and realized I didn't need to take it personally. There simply needed to be an inner adjustment. I would tell her that the performance of her work tasks needed to improve and I would help in any way I could to facilitate that improvement. Whew! I began to feel more balanced even though I knew that I couldn't anticipate her reaction to this news.*

By dissolving the significance a little at a time, your heart helps release the locked up energy and unravels old patterns, giving you new insight into unsolved mysteries of your emotional history. Just try to soak and dissolve any uncomfortable feelings in the warmth and compassion of the heart until you feel a release. Ease them out, and let the coherence of the heart work for you.

Take your time with this step. Most emotional histories are deeply ingrained in your neural circuitry. Depending on how deep these feelings go and how much vanity reinforcement they've had, you may find a lot of emotional energy stored in them. Using the coherent heart in this way helps erase the unproductive emotional patterning in your unconscious memory.

As you focus on taking significance out of a pattern and transforming the energy locked up there, you release the incoherence, resulting in more peace and satisfaction. Just keep focusing in the area around your heart, taking uncomfortable or perplexing feelings back to the heart area and soaking them there to dissolve the significance. This requires relaxing and letting go of resistances you may be feeling. Allow resistances that won't go away to simply soak in the energy of the heart. Feeling compassion for yourself as you soak in the heart helps increase your coherent power.

This step is like using spot remover to get the density of a stain out or soaking dishes overnight in detergent to dissolve the sticky encrustation. The next day some residue may remain. So you repeat the process. Each time you do, more of the buildup is gone. You may find other analogies as you practice.

Long-held hurt, emotional trauma, resentment, guilt, or vanity can produce a few tears as the negative feelings or thoughts leave your system. That's part of the process. A few tears from the heart as feelings release are much different from crying that has a lot of anger and self-pity mixed in. The difference is obvious in young children. Disappointment can produce a little crying or can become a total tantrum for a child who cannot let go of what he or she wanted. Adults can have inner tantrums, too. As you practice removing the significance and soaking the issue in your heart, new understandings will wipe away years of stress and disappointment. As stress leaves your system, peace returns. Hold to any peace you find, even if it is not a complete peace. This is your springboard to new intelligence.

STEP 6:
After taking out as much significance as you can, from your deep heart sincerely ask for appropriate guidance or insight. If you don't get an answer, find something to appreciate for a while.

Now, after having done *Steps 1* through *5*, you are more easily able to hear your heart intuition. When using Cut-Thru, you won't always get an insight right away or even the same day. Intuition often comes in after letting go and forgetting about the issue. Some of the greatest inspirations occur, not while in the midst of tussling with an issue, but after the fact, while at peace taking a walk or enjoying nature. That's why many advise, "sleep on the problem," not realizing that during deep sleep more coherence comes into our heart rhythms and we sometimes wake up with intuitive clarity. By going through the Cut-Thru steps, you increase coherence consciously, which makes intuition more available to you.

The heart doesn't always flash its answer on a neon sign. A lot of times the heart answers softly and subtly. When people talk about the "still, small voice" of the heart, they are saying that the heart communicates through delicate intuitive feeling or subtle knowing. It's important to follow even fleeting heart perceptions. If a perception is peaceful and feels good to you, that's your signal to follow it, even if it seems too simple or easy.

The heart signal is often weaker than the mind at first, so you have to listen deeply. You may have to pull the answer out amid the noise of the mind, which sometimes tries to jump in and mask the voice of the heart with "yeah, buts" especially when the answer isn't something the mind wants to hear. Heart intuition can also work the other way and be loud and clear. Respect both ways, and have the awareness to know that the process of learning to listen to the heart takes refinement.

Here's Tracy's experience:

> After I removed all the significance that I could feel and think of, I sincerely asked my heart to help me write the evaluation. I also asked for instructions on how to proceed in the meeting. The most difficult part was done—letting go of the anxiety that kept me from moving forward effectively. Writing the evaluation was a lot easier once I released the anxious feelings. I knew intuitively what to write and felt good about what I said. The review, although not perfect, was smoother than I expected. We addressed the issues and set new goals: she agreed to do some extra training, which she went ahead and took.

Don't despair if you can't always release an uncomfortable feeling all the way or if you don't get an intuitive answer on the spot. Sincerely ask your heart to help, as Tracy did, and let intuition come to you.

Then find something to appreciate. Take whatever new peace or release you have gained from using the six Cut-Thru steps and appreciate that or find something in your life to appreciate. Appreciation of anything increases coherence and can keep you from being pulled back into the old pattern of identity with your issue. Feeling appreciation often brings new intuitive clarity on other issues you were working on as well. So it's a productive use of your time and energy. Try to find something, anything, to sincerely appreciate for at least 30 to 60 seconds. Then, let go of the issue you've been asking about and move onto something else. Additional insights often come to you later as you put your attention elsewhere.

Repeat the steps of Cut-Thru as needed. Many emotions can be Cut-Thru in one sitting. Others will take time, depending on how intense they are or if they are related to issues that have built up over a long period. If the same unpleasant feelings keep coming up, have patience. Assign them to soak in the compassion of your heart as you go about your activities between your Cut-Thru practice sessions. With consistent practice, you will eliminate them completely. Here are the steps once again:

THE CUT-THRU TECHNIQUE

- **Step 1:** Be aware of *how you feel* about the issue at hand.

- **Step 2:** Focus in the heart and solar plexus— *Breathe love and appreciation* through this area for 30 seconds or more to help anchor your attention there.

- **Step 3:** *Assume objectivity* about the feeling or issue—as if it were someone else's problem.

- **Step 4:** *Rest in neutral*—in your rational, mature heart.

- **Step 5:** *Soak and relax* any disturbed or perplexing feelings in the compassion of the heart. Dissolve the significance a little at a time. Remember it's not the problem that causes energy drain as much as the significance you assign to the problem.

- **Step 6:** After taking out as much significance as you can, *from your deep heart sincerely ask* for appropriate guidance or insight. If you don't get an answer, *find something to appreciate for a while*.

APPLYING THE STEPS

You might want to tape-record the steps of Cut-Thru at a pace that feels right to you. Then you can listen to the tape and guide yourself through the steps without being distracted by reading them. Have a pencil and paper in front of you to write down your feelings and your insights. You can keep a journal of your progress to help you become more aware of your feeling world and to remind you of what your heart is telling you.

The next step in learning the technique is to identify some of your emotional habits, reactions, or moods that you'd like to Cut-Thru. If you're not yet conscious of your emotional habits, review the feeling states listed below to see which ones apply to you. Consider what issues or situations in your life frequently evoke those feelings. These are the issues that would benefit from more emotional management. If you experience one or more of these moods frequently, but can't associate any particular issue with it, just take the feeling into your Cut-Thru practice as the issue at hand, and go through the steps to help you gain insight and release.

- Tense
- Edgy
- Overwhelmed
- Full of angst
- Enraged
- Guilty
- Apathetic
- Hurt
- Sad/Low
- Energy/Fatigue
- Overcaring
- Resentful
- Worried
- Angry
- Anxious
- Self-blaming
- Depressed
- Fearful
- Blaming
- Numb
- Resistant
- Blocked
- Uncaring
- Bored

Find a place where you can practice the Cut-Thru steps for 15 to 30 minute sessions several days a week, by yourself with no distractions. This is your time to emotionally care for yourself. Use the technique on the moods or issues you identified, one at time. Let your heart guide you on which to pick. Practice doing what your heart gives you as appropriate guidance or insight. Watch yourself grow into new levels of emotional coherence and clarity within a short time period.

Participants in a research study who practiced the Cut-Thru Technique thirty minutes a day, five days a week, for thirty days experienced reduced anxiety, guilt, burnout, stress, and hostility, along with increased caring, contentment, warmhearted emotions, and vigor.[3]

Remember to give yourself full-service care. Don't short-change yourself. If you "sort of" use the technique—make a gesture in that direction but then hedge on really applying it—you won't get the mileage it can give you. Realize that Cut-Thru is carefully designed to transform your ineffective emotional patterns. When you make sincere efforts to gain a more coherent, peaceful state, more of your true spirit can come through to help. Then you can fully enjoy the rewards of self-care.

To facilitate your practice, you can do the steps while listening to Doc's music *Speed of Balance*.[4] Used in the Cut-Thru study, this music was designed in the laboratory to facilitate emotional regeneration and release from cellular patterns.[5] You can also use the Cut-Thru worksheet in the Appendix to help focus your practice sessions. Again, don't start with your most emotionally challenging situation. Pick something that you don't have too much emotional investment in until you get the hang of it.

PRACTICE MAKES PERMANENT

With practice, you'll be increasing access to your heart intelligence as easily as you now turn on your computer each morning. You'll find that you move in a more liquid flow through life even in the midst of challenging situations, opening windows to new, intuitive intelligence as you go. The more you use the Cut-Thru, the easier it gets.

It's well worth the time it takes to memorize the steps and create reminders for yourself so you practice them. Try writing the key words of each step on 3" x 5" sticky notes and place them on your computer screen at work, on your bathroom mirror or your refrigerator at home, and in other convenient places to remind you to use the steps in the moment when you need them.

Alexis explains how this helped her:

> *"Moving quickly through the key words of the Cut-Thru steps helps get my mind and heart working together when I'm on the run. Usually I go through all six steps in a row, but sometimes my heart just pops in with which one to use for a particular issue.*

Each of the Cut-Thru steps, by itself, can induce profound changes in your psychological and physical well-being. Spending some time with each one will allow you to establish a healthy personal foundation for emotional self-care. You might spend a day or two focusing on just one step in order to gain a deeper understanding of how it feels and to anchor your understanding of how it works. In Chapter 7, we'll take a deeper look at how to use each step as a Cut-Thru *Tool in Action*.

Bringing in new intelligence involves increasing the ratio of time you spend in your heart (at peace and in an intuitive flow) as compared to out of your heart (stuck in your head and emotional reactions) throughout a day. Life can be viewed as a video game. There is always a new level of challenge to master and reward to gain. Cut-Thru builds flexibility and prevents you from having to repeat the same old stresses again and again. It brings you back to your care-free childlike spirit.

You'll surprise yourself at how adept you can become at managing and directing emotional energy. With practice, you can do it instinctively anytime, anywhere. As you increase your coherence and retrain your emotional reactions, you'll find that you are recreating your life. You'll reach a place where you'll know some of those things you've been "working on" and "working out" for a long time are finally over.

Chapter 6

THE HEART LOCK-IN
TECHNIQUE

*The higher order of logic and understanding
that is capable of meaningfully reflecting the soul
comes from the heart.*

—GARY ZUKAV

Heart Lock-In is a powerful technique for sustaining coherent heart power. Practicing Heart Lock-In for even five minutes a day will increase your capacity to get back to coherence faster when you get out. It will also help you create your deepest heart's desires.

Just as the mind needs to be exercised to build strength and flexibility, so does the heart. Practicing Heart Lock-In builds "muscle" to stay in your heart and not keep drifting back up into your head. You do this by locking into and sending core heart feelings to yourself, your body, other people, or issues for five to ten minutes (or longer).

Core heart feelings like love, care, appreciation, compassion, and forgiveness give us power to *live* our core values. But so often, an initial, genuine feeling of love or care gets compromised. Add a little insecurity to your feeling of love for your boyfriend, and your head can take you right into clingy over-attachment, jealousy, or paralyzing fear. Get too identified with what you care about—your job, children, or

99

some issue—and if things don't go your way, you can get drained from overcare and anxiety.

Love and care that get compromised by insecurity turn into "lower heart feelings." You're still caring—about your mate or your job—so you still feel some heart. But you also feel pulled by overcares or over-attachments that generate a sense of fear or threat. Lower heart feelings send the body "fight or flight" signals, drawing your energy down into the solar plexus and propelling you to glom onto what you are attached to or to close your heart in self-protection. Love turns to jealousy or even hate, care turns to worry, and appreciation goes out the window often turning into blame.

When you enter this state of mixed heart feelings, your sense of who you really are gets compromised. Your emotional vanity flares up and the heart usually gets the blame for it. After all, it really seems like your heart led you down that road. Understanding the distinction between the core heart feelings of love or care that feel wonderful and lower heart feelings of overcare and over-attachment that feel uncomfortable, draining or painful, can clear up a lot of confusion about the heart.

But my heart does *get me into trouble*, you may say. Many believe their hearts are not trustworthy because they've been hurt. Where the heart gets blamed for our problems is when our genuine feelings of love or care become compromised by our overcare, over-identity, and over-attachment. When attachments are broken and expectations aren't met, it's our beliefs and emotional vanities, not our real heart that gets broken. The brain sends out distress signals, and we feel the pain of hurt, rejection, even betrayal in the heart and solar plexus. The more emotional energy we have invested in an attachment or expectation, the deeper the hurt. The heart, being the sensitive organ that it is, feels the pain and gets the blame.

Even in the midst of emotional pain, some love or care can still be flowing toward the person who hurt us, unless we've shut our heart totally down. That's where love can get so confusing. Most people want to love or care more, but they don't know what gets in the way. An important benefit of the Cut-Thru and Heart Lock-In Techniques is that they empower your love and care to repair those broken patterns and sustain more clarity through painful situations. The coherence of the heart can mend the incoherence and repattern your neural circuitry with intuitive understanding that will facilitate more emotionally mature attitudes and responses in future situations.

The Heart Lock-In Technique shows you how to spend time in your heart so that you can distinguish the difference between higher and lower heart feelings in yourself to better understand the language of your feeling world. You'll get to see how the mind and unmanaged emotions create the over-care and over-identities that compromise *who* you really are.

Vanessa expressed her anger and resentment at getting older, of having no control over this inevitable part of life, feeling she had so much vitality inside; so much she wanted to do. "I'm attached to having smooth skin and my naturally dark hair. I hate the wrinkles, the gray coarse hair coming in, and double chin. I see a stranger when I look in the mirror. Then she tried the Heart Lock-In, sending sincere compassion and love to herself following the steps of the technique. She found a deeper, secure place in the heart and began to feel a certain peace. As she began to make peace with what is, appreciating all that she had done in her life and how she could be alive in each moment, she truly began to have a breakthrough. "I surrendered to my heart's intuitive messages and began to feel my own inner beauty. I decided that each morning as I got up, I would start the day appreciating—the birds, the sunshine, my friends, and use the Heart Lock-In to find this peace in my heart, then deal with what is each day." A few weeks later she called to tell us how much she was enjoying her new-found freedom, "The years will still roll by," she said, "but at least they won't run over me. I have the choice and I choose the heart way." Vanessa found the power to live her core values—the power of the coherent heart.

Using the Heart Lock-In and sincerely radiating core heart feelings, such as love, appreciation, or compassion for even five minutes to people, situations or yourself feels good to your entire system and can help you get out of excessive self-absorption with problems. It adds buoyancy and regenerative energy that also increases immune system activity.[1] Most importantly, the Heart Lock-In will help you build a solid baseline of heart coherence, making it easier to Cut-Thru limiting emotional and mental habits and access heart intuition more quickly. This accelerates healing inside you and between you and others.

Heart Lock-In brings in more of your spirit to help you build and sustain coherence between your spirit, emotions, mind, and body. As such, it can facilitate any other practice you may do, like prayer, meditation, affirmations, healing methods, etc. Practicing Heart Lock-In while listening to background music that lifts your spirit can increase its positive effects.[1, 2]

Some people enjoy using Heart Lock-In in the morning to start their day in coherence before work or getting the kids up. Others use it later in the day as an energy refresher. You can also do a Heart Lock-In at the end of your Cut-Thru practice to help instate a new feeling or attitude in your system. Experiment with different times to see what suits you most.

The Heart Lock-In Technique

1. Find a quiet place where you can relax for five to ten minutes and close your eyes.

2. Gently shift your attention away from the mind and emotions and focus in the heart area. Allow yourself to breathe slowly through the heart/chest area throughout this technique. For some, it helps to place your hand over your heart for easier focus, yet it isn't necessary.

3. Now, focus on creating a genuine feeling of appreciation and care for someone or something positive in your life. Really try to *feel* the emotions of appreciation and care, as this anchors you more deeply in the heart.

4. While maintaining your focus in the heart area, gently send positive feelings of appreciation, care and love to yourself or others. As you catch your mind wandering, gently refocus your breathing back through the heart and reconnect with the attitude of care and appreciation. If disturbed feelings are activated by something from the past, relax and refocus on breathing appreciation. This helps to release stored and repressed emotional hurt and pain.

5. After you've finished doing the Heart Lock-In, try to sincerely sustain those feelings of appreciation, care, and love as long as you can. This will act as a cushion against recurring stress or anxiety.

Do the Heart Lock-In with the aim of going deep inside your heart and staying there. It's fine to visualize a person or situation, like a child you love or a vacation in Maui you appreciated, in order to get a sincere feeling or attitude of appreciation, care, or love going. But it's important to then let the visualization go and focus on radiating that feeling or attitude.

Powering up isn't about always experiencing a wonderful heart feeling during the *Lock-In*. But you can always put out the *attitude* of a core heart feeling, like the attitude of appreciation or love. As long as you're sincere, you'll gain the benefit of increased coherence. Similarly, powering up in life isn't about how often things go your way or how often you score. It's about how fast you can make peace within yourself when things don't go your way or you don't get clarity right away. You don't want to use the time you spend in Heart Lock-In to mentally plan your next move or to plan your day. You'll gain the most from a Heart Lock-In when you don't look for answers with your mind, but stay centered in your heart and let intuition or inspiration find you when it will. If you can, write down any intuitive feelings or thoughts that are accompanied by a sense of inner knowing or peace. This will help you remember to act on them.

The more you can enter the state of coherence, the more easily your brain's neural circuits may be retrained to operate from a healthier baseline of functioning. Practicing the Heart Lock-In daily or several times a week will power up your practice of Cut-Thru as well.

For example, if your over-attachment to someone or something is causing you insecurity, and you can't get out of it, you can use Cut-Thru and Heart Lock-In together to power up more coherence. Practice Cut-Thru *Steps 1–4* and try to rest in neutral in your rational, mature heart. Neutral doesn't resolve anything, but it does prepare you for resolution. Then do a Heart Lock-In and find something to love or appreciate. Choose something that is easy for you—something where your security is not threatened. Enjoy that core heart feeling of love for a few moments to bring your system back into balance. Then go onto *Steps 5 and 6* of Cut-Thru. Ask your heart sincerely for a balanced perspective on the attachment; this will help dissolve the insecurity or fear associated with it. If the attachment is strong, you may have to do this combination practice several times to gain new light on the issue. Once you see a new perspective, you get a boost of free energy and a sense of discovery, which leads to more freedom.

Your system will get used to what coherence feels like, mentally, emotionally, and physically, as you progress with your practice of Heart Lock-In. Remember, it's increasing and sustaining your coherent heart power that brings your entire system into coherence. You will build new internal references of focus that make it easier to manage your emotions and mind so you can come back to a flow more often throughout your day.

When overcare emotions, like worry, guilt, or frustration, are constantly repeated and reinforced they become traits. The problem with all traits is that we default to neural circuits and mental programs that have been burned into our brains over many years even though they no longer serve us. These old programs are now *presets*—ingrained perceptions and reactions from the past that condition how we see situations in the present. Like radio stations that are programmed or preset to come on at the push of a button, presets mechanically come on when something triggers them. Presets feed the emotions and determine your emotional set-point for overreaction.

Presets form a convincing sense of reality. We're not bad to have presets. They are part of being human, and some presets serve as assets to protect us from real danger. We don't have to think about how to drive a car once driving becomes a preset behavior. We learn not to touch a hot stove because a preset reminds us that it will hurt.

However, presets often end up as deficits and energy drains. Presets built from strong negative memories allow our past to intrude upon the present, putting a negative slant on our current perceptions. They block us from being fully present in the moment where we might see something differently. Presets can impose an edited script, a main character, a plot, and a predicted outcome onto the present so that we mechanically keep creating and projecting that same old movie as our reality.[3]

Examples of presets are when we hear ourselves repeating, "I knew she was going to do that," or "If I walk in there, they're all going to judge me," or "I just know how this is going to turn out." Most negative presets project a "worst-case scenario." Many presets are handed down from parents, friends, and society. We take them on as our own.

Presets box us into predictable behaviors. We limit ourselves to the uncomfortable "comfort zone" of what we believe we know. Without the coherent strength of the heart, we cannot see outside the box, and our presets, instead of serving our deeper heart's desires, continue to limit our thinking and define our behaviors.

Practicing Cut-Thru and Heart Lock-In will reveal your particular preset patterns to you. You will become more aware of how many of your emotional reactions are learned responses that are unconsciously dictating how you perceive and behave. *Because you learned them, you can unlearn them.*

Once you recognize a preset, the Cut-Thru and Heart Lock-In Techniques are effective tools to soften the rigid and outdated pattern. Gina tells how she used these tools to release an old vanity preset that had affected her strongly throughout her life:

"I had become aware of a subtle preset where I told myself that 'I had to work hard in life to be worthy of love and attention.'"

Gina wanted to know what lay at the core of that belief, so she used the Cut-Thru Technique and spent most of her time in *Step* 5 and 6, dissolving the significance and sincerely asking her heart for help. She followed up, the next day, with a Heart Lock-In, and during that time she received an intuitive picture of an event from many years earlier.

"With wrenching pain I saw someone I loved and admired slipping away from me and forming a close bond with someone else. In my Lock-In, I soaked this picture and this pain in the solvent of my heart and just sent it love."

Gina found that continuing to soak the memory in love began to change her feelings about it.

"I found I was coming into a neutral feeling about it and became open to a possibility that maybe what had happened was really just right. What if it was? And what if it wasn't the result of some big misstep on my part?"

She began to realize that her pain had been made up of feeling that she should have said or done more to create the closeness she'd wanted with this person. It occurred to her that perhaps, after all, what had happened was really okay in the large scheme of things.

"Pondering this possibility, my intuition showed me the origins of this pattern. As a child, I'd adored my father, yet was shy. When I was a young teen, my father suddenly began to devote his attention to my younger brother. I felt shut out. I was hurt and shocked, then resentful and hardened. I turned to making good grades to get the acknowledgment that I needed."

Soaking these memories in her heart, Gina received another insight.

"Yes, my brother had gotten the attention, but he'd also gotten the heat. He carries the baggage of that now and its scars, and I carried only a little of it—I had been left alone, but peacefully so. My heart began to melt as I felt a new care and tenderness for my brother who had been 'on the front lines'. I have a deeper respect for my brother now. I also have new respect for myself and more peace and appreciation inside for this journey of life I've been on. I still work hard, but I have more internal balance and flow as I work, and I don't drive myself so much. It's no longer a way of earning a feeling of self-worth, but a way of giving to something larger than myself that I enjoy."

Using Cut-Thru and Heart Lock-In together empowered Gina to uncover and eliminate an ego vanity preset that was causing her emotional distress.

Many psychologists find Cut-Thru combined with Heart Lock-In a useful adjunct to therapy. Dr. Pam Aasen says:

"I tell patients that Heart Lock-In is like taking your daily vitamins for increased health. It decreases negative transference, and keeps the power with the client rather than with the doctor or psychologist. . . . When I do a Heart Lock-In with clients, not only do they get relief, but also I see more ways to help them. Sometimes a lot of emotions come up because they are feeling safe enough to allow the feelings to resurface. Afterwards, they always report feeling better. With Heart Lock-In or Cut-Thru, some people think they're being told they shouldn't cry, be angry or whatever. But that's not the case. What these tools help patients see is they can allow the feelings to come up and release without having to stay in these states endlessly. The tools help them rebuild their faith in themselves."

Preoccupations are presets that get stuck on "repeat" like a broken record. Overcare about performance, insecurities about what others think of us, worries that we might not get what we want are usually involved. Preoccupations drain our emotional energy reserve, and when that's used up they start draining our nerve energy as well. They exhaust and age us before our time.

The next frontier in anti-aging will be extending the emotional quality of life. People still want to see, touch or taste things to prevent aging because emotional intervention can seem intangible. Yet emotional quality of life will become an ever more important issue as people live longer.

Clearing out presets actually becomes fun once you get a feeling of how it works. You can start now. Pause for a moment and consider what presets or preoccupations may be draining your energy. Start with thoughts and feelings that arise when you wake up in the morning, then scan through a typical day until you go to bed. See if you can notice any correlation between a preoccupation about someone or something and energy drains you typically experience throughout a day or week. You might want to keep a notepad to write them down.

By consciously identifying your presets and preoccupations, you can start to do something about them to stop the premature aging they cause. Use the Cut-Thru and Heart Lock-In Techniques to gain freedom from them. At first you may not notice a substantial change. Then soon, out of nowhere, you may see a preset start to form in your thoughts and reactions, so you shift to your heart, and suddenly see the situation in a whole new light. It's like a kaleidoscope that has turned to a new view. Eliminating the influence of even one preset or preoccupation can save untold amounts of energy, and then power you up to a new level of effectiveness in achieving your goals.

Seeing through one preset makes it easier to catch the next one and diminish its hold over you. The energy you save and the intelligence you gain spark a zest and a knowing that you *can* do this, so you want to find more of them to Cut-Thru. You'll increase your coherence and flow with every incoherent pattern that you release. This gives you added strength to clear out the next preset pattern. It works as fast as you practice.

Kara entered a period in her life when everything seemed to be falling apart around her. Feelings of worthlessness she'd experienced throughout life preoccupied her. Around that time, Kara learned and began applying Cut-Thru to what she called "the layered silt of my feeling world." It was during her very first Cut-Thru practice that she came to know in her deepest being that she was not her preset pattern!

"It was when I used the objectivity step," Kara says, " I saw clearly, as on a movie screen, the patterns of worthlessness built over years that were embedded in my neurons and how I had identified 'self' as those patterns. In this moment I could see clearly that these were not who I really was. Checkmate."

Kara then began to ask deeply, "If I am not my lifelong patterns of thought and feeling, then what am I?" Immediately, she felt buoyancy, a feeling of fullness in the area around her heart, "a joyfulness so profound that it can't be completely expressed. I breathed through my heart and solar plexus to anchor these feelings of my real self."

Since then, nothing has been quite the same for Kara. "I can no longer pretend, for very long, that I am a victim of my old feeling patterns. I have experienced the difference and know that I have the choice to go to my heart, or not, to be alive or to diminish myself by identification with what is not real. I am so much larger than a set of biochemical patterns that don't serve me!"

It required deep sincerity and courage for Kara to face her old patterns and let them go, but she felt she could no longer afford the energy required to hold onto them. "It's no longer acceptable to me to sit in the cloud of my old feelings, because I know what the other side feels like. There's no contest!"

Many times since her initial breakthrough, Kara admits, she has "sunk beneath the waves" of emotion. "But kind of like a beach ball, I'm not down long before the buoyancy of my heart pops me through again. I remember, daily, that disturbed emotional patterns are only feelings that are out of coherence with my heart and to which I have added significance. I made them 'real' by adding the significance over the years, so I regularly take the significance out when the remnants of those patterns come back up."

As you get presets out of the way, you get clearer answers from your heart. You get more plugged into your source or spirit. Getting clear answers from heart intelligence is what people have been seeking for thousands of years.

The amount of coherent heart power it will take to completely release a preset has to be equal to or greater than the amount of emotional energy you invested in creating and reinforcing that pattern. It's just physics at the personal level. The good news is that coherence is more powerful than incoherence; so it can take much less time to undo presets than it did to create them, as in Kara's case. Because coherent heart energy is so laser-like, building the coherence you need with Cut-Thru, then sustaining it with Heart Lock-In, can happen quickly as you practice.

Learning to sustain the power of heart coherence will optimize creative abilities, as well as intuitive abilities. Intuition is a user-friendly, convenient guidance system for decision-making, and is readily accessed through the heart. Love, care, appreciation, compassion, and forgiveness (any core heart feeling) serve as carrier waves for intuition. Radiating your core heart feelings helps sustain your connection so you don't get off course.

Like radar tracking of a signal, we call tuning to intuition "heart tracking" and distinguish it from mind tracking where you follow the same old thoughts and emotional reactions. The mind comes into its highest potential as it translates intuition from the heart into new thoughts and ideas, then applies its rational abilities to doing what the heart says.

There will be times where you aren't sure if it's your heart or mind guiding you. Through practice of Cut-Thru and Heart Lock-In, you'll come to see that dwelling on what your presets mentally and emotionally offer you *feels* different than intuition from the heart. You'll be able to track what's going on in your emotions and mind, then lock onto an intuitive flow for deeper understanding. Heart coherence provides the lens through which you can decipher the language of your feeling world more consistently and see life more completely.

Neuroscientist Dr. Karl Pribram, director of Stanford University brain research for thirty years, explains how focusing in the area of the heart, and feeling love or appreciation, is like adding a lens to the heart's system. He says, "You've got to have eyes to see, you've got to have the heart to feel. The 'lens' of positive heart feelings like love, care, and appreciation bring intuitive perception. Love increases coherence and clarity. When you use tools like Cut-Thru and Heart Lock-In to stop all the nonsense (mental and emotional nonsense) for awhile, it's like focusing the lens of heart perception."

Debbie shared how using Cut-Thru and Heart Lock-In helped her get on the heart track. Some years ago she wrote in a journal, "Heart tracking is a bullet train to get where you want to go. It's high speed and makes few stops. Mind tracking is a slow train with lots of stops and chances to go off on tangents. I realized this when I was on a writing deadline and kept hitting a wall. My mind would try this idea and that idea but nothing was coming together. My heart kept saying, let it go and pick it up later when you have clarity. Part of me doubted I would get any clarity by the time I needed it. But I wasn't getting anywhere trying to write, so I decided to put it all on *soak*, asking my heart to give me clarity on my next step."

The next day she went on a fun shopping trip with her mother where they spent quite a bit of money. Lying in bed that night, Debbie felt worried and guilty that they might have spent too much. She could not shut off her mind about what they bought, whether they needed it, and on and on. Her mind kept going in circles like an endless tape as she tossed and turned for over an hour. Finally, tired as she felt, she decided to sit up and do a Heart Lock-In to see if she could change the runaway mind program. She put on the music, *Speed of Balance,* focused deep in her heart, and radiated appreciation for her mother and for other things in her life.

"In a very short time, my heart came online and said, 'Let go, everything will be all right, it's never as bad as you think it is,' dismissing my previous concerns. My mind wanted to say, 'Oh sure, how can that be?' but I stopped it. I'd had too much prior experience of my heart working things out in surprising ways not to listen." Within moments, Debbie watched herself jump onto an entirely different track. "I was suddenly tuning into a totally different train of thought than what my mind had been serving up to me just moments before. Intuitive ideas related to my writing unexpectedly began to download into my mind like a laser printer, as if they'd been waiting in line for me to tune into them. I realized how my preoccupation had been *preset mind tracking and this was now intuitive heart tracking.*"

"I was able to ask questions and track answers that seemed to have a higher order of logic and refinement than what I was used to thinking. I found myself going back and forth between non-linear intuitive ideas and linear logic that put it all together. This was accompanied by an uplifting feeling where I felt like my heart and mind were one and the same and this was my higher self."

Debbie's description of going back and forth between non-linear intuition and linear logic illustrates how the mind in alignment with the heart becomes higher mind. "As the inflow of intuitive discovery continued," Debbie wrote, "I had to focus deeper in my heart to lock onto the tracking and not allow my mind to wander off on some old thoughts that were trying to intrude. After the music finished, I softly laid my head on the pillow and fell right to sleep. The next day, just as my heart said, everything was just fine. My mother thanked me for the shopping trip and money wasn't an issue."

Aligning the power of the mind with the power of the heart unlocks creativity and fulfillment. You hone your creative problem solving skills and start to draw to you more people, situations, and events that are fulfilling to your mind and heart. You'll draw more of your real heart's desires to you as you understand the language of your feeling world and feel secure in following your heart. Cut-Thru and Heart Lock-In are like training wheels on a bike that guide you to a place of deep surrender and love toward yourself. This is a place in the heart where you can "be still and know," where you can connect more with the spirit of love and reenergize your system with wholeness.

During a Heart Lock-In, one of the most powerful core heart feelings that you can send to yourself or others is forgiveness. It is probably the most potent attitude for restoring mental, emotional, and spiritual health. Yet forgiveness is one of the hardest feelings to sustain. People can invest a lot in various personal growth or spiritual practices yet be holding themselves back in areas they haven't been able to reconcile or completely forgive.

Forgiveness means totally releasing an issue that has hurt you or hardened your heart—really letting go of the issue, the resentment, and the judgment completely. On minor offenses, releasing a grudge is easy. Major offenses are another matter, whether personal, ethnic, religious, or political. Events that have caused the deepest hurts can seem so unfair and unforgivable. We can feel the urge to forgive, and in a heartfelt moment we initiate the process, but soon the same nagging feelings of anger or breach of trust creep back in, sometimes stronger than before. Even if our mind has forgiven, our cells can still cry out, "How could he have done this to me?" or "How could God have allowed it?" Underneath those persistent questions, lodged in our psyche and cells, are judgments toward someone else, toward God or life, or toward us. To forgive, we need to dislodge those judgments, even before we fully understand why things happened. But we want to have understanding before we forgive something so hurtful. It's a catch-22. This is what makes forgiveness so difficult and why people so often fail at it. After a while it seems easier to live in a state of pout, disdain, or revenge than to try the forgiveness process again.

A main reason that forgiveness doesn't often reach completion is because there's not enough depth of emotional commitment and heart coherence to extract the underlying judgments from their cellular storage centers. The judgments keep the hurt locked away in a vault, so it keeps resurfacing. Someone hurts you with words or deeds. After time has healed the pain somewhat, you decide to forgive and you believe you did. Later you see the person do something that annoys you—and wham! It *retriggers* the cellular memory of what you'd already forgiven them for, and you relive the same hurt and betrayed feelings you had previously experienced. You start judging them again, perhaps with even more vengeance. This happens daily inside thousands of people.

Or maybe it works like this for you: You've finally let go of some issue, and you think, "I finally forgave. I finally did it." Then, later, you notice afterthoughts like, "But don't get me wrong, I'm going to be hurt for a long time still," or "Yes, I forgave him, but I never want to see him again," or "Something told me to let it go, but that's not what I really want to do!" See if you are taking three steps forward in forgiveness and two steps backward at the very same time.

Often we don't complete the process of forgiving because we do not hold the emotional commitment to see it through to the end. Keep practicing until you extract all the energy from your subconscious and cellular storage centers. You have to care enough to want to take all the old patterns out of your system. Deeper sincerity to keep forgiving builds the sustained coherence needed to dislodge them.

Another reason many don't forgive is because they consider the deed so bad or evil. It can be easy to feel morally justified in not forgiving. We may tell ourselves, "I'll never forgive that." Or, "I would forgive, but because of the principle of the matter I can't." Sometimes we fear if we forgive, we'll forget and allow the same evil to continue, whether personal or societal. But as we go deeper into the heart to find deeper care, the heart's connection to higher intelligence can show us what's needed to prevent the evil from happening again. Sometimes people will say, "Well, I forgive the doer but not the deed." We don't have to approve of the deed, but we have to be able to forgive without compromise if we want to be whole and create a hopeful future. It's these unforgiven hurts that perpetuate aggression, suicidal thoughts, or terrorism in all its forms.

Some people don't forgive themselves because they feel they must keep remembering a wrong or they will not learn from it. They ask God or other people to forgive them but won't forgive themselves. Through forgiving ourselves, the wrong releases its emotional stranglehold on us so that we can learn from it and we become open to receiving others' forgiveness. Whether other people forgive us or not, through the power of the heart, our forgiveness will bring in intuitive intelligence to address the situation more effectively.

More often than not, forgiveness lacks completion because it was attempted as an act of duty from the mind. "I know I should forgive," we say, but we can tell even as we say it that there is no feeling behind it. We lack the sincere heart commitment that would motivate us to want a clean release at mental, emotional, and cellular levels. Forgiving as a duty often just serves the ego vanity, acting as a tonic for moral righteousness. It leaves us feeling as if we've done some good, even if it's only superficial. By taking the insecurity and ego vanities out of forgiving, we will be more aligned with our spirit and more mentally and emotionally at peace.

Practicing Cut-Thru and Heart Lock-In can develop the spiritual and emotional integrity it takes to expunge all the old bitterness and find new peace and personal restoration.[4] To forgive completely starts with heart vulnerability. Use the steps of Cut-Thru, and sincerely ask your heart to help you forgive. Even when you can't understand why something had to happen the way it did, know that you need to make peace with it first to bring in more of your spirit and recoup your lost energy. Practice forgiveness for your sake, not for someone else's. Then practice Heart

Lock-In, radiating an attitude of forgiveness to your cells and to the people or issues involved. Judgments may pop in that you can't completely release at the feeling level but as you maintain the emotional commitment to keep sending forgiveness, you will start to track the intuitive understanding you need.

At times the heart will nudge us to talk to the very person we are trying to forgive. This can be especially hard. When it's someone we love or whose approval we still want, we have to overcome fear of rejection and fear of being judged. Be sincere in the heart before you speak. Have the courage to tell the person that you are afraid he or she may judge you and why. Whatever the response, stay neutral in the heart and express yourself authentically. Don't clam up as you try to reconcile your differences. This act of heart vulnerability and courage ushers your spirit in to give you more understanding. Whether you come away closer to the person or realize that he or she is not going to change, use it as an opportunity to gain more power to release fear, forgive, and let go.

In learning forgiveness for emotional or spiritual health, we have to unlearn the idea that forgiving does *someone else* a favor. Realize that when you unconditionally forgive, it's you who profits most because you have cleansed and released your emotional nature and realigned with the nature of your real heart. Your entire system moves into a rhythm of synchronicity, back in the flow and alignment with your spirit.

Chapter 7

TOOLS IN ACTION

*We know the truth,
not only by reason,
but also by the heart.*

— BLAISE PASCAL

Each step of the Cut-Thru Technique is actually a tool in and of itself. Different situations can pop up during a day or night where using just one of the Cut-Thru steps as a *Tool in Action* is all you'll need to come back to coherence.

In this chapter, we'll describe each Cut-Thru step as a *Tool in Action* with examples of how to use it. Be sure to note examples that apply most to you, and practice the appropriate *Tool in Action*. On major issues, or when emotional unrest just won't go away, use all six Cut-Thru steps to find new heart-intelligence.

STEP 1:
Be aware of how you feel
about the issue at hand.

119

OPENING THE HEART: HEART VULNERABILITY

To start using *Step 1* as Tool in Action, periodically throughout the day, simply pause and notice how you feel. It only takes a second to ask yourself, "What am I feeling?" Open your heart to whatever feeling is there. Notice trigger reactions that dart out toward others or even toward your own thoughts. Discover the currents in your feeling world. You educate yourself in the language of the feeling world by "Opening the Heart."

NOTICE AND EASE

When you notice a feeling that is resistant, raw, or disturbing, relax and ease the feeling out through the heart. Tell yourself to *e-a-s-e* as you gently focus in your heart, relax, and ease the stress out. Telling yourself to "Notice and Ease" can quickly bring you more balance and calm.

BE IN THE NOW

Our feeling world is dynamic and alive. Only in the present can we gather and direct our energy to make our next moments more enriched. To help eliminate living in the future or in the past, ask your heart, "What am I intending with my feelings and thoughts right now?" By pausing to sincerely ask this question, your heart intelligence can bring you back to the now, give you more awareness, and show you other options. Your future—your next now—opens to new potentials.

The practice of Opening the Heart, Notice and Ease, and Be in the Now will train you to come back to the present moment and develop emotional awareness to release overcare, over-identity, or over-attachment. Use these key phrases as reminders; use them as coherence building tools in the moment. They will increase your presence, giving you more power to connect with the people and world around you.

Exercises on Step 1 as a Tool in Action

Most people tend to notice other people's energy and actions before they notice their own. They become preoccupied with what others are doing or not doing, projecting their ideas about why they are that way. They carry on with criticism or comparisons, while their deeper feelings go unattended.

This first step for gaining intuitive insight about any issue while you're moving through your day is to become aware of what's going on in *your* feeling world. If you're reacting to something or in denial about it, you can't transform it. "Whoa!" you might say. "I don't want to open my heart to my deeper feelings, especially not during my workday. What if I get stuck there?" Closing down the heart is a natural, human defense mechanism when we feel too vulnerable. But we have to walk through that doorway of defense to build our emotional power.

When we open our heart to ourselves we become *heart vulnerable*—open to our feeling world and what's really going on inside. It's not being emotionally vulnerable or sentimental. It does not mean losing control or being weak; neither does it mean parading your feelings before others and opening yourself to criticism or attack. Heart vulnerability means being sincere and honest with *yourself* about

121

whatever you are feeling. It's the honest acknowledgment of what's going on that then allows your heart intelligence to reclaim that trapped emotional energy and bring it back into coherence. This self-admittance opens you to hidden authentic power and to the wisdom of your heart.

Heart vulnerability starts by making a listening agreement with yourself—that you will listen more sincerely to your feelings. This is not a posture you assume; it's simply an agreement to listen more deeply inside, to your own heart. You do this by focusing your attention in the area of your heart and *feeling*. You collect your energies and ask yourself, "What am I really feeling about this upcoming conversation, a meeting that's been dragging on and on, the way my son rudely spoke to my wife?" Is it pain, hurt, anger, confusion? Taking a moment to do this allows you to become aware of underlying feeling currents that may be motivating your choices without your knowing it. Heart vulnerability gives you the key to see and then you can take responsibility. Pretend your ears and eyes are inside your heart then *feel* with your heart. This will help you become more aware and bring in more coherence. Notice and Ease whatever you are feeling, then listen to your heart for intuitive direction.

Anne Marie found that Notice and Ease helps her stay connected with her inner power and creative flow. "During the day I frequently stop and use Notice and Ease as a personal check-in. Sometimes I see that I'm in my head with too many thoughts or pushing too hard or that I have an underlying worry that needs attention. Other times I discover I have feelings of joy I was not fully appreciating. Quite often Notice and Ease is all I need to recalibrate and find new insight."

Real power lies in the *now*. Tremendous energy is locked in our feelings, thoughts and body. You can gather that power into more coherence as you tell yourself, "Notice and

Ease and Be in the Now." You'll be less distracted and more fully present to others. As you increase your presence, your listening improves. People with presence are more magnetic. We like to be around them. They know how to live in the now.

STEP 2:

Focus in the heart and solar plexus:
Breathe love and appreciation through
this area for 30 seconds or more
to help anchor your attention there.

ATTITUDINAL BREATHING

Using *Step 2* as a Tool in Action is powerful. It bootstraps your power to quickly shift a mood or attitude. Effective emergency workers have to learn to shift out of emotional reactivity fast, or the energy drain will block their ability to make fast, accurate decisions and lead to burnout. They develop the capacity to focus their energies in the heart and solar plexus to prevent over-identifying with the victims they're helping. Care and compassion from the heart help them renew energy, but it's anchoring in the solar plexus that keeps them from becoming an emotional wreck from over-identity. When you use heart and solar plexus anchoring, the mind and feelings might still react at first, but the excess emotion is taken out. You stay centered and see calmly and clearly how best to respond.

When you find yourself getting caught up in an area of emotional reaction, preoccupation with worry or in negative thinking, shift your focus to your heart and breathe an *attitude* of love, appreciation, or any other higher heart feeling, such

123

as care, compassion, balance, forgiveness, etc. Breathe that attitude through the heart and solar plexus area for thirty seconds or longer to create coherence. Tell yourself, "Breathe Love," "Breathe Appreciation," or "Breathe Balance." We call this "Attitudinal Breathing."

Exercises on Step 2 as a Tool in Action

Extreme emotional reactions like rage, jealousy, or envy can be very hard to shift, no matter how much you try. Attitudinal Breathing will help by anchoring your power in the heart. It will take the "fire" out of negative thoughts and emotions so they have less fuel.

Try staying focused in the heart and solar plexus area as you go about your daily activities. At first you may feel like a rubber band is operating inside you; you try to go to your heart and mental or emotional habits keep pulling you back into your head. But the more you keep breathing through the heart and solar plexus and hold more of your attention in that area, the easier it will be to stay there. Eventually you'll reach the point where your center of action is mostly in the heart and you'll no longer feel the rubber band pull back to the head. You can also breathe other positive qualities, like "Breathe Ease" or "Breathe Neutral," through the heart and solar plexus or breathe an insight you've gained to help anchor it. As you breathe, ask your heart to help you mark that insight and not forget it.

"Attitudinal Breathing" is one of the most universally applicable tools for shifting moods and attitudes fast. It can be used in a wide variety of situations. Here are some key times to use it:

CLEARING OUT MORNING FUNK

What we do in our early morning hours can set the tone for our entire day. Many of us wake up in a funk. Before we open our eyes, we've got worries and judgments swirling around inside, having surfaced from their storage banks during the night. That's where the expression "getting up on the wrong side of the bed" comes from. As soon as we start thinking about these unresolved issues, we ignite residual negative feelings like anger or hurt. Our heart rhythms become irregular, our body increases production of the stress hormone cortisol in response, and we haven't even talked to anyone yet.

Elizabeth found that most of her morning funk came to the surface and woke her up around 3 A.M. She decided to use "Attitudinal Breathing" as soon as she awoke. Elizabeth found that breathing in love and breathing out the funk through her heart and solar plexus started to melt it away. "The funk has less impact. I can tell it's dissipating, and I fall back to sleep with more peace."

Long-standing traumatic memories or yesterday's resentments can resurface during the night. In our half-awake state we start replaying an incident with someone and blame the person all over again. We are judging and draining energy and we haven't even got out of bed. We've lost the race before we started the day.

Use "Attitudinal Breathing" for one to three minutes when you're tossing and turning at night or when negative thoughts or funky feelings greet you as you wake up in the morning.

STOPPING PROJECTIONS

Negative projections about what might happen today or tomorrow can surface anytime, but most of us are more vulnerable to them in the early morning or when we haven't taken a break and are tired in the afternoon. We spend energy and time emotionally reacting to all the problems we think we're going to encounter—too much work, never enough time, having to talk to someone we don't like, another hard day like yesterday. We project our insecurities into the future, which tends to bring up other insecurities. The resulting energy drain is like paying a projection tax. When you tally the accumulated tax from all your projections by the end of a day, you can see why you may feel a bit down or don't feel as good as you should, even if it was a pretty good day overall.

To prevent projecting into the future, as soon as you notice a projection taking hold, stop and use "Attitudinal Breathing" for a few moments. Find something to appreciate and breathe an attitude of appreciation through your heart and solar plexus to prepare yourself for whatever might happen next. It could be better than you think. Doing this for thirty seconds or longer will build your energy reserves and serve as a reference place to come back to if a projection starts up again. When you see yourself starting to squander your energy in a projection, ask your heart intelligence to come in and say, "No, don't go there. I can't afford it. It'll be too much tax, and I've already paid that one."

Janice talks about how she got over her habit of projecting anxieties into the future. "I used to get ready for work in a totally preoccupied state, running a steady stream of thoughts about what was going to happen that day." After tiring—literally—of the process, she decided to try "Attitudinal Breathing." "Now, as soon as I get up and start moving around the room, while my husband sleeps, this is my time to love and appreciate life. I tell myself, Breathe Love and Appreciation and negative thoughts and feelings aren't allowed. Only love and appreciation." Janice admits, "Of course, it's not perfect; other thoughts and feelings do come up. But I stop them as soon as I can and don't give them any more energy. I just take them right back to the heart and breathe." The results have been subtle yet unmistakable. "It's not like I get into a great burst of love every morning. Most of the time, it's just a soft, gentle feeling—but a good one. This is a special time in which I get in touch with myself and muster up some of the best inside me before I start my day."

DEFOGGING

We can't be or do our best when we're in a mental fog, whether the fog is caused by not taking a break, too little sleep, the weather, or a preoccupation. A mental fog feels like a gray pallor cast over your brain and your eyes. You can't focus in the now or remember what was said even a few minutes before without a lot of extra effort. Typical times that people go into fog are during meetings, while listening to others talk, while trying to compose their thoughts to write or speak, and when work becomes drudgery. Other times the fog just seems to settle in from nowhere as we go about our regular tasks. Fog moves in when our mind and feelings are out of sync.

To defog, shift focus to the heart and solar plexus, and tell yourself to "Breathe Balance" through that area for one to two minutes. It's similar to the shift you feel when first getting into cold water. You automatically brace yourself. Breathing an attitude of balance through the heart and solar plexus is like bracing yourself emotionally. As you try this, you will start to see your inner mental and emotional screen clear and come into new focus.

RELEASING TENSION FAST

An indicator of being out of balance is that all too familiar buildup of tension. Some of us accumulate tension in the area of the heart. We may experience shortness of

127

breath, heart palpitations, or irregular heartbeats. Others experience tension as a headache or a knot in the stomach, back, neck, or shoulders. To release tension in any part of the body, use "Attitudinal Breathing" and breathe the attitude of balance for thirty seconds or longer. As you do this, ask yourself, "What would be a more balanced feeling or approach to what I'm doing?" Once you feel more emotionally balanced, then breathe the feeling of balance through the area of physical tension. You'll start to feel the tension release as more coherent heart energy moves through that area.

Gwen shared her experience using this tool in action: "In my public relations job, the tension gets so high at times that every question asked of me or new demand on my time makes me lock up inside like a muscle going into spasm. The tension goes to my head in migraines and to my legs in cramps. I tried breathing exercises, but the tension would come back after I stopped the exercise and I couldn't be huffing and puffing all day. Breathing through the heart/solar plexus area with a conscious intention to breathe the attitude of balance through the areas of physical tension works for me. First it's easier and more interesting to do. Second, after a few days of doing it, I noticed the rhythm of my day changing. I was moving through demands with less tension and my body was much more relaxed."

STEP 3:
Assume objectivity about the feeling or issue,
as if it were someone else's problem.

INCREASING COMPASSION

You can use *Step 3* as a Tool in Action to release over-identity and find more objectivity by "Increasing Compassion." Start by focusing your energy in the heart. Find a feeling of compassion for yourself and everyone involved. Then pretend you are observing the situation from an elevator that rises above the ground or from a helicopter that lifts you above the maze. Look at yourself down below with compassion as if you were watching someone else. This will help you disengage from your mind and emotions and see a bigger picture. Insight or wisdom often follows.

When we can look at ourselves as though we were someone else, it tends to increase compassion, which activates the wisdom of the heart. We see the whys and wherefores from a larger perspective and have more clarity. Being able to increase compassion to become more objective right in the middle of an argument or difficult communication is an important skill.

Exercises on Step 3 as a Tool in Action

We've been taught that to be objective we must get the cold, hard facts, and subject them to analysis. However, true objectivity is only possible when we get heart and mind in sync before we assess a situation. Then we can see all sides of the issue. Otherwise, the mind's linear reasoning can be colored by biased beliefs, fair and unfair comparisons, projections, and assumptions. As the mind tries to reason the why, what, and how of the issue, it blocks out the bigger picture. As soon as the mind perceives "a wrong," its tendency is to start fault finding and looking for someone to blame. If we buy into one of those tendencies, we will react and move into despairing attitudes like "other people have it better than I do," or projecting worst-case scenarios based on anger or fear. Then, in self-defense, we close our heart or assume a stiff upper lip.

Using *Step 3* as a Tool in Action can take you to a bigger picture right in the middle of action, like looking through one of those wide-angle lenses. Tell yourself, "Increase Compassion" and "Assume Objectivity" when negotiating a business contract, working with a project team, during an argument with your spouse, or negotiating curfew time with your teenager. As you start to increase compassion and find a bigger picture in one problematic area, it tends to show you a bigger picture perspective in other areas of your life as well.

STEP 4:

Rest in neutral:
in your rational, mature heart.

HOLD TO NEUTRAL

Resting in neutral isn't always that easy. More often than not, our vanity does not have the patience. Our mind is convinced it knows and wants to be confirmed in that. Telling yourself, "Hold to Neutral," and don't go one-way or the other in an emotionally charged situation helps you build patience.

"Hold to Neutral" involves making peace with what isn't peaceful—which means making peace with an issue *before* you gain understanding of it. You know you've achieved neutral when you can honestly admit you don't know all the whys or wherefores and thus you're not going to react. Neutral depersonalizes the issue. You say to yourself, "I don't know" or "What if it could be this way or that way or another way completely?" "Hold to Neutral" is not about freezing up or becoming numb to feelings. It's about taking the charge out of feelings so that you can address them maturely.

"I CAN'T AFFORD THIS"

Resting in neutral, in your rational, mature heart leads to what we call "business heart." It's an aspect of heart intelligence that "means business," where you know and say to yourself, "I can't afford this anymore." To apply business heart, realize that you are accountable for your energies. Tell yourself, "I Can't Afford This," then go to your heart. Hold and rest in neutral if nothing else. If the old pull comes back, keep going back to your rational, mature heart, telling yourself, "I don't need this anymore. I absolutely cannot afford it." Then use Attitudinal Breathing to stay anchored in the heart as you move on to your next activity.

Many parents and teachers have adopted the term "tough love" when applying business heart with children. Tough love means holding limits for children because it's best for them. When it comes to our own difficult emotions, we need to give ourselves some tough love. A firm limit needs to be set on things you've done and keep on doing, even though you really know better. Tell yourself you can't afford to do that anymore because you don't want to have to pick up the pieces every time. Each time you just say no and follow through, you build your heart power. Once the ratio of saying no versus caving in gets above 51 percent of the time, the process gets easier.

Exercises on Step 4 as a Tool in Action

To "Hold to Neutral" you don't have to let go of what you think or agree with anyone else's point of view. When you're in a polarized perspective, it's harder to feel neutral because the mind believes things are the way it perceives them to be. After all, it's right a lot of the time, and so it must be right now. "Hold to Neutral" allows for more possibilities to emerge. It's a place to go where emotional maturity grows.

As Ginger tells it, "I used to find myself feeling misunderstood all the time. I'd try to be neutral, but could hear myself saying to others, 'Well, all I meant was . . .' I was so convinced that I knew what others were thinking of me that I was constantly defending myself and my ideas." Ginger decided to practice *Step 4* as a Tool in Action by telling herself, "Hold to Neutral." She would stay centered in her heart and ask herself, "What if it's not like I'm thinking it is?" Asking the question began to unlock her vanity. "I began to see waves of assumptions come up in my mind that I never realized were behind a lot of my thoughts," she says. "But I really had to be solid in my heart and hold onto neutral to see this." The neutral place Ginger found is actually a place of freedom. Freedom to see and experience one's reactions—and freedom to choose not to buy into them. Neutral is a place where one has real choice.

So often we assume we have freedom of choice when really we're chained to our vanity habits. When we hear ourselves say, *I just want to be understood* or *I just want to understand*, it's often because we're already hurt or have already decided that something wasn't fair. If you find yourself there, try to "Hold to Neutral" so that you don't add energy to the situation, then allow the mind and emotions to settle so you can rest in neutral in the heart. When the mind is running at full speed or when it feels stuck in a corner, it can get very manipulative with ideas and plans of its own on how to get what it wants—without the input of the heart. By learning to "Hold to Neutral" you will have more power to apply business heart, telling yourself "I Can't Afford This" and really meaning it.

STEP 5:
Soak and relax any disturbed or perplexing
feelings in the compassion of the heart.
Dissolve the significance a little at a time.
Remember, it's not the problem that causes energy drain
as much as the significance you assign to the problem.

Using *Step 5* as a Tool in Action is one of the most soothing things you can do when a disturbed feeling just won't go away.

HEART SOAK

Find a place inside the heart that feels soft, warm, or gentle. Relax and soak in this soft heart state for a while. Heart soaking is balancing and soothing to the nervous and hormonal systems. Keep surrendering mind to heart, find some compassion for yourself, and let the Heart Soak take over. Soaking in the compassion of the heart will allow you to deal with the issue later with more objectivity.

Whether or not you know why you're feeling disturbed, *assigning* disturbances or a problem to soak in the compassion of the heart slows down the drain on your energy and releases some of the incoherence. Just keep your energy in the heart, even if it feels uncomfortable, and let the heart do its work.

TAKE THE SIGNIFICANCE OUT

When you dissolve the significance, or "Take the Significance Out," you're withdrawing the mental and emotional energy you've previously invested in your issue. This is a potent Tool in Action because of the depth of release that it can bring.

Tell yourself "Take the Significance Out" anytime you feel overloaded or overwhelmed. Sincerely consider that the situation may not warrant all the mental or emotional energy you've been putting into it. Make a sincere heart effort to release your over-identity with the issue, and then stop over-investing your mental and emotional energy.

"Take the Significance Out" is especially helpful if you tend to be overly self-conscious—always running over a social interaction in your mind after the fact, wondering if you said or did the right thing, or how you were perceived. "Take the Significance Out" helps you ease things back to their proper balance and proportion. This can be essential in the workplace where time pressures, work overload, and over-identity with projects and outcomes can seriously tax your energy and reduce your productivity.

Exercises on Step 5 as a Tool in Action

It could be scary if we saw a computer read-out of all the energy we waste over-identifying with issues, projects, people, and situations. One over-identity usually attracts another until the stack consumes most of our energy. By telling ourselves "Take the Significance Out" we learn how to stop that drain. Use "Take the Significance Out" on both the small stuff and on more deeply rooted emotional issues that preoccupy you during the day to lessen their hold. Make note of what really is just "the small stuff" and what's the more important stuff that you need to address with deeper Cut-Thru practice.

Taylor wrote, "My usual 3 P.M. mental state is too much to do, not getting things done fast enough, and feeling used up with hours to go before the workday will be over. Through practicing the Cut-Thru Technique, I got to a place where I understood it was my perception of too much to do that was causing me more drain than the number of projects. Then I realized I had to go past conceptually knowing this and use the technique in real time." Taylor decided to ask his heart to cue him up to "Take the Significance Out" as soon as overload started. "My projects are still abundant," he says, "but my attitude has changed. I may feel a little tired sometimes, but I know that the increasing ease that has come from not putting so much significance on everything has improved my outlook and my efficiency. I've come to see that so much of what I was putting significance on didn't really warrant it."

STEP 6:

After taking out as much significance as you can, from your deep heart sincerely ask for appropriate guidance or insight. If you don't get an answer, find something to appreciate for a while.

Using *Step 6* as a Tool in Action involves "Sincerity in Asking." Pause, at any time during the day, to ask your heart sincerely for appropriate guidance or insight. Accessing the heart requires simply focusing our thoughts and energy in the heart, finding a feeling of sincerity, activating a sense of care, compassion, or appreciation to generate heart coherence, and then asking a question sincerely so our mind can receive a coherent answer. Remember that you may not get an answer right away, but you can Hold to Neutral until you do.

Often we get so busy we forget to pause, go to the heart, and *ask*. Our heart is always there, like a best friend, waiting to give advice about anything. If we ask just from the mind, we probably won't get a clear answer. If we first access the heart, we have a much better chance. When you've been running fast or overly processing an issue, it may be harder for you to decipher what the heart says. Focus more deeply in the heart, pull in more of your spirit and really ask. Ask your heart to speak to you clearly, so you understand.

SINCERITY IN APPRECIATING

When using "Sincerity in Appreciating" as a Tool in Action, watch for subtle afterthoughts like, "Don't get me wrong, I really appreciate all he's done, however . . . ." The *howevers* usually end up with a judgment or blame tagged on, and your appreciative intent and energy will get drained away. *Howevers* punch holes in our sincerity, and then we wonder why people don't feel appreciative of our appreciation. *Howevers* can quietly go on under the surface while we voice appreciation. If you sense them, go deeper in your heart to find real sincerity when you are appreciating. Then ask your heart intelligence to guide you how to release the *howevers* so you don't keep carrying them.

Whenever you feel like you're stuck, going backward, or even falling apart, use "Sincerity in Appreciating" as a power tool to create a parachute so that you don't have to fall as hard or as fast. Even a little sincere appreciation will help you recalibrate and maybe give your system a shot of good feeling. It can also help you sustain heart tracking of insights you've previously had. "Sincerity in Appreciating" brings coherence to heart rhythms quicker than any other tool we've tested.

HEART LOCK-IN AS A TOOL IN ACTION

You can use "Heart Lock-In" as a Tool in Action when you feel you're getting too self-absorbed or when your emotions are getting pulled by other people's anger, blame, or negativity. You can even do this while you're reading or watching TV.

Shift your attention away from your mind or emotions, and focus in your heart. Try sending a feeling or attitude of love, care, appreciation, compassion, or forgiveness to your environment and to yourself. This will help protect you from others' negativity and can at times help those around you come to more balance.

Using the Tools in Action builds emotional fitness. Start by picking one Tool in Action at a time to practice in different situations until you find which ones work best for you. To advance in emotional empowerment, play a game called "How Fast Can You Shift?" Record how long it takes you to shift back into balance and coherence. Challenge yourself to beat your previous time. That's energy economy. Anchor your insights with Attitudinal Breathing and put them into action. As you bring more heart into each moment and refuse to contribute to emotional chaos inside or around you, you invite in more of your spirit. Your appreciation for life will increase as your downtime and energy recovery decreases. The result will be that your activities will take on more value and positive meaning. You will become more of who you really are.

Chapter 8

MANAGING OVERWHELM

The mass of men lead lives
of quiet desperation.

— THOREAU

The next three chapters address health issues that can arise from too much overcare, over-identity, and over-attachment. A sense of overwhelm is often the first indicator of a health alert. When overwhelm becomes the "norm," then anxiety, low-energy fatigue, or despair can take over. If these symptoms aren't remedied, your body can bottom out in depression. Too many are on this downward spiral, not realizing that by increasing heart rhythm coherence, they could bring themselves back to more balance with relative ease. Anyone can stop the overwhelm momentum without sacrificing getting things done, and make it fun.

Haley's job responsibilities had increased tremendously. When a large and detailed project with a critical timetable was put on her plate, she knew it was going to take a concerted effort to keep her balance. Then another huge project was loaded on, right on top of the first one. Haley was overwhelmed. "I felt an intense momentum mounting inside me," she said. "I felt I was going to explode, not from anger but from being pumped with stress. I thought desperately, 'This is only the third day into the launch, and I've got six more weeks!'" Every time someone would ask her a question, Haley felt something locking up inside.

Overwhelm starts when the mind takes in too many things at once that seem important and doesn't see how it can possibly do them all within the time period it projects. At first you might just call it time pressure or overload. But if you do not address the feeling world at this stage, overload will cascade into overwhelm much like Haley's or worse.

People often have an underlying river of negative self-projections, projections on others or comparisons running in their feeling world that they don't associate with over-whelm. That's because there are two rivers flowing at the same time. The top river is made of obvious thoughts and emotions that we are aware of, then underlying that is a river of feelings that only surfaces once in awhile. Overwhelm sneaks into the feeling world more subtly than anger or anxiety, and it can disguise itself as feelings of defeat, resignation, or *soldiering on* just because you have to.

It's easy to justify staying overwhelmed because the mind is convinced there's no way out. We may even deny we're in overwhelm until we give out in anxiety or fatigue. Underneath is an over-identity, which causes us to put too much significance on small stuff, create self-imposed dead-lines, or project worst-case scenarios. If overwhelm is a problem for you, find the over-identity and take it out. You don't have to do it perfectly. Do it in stages and make it fun. Even taking out a little bit of over-identity can go a long way in reducing overwhelm and preventing health problems.

After trying Cut-Thru a couple of times, Haley realized her over-identity wasn't a sense of accomplishment, as she'd thought, but an ego vanity of being "not good enough" was underneath. "This surprised me," said Haley. "If I could juggle numerous balls in the air at once, somehow I thought this would make me a better human being. Once I identified the vanity and began to 'Take the Significance Out,' I was able to put things in perspective. I had to admit that it just wasn't humanly possible for one person to handle everything on my plate. In fact, it was a joke. In taking the significance out and finding humor in the situation, I was able to see what I could let go of."

The pace of change and uncertainty in society has caused an epidemic of overwhelm. People are trying to survive the ups and downs. They stay pumped up with caffeine or other stimulants just to stay afloat. For many there is an emotional dryness and fatigue that's so standard it feels "normal." They have forgotten how much better life could feel. If this isn't you, realize that you can still have overwhelm draining your energy.

Once your emotional energy reserves become exhausted, if you continue to drive yourself you'll end up running on "raw nerve" energy. That's when you finally know you're on edge or tell others that your nerves are frayed or fried. It *feels* like electricity is coursing through your system without enough salve or coating on the wires. And it is—a short circuit *is* going on. As emotional energy gets exhausted, your heart's electrical rhythms become more incoherent, your brain can't function properly, and you see no way out. You need to renew your emotional buoyancy in order to buffer the nervous system so that proper communication can flow through your neural networks.

Overwhelm left unattended will produce cycles of diminished hope, fatigue, and temporary despair or depression. The nervous system will keep sending you messages in the form of symptoms, trying to tell you to make a shift in attitude and self-care to recoup lost energy. After sustained bouts the symptoms can become chronic. Of course, there can be other clinical or biological factors involved. But overwhelm so often produces or exacerbates these symptoms that it's an intelligent first place to look.

After the World Trade Center tragedy and the emotional chaos it caused, millions of Americans reevaluated their lives practically overnight. The overwhelm grind no longer seemed worth it. People gave up being as enslaved to time, ambition and other vanities, once they realized there was a much bigger global drama going on over which they had very little control. When people are backed into a corner, they go to the heart to recoup because there is nowhere else to go. The war on terrorism was a wake-up call to let go of vanity excuses and listen more deeply to the heart. Often it was family, friendships, or taking time just to be still that renewed people's spent emotional energy.

Joel was sitting next to Debbie on an airplane a few weeks after the World Trade Center collapsed. Before take-off he initiated a conversation, "I'm a tax man and life has sure been different since September 11. I don't work the long hours anymore. The same things don't matter. I go home to be with my family. How about you?"

Sensitivity to overwhelm increases as emotional chaos increases. You don't have to wait for a crisis to occur before you go to your heart. Take stock of your life and start looking at whether—and how often—the following symptoms happen to you.

Common Symptoms of Overwhelm

- Time pressure: always rushed, too much to do, not enough time.

- Tunnel vision: reacting in irritation to anyone or anything that breaks your focus.

- Internal pressure: raw or gnawing feeling in your gut, knot in your stomach.

- Impatience: lack of compassion for self and others, judgmental thinking.

- Feeling a constant slow burn inside.

- Low-grade shock and strain.

- Zombie-like numbness: no feelings positive or negative; mental or emotional paralysis.

- Feeling disconnected from life.

- Decreased enjoyment of projects, relationships, or life in general.

- Feeling the all consuming alarm and dread.

One more area to look out for—you can also get overwhelmed from too much positive stimulation, like overdoing it at a party or at the sports arena. Many adults and children stay on stimulation overload. They move from stimulation to stimulation: coffee, food, shopping, hauling themselves and their kids to too many activities, computer games, the Internet, movies, TV, and so forth. Advertisers keep raising the ante to keep us stimulation-hooked. There are so many things to do and buy. If it's not new or different, it's blasé. We often get intuitive signals from the heart to chill or slow down. But when we're on the fast track, our mind can disregard what our heart intuition is trying to say.

We can also get too much stimulation from a continual barrage of information. We go into a state of "information overload" where it feels like there's no room to stuff in anything more, the mind shuts down and we can't remember what we were thinking a few minutes ago. People over 40 like to call these "senior moments," not realizing that many in their twenties are describing the same phenomenon.

Information overload nearly pushed Amber, an advertising clerk, over the edge. "I was asked to keep up with developments in my market via Internet search engines to create weekly reports for my group. At first it was fun. I stayed up half the night hooked on the Net and on caffeine. After a few weeks, I realized there was too much information to keep up with. I was starting to overload." Amber couldn't stop her pace. She was losing sleep, which affected her ability to focus. Her over-attachment to the stimulation of information became an addiction. Finally Amber went into burnout. She could barely make it through a workday and went home every night, unable to do much but heat up a prepackaged dinner in the microwave then crawl into bed. She says, "The extremity of the situation finally made it obvious that I had to do something."

For many, overload never seems to stop. If this is you, try using the *Tools in Action* "Notice and Ease," "Attitudinal Breathing" (tell yourself to "Breathe Balance"), and "Take the Significance Out" as you move through a busy life. Using these three Tools in Action together will help you see new ways of doing things and find a stride. Use your feeling world to cue you. As soon as you start to feel the strain of too many things hitting at once, tell yourself, "Notice and Ease," "Breathe Balance," then "Take the

Significance Out." Release the over-identity and shift right back to the heart to move forward in ease.

Amber found, "Breathing Balance" and "Taking the Significance Out" several times during the day helped her stay centered. "A strong inner voice told me that I no longer could afford the luxury of living on the information edge, losing my ability to focus, getting irritable with others and draining my life away. I had to discipline myself to take the significance out of this over-attachment to the Net, and use my heart to sort out what I really needed to do." Whenever Amber listened to her heart directives, things would ease up, and when she didn't, she was back in the overwhelm addiction game.

When your mind assigns too much importance to something for whatever reason, it has to draw energy from your emotional reserves to sustain the importance. The more important something feels, the more emotional energy it draws. If your mind has assigned major importance to several areas at the same time (job issue, relationship issue, financial issue), then the energy draw on your emotions can exhaust your reserves very fast. Mind fuels emotion and emotion fuels mind, until you are thoroughly invested in the issue.

The mind usually assigns too much significance for one or more of the following reasons:

- Overcare: "I have to take care of everyone and everything, because no one else will."

- Future projections, worst-case scenarios: "If I don't do it all, I could lose my job."

- Approval vanity: "This is an important project that makes me important" or "Anyone who can handle this much responsibility is more valuable."

- Comparison vanity: "Everyone else is over-whelmed so I have to be or I won't measure up."

- Desire vanity: "I've got to get it done to get what I want" or "I've got to have what I want to be happy and I'll do anything to get it."

- Good that gets in the way: "I'm a good person to work so hard."

Ask yourself, do you see yourself in any of the above examples? Think of areas and reasons why you assign significance.

The reasons behind overwhelm aren't always obvious. Sometimes it takes a little digging. If you use the three Tools in Action together, one-minute at a time, four or five times during a day, you'll start to see the reasons why and recoup spent energy, then you can manage the overwhelm.

Ann identified performance vanity behind her over-whelm. When her boss asked her if there was anything he needed to know, she felt a tightening in her solar plexus and a feeling of "doesn't he know I haven't had time to pre-pare." She answered feebly, and he said they'd talk later. As she walked away she told herself, *e-a-s-e and "Breathe Balance" and "Take the Significance Out."* Within a few moments her attitude shifted and she realized she'd over-personalized his question. In her heart she knew everything was fine, he was just genuinely asking the question and didn't mean to put any pressure on her. It was an old vanity of performance identity that had reared its head. "By using the Tools in Action, a river of heart knowing transformed the undercurrent of performance identity. When the two rivers merged I saw his heart," Ann said.

Heart coherence can help you depersonalize situations and transform mental and emotional undercurrents that sabotage you. As you move through your to-do lists, tell yourself to *e-a-s-e*, and gently focus in your heart and relax. "Breathe Balance" and repeat to yourself, "Take the Significance Out" to bring in heart coherence when unexpected pressures come up during the day. Then it takes actually *making an attitude shift* to a new perspective to recapture the emotional energy spent on too much significance. You'll prevent yourself from getting too far out of whack by regulating how much emotion goes into your perceptions of every little thing. When you can make it all small stuff and depersonalize a situation, you'll see a more efficient way to go. That's self-care.

One of the chief contributors to overwhelm is project over-identity. You invest mental energy in a project—and, without realizing it, a lot of emotional energy also. All that energy going into one project can create tunnel vision, blocking out other important things in your life. It's a rare person who has never suffered from project over-identity. A key symptom is when you find yourself feeling irritated if anything or anyone interferes with the project you are focused on. If this happens regularly, project quality suffers.

Whether you are writing a report, preparing a meal, helping your children with homework or planting a garden, you can see new ways to accomplish the project and enjoy it more if you stop for a few minutes to use the three Tools in Action. Heart intelligence will guide you to a larger picture and show you things you couldn't see before. It also renews your heart connection with others. Then your energy reserves automatically start to fill back up, too.

Many people believe that their project over-identity is due to simply not having enough time to get everything done. They feel they have to push everyone away to press on. But it's a serious act of self-care to improve the *quality* of time you spend doing anything. Time pressures actually subside when you shift to heart perception. It's only the unmanaged mind and emotions that turn time into an opponent and make life a rat race. Managing time with heart is the ultimate time management tool. Otherwise you'll be controlled by time and led around by the nose by your to-do lists. And that's no fun.

The world is speeding up and so is the sense of time. This acceleration can be a curse or a blessing, depending on your emotional state. Managing the *quality of a moment* is what brings more fulfillment. It defines the quality of your next moments. When you're in your heart, there's more rest and more space, even though everything's going fast around you. Hidden resistances and repressed emotional issues can surface in this space. Because you are more present, your heart brings them up to be addressed. Don't let that dissuade you. Now you have the tools to address unresolved issues. Look at it as a fun opportunity to transform what surfaces into free energy, because left unresolved it will keep dragging you down.

Your heart intelligence can organize time into a flow and everything that really needs to get done actually does. You find a rhythm through pressure and resistances. Take Patti, for example. She lived in time conflicts that made her feel like she was starting and stopping in fits. "My days were herky-jerky. I asked my heart to show me what was blocking me from an easier flow. What surfaced was an attitude I've had most of my life, 'If you want to do something of quality, you need to have adequate time to really do it right.'"

This preset known to millions had operated constantly in Patti's life. She had been known to start her Christmas shopping in July to be sure she got just the right presents, and she often felt that to really appreciate a good meal, it needed to be a long, leisurely meal. But in her job Patti could not afford to spend that kind of time on everything. It just wasn't practical or appropriate. "I thought I had sped up to match the challenge," Patti said, "but I had not let go of the preset. So I was constantly starting and stopping." But if she faced a deadline where she felt there wasn't enough time, she would become insecure and procrastinate.

"Seeing this started to explain a lot of my reactions to people and things. I could start a day feeling good, enjoying the people around me, but each little event where I felt there was not enough time would drain me. People would ask me for help, and while a part of me would have the impulse to care, a quick mechanical resistance would often override it, and I'd tell them that I didn't have time. These stacked up and led to a high percent of days where I felt time deprived and frazzled by the day's end."

Patti really wanted to change this pattern. "I started a game for myself where each day as I got ready for work in the morning I'd use 'Attitudinal Breathing.' I'd say to myself, 'Breathe Love' and 'Love is more important than time. Today, let's put loving people first. Choose love instead of time.'" She was able to see her choices moment to moment and stay more consistently in an easy flow.

About a week into her game, she hit an especially difficult time-crunched day. "My company was processing month-end, year-end, and payroll deadlines all at once. My co-worker said, 'Jeannie is out sick today . . .,' and before she could finish her sentence, I knew I was going to be asked to fill in for one of her tasks that isn't easy for me." Patti felt her mind start to scroll through how much time it would eat up. Her mechanical resistance started. "But I remembered my game. What happened next was so interesting," Patti said. "Time slowed down, and the moment got really long." Patti clearly saw her choice: "Choose my old, reactive, mind pattern, or choose the deeper heart. My heart came in swiftly with a directive, 'Say yes to the job! Choose love now!' About that time, my co-worker was finishing her sentence, asking me to do the job, and I said yes right away—no resistance, no hesitation."

As Patti did the job, she noticed a warm feeling inside from having shifted her time preset. "I felt a real surge of power in my heart and a satisfaction from acting from a place of empowerment." Patti reflected, "The heart was not aggressive, and that surprised me. My heart didn't push my mind out of the way, so that it could speak. It spoke underneath the mind in a poised, graceful way. That came from practicing putting love first. There is a beauty and grace to this that is very rich."

When we improve the quality of a moment, we are achieving what is called a *time shift*. It creates a different day and a different future. Here's another example of how it works:

> When you yield to frustration in a traffic jam on the way to work, it's likely you'll carry over that frustration into the workplace and react with irritability throughout the day. The quality of your time during the day will be negatively affected. Then instead of going home to a welcome retreat at the end of the day, you're more vulnerable to feeling annoyed by the parking place in front of your house that a neighbor has chosen for his truck, getting into conflict with your spouse if the house is a mess, and arguing with the kids over chores. When irritated, you often say things you later regret that can take hours or even days to clean up. You've lost energy and time through that whole negative progression of events.

If you balance your emotions at the first irritation in the traffic jam, you save all that energy and stress. You divert those negative emotions so they don't play out in stressful scenarios at work and then at home. That's energy saved, but more importantly, you've changed the course of events throughout the day. A *time shift* occurs anytime you make an efficient choice in a moment of indecision, when you could have gone another way. You establish more effectiveness within a time span, which changes the course of your next moment and those that follow. When we're overwhelmed, our choices for who to call, what to do next, what to say to someone, and so forth are confined to narrow perceptions. We're also more prone to accidents. One tool used to balance your emotions can stop a chain reaction of choices that lead to wasted time and energy, or create events that you later regret. Balancing your emotions from heart coherence clears the static from your mental screen and allows you to time shift into new possibilities.

Dan says of his experience with time shifting, "When I'm going too fast, it's usually because I'm trying to get something over with so I can get onto something I'd rather be doing. That's when I get into overload. I move too quickly and get ahead of myself, maybe spill something or have to do something twice. Now, when I see myself going too fast, I try to remember to get back in my heart to check-in earlier. Sometimes my heart tells me to stop and do what I'd rather be doing, then come back and finish the other task later. Other times, I need to finish what I'm doing first, but just making peace with that allows me to enjoy it more."

Cutting-Thru to heart intelligence can create a time shift at any moment. Don't think you've blown it if you forget to use a tool until after the first or second frustration about how much you have to do. Even if you forget until you've slid right into a full-blown case of panic, use a tool then. Soon you'll remember to manage overwhelm at earlier stages in the chain reaction.

Using the Tools in Action provides the same centering effect adults naturally try to help children achieve when they're rushing too fast or when their emotions are out of control. Be open to going against a momentum of resistance from inside yourself or from overwhelmed people around you. You can find quicker time shifts at times by looking out the window at nature or at an inspiring picture as you use a Tool in Action.

As you learn to stack up time shifts, you build a platform inside of basic peace that renews your spirit. Your brain receives the first assignment of energy or spirit from the heart. The brain then acts like a general that distributes the energy of spirit through your central nervous system to your organs and body. Children have a steady flow of "spirit" regenerating their nervous systems and bodies until they begin to stress out through emotional mismanagement.

The human nervous system can develop electrical spurs from lack of emotional management and overwhelm that short circuit the flow of spirit. That's when you start to feel a sense of disconnect from others or from life. Overcares, unresolved hurts, guilt, vanity presets, and subconscious emotional processing form these spurs. As the energy of spirit tries to flow through the nervous system enroute to the cells, the spurs cause incoherence and resistance, so communication from your spirit loses focus and potency. Then the weight of emotional habit floods back in. You adapt back to old presets and attitudes and thus perpetuate overwhelm.

Increasing your heart coherence enables spirit to fire more coherently through the brain and central nervous system to your cells. Higher heart feelings of love, appreciation, care, kindness, and balance, act as a tonic to the brain and as oil to the nervous system. They will boost your immune system and establish new hormonal patterns so you operate at a higher-octane level, producing richer emotional textures and experiences. By bringing the nervous system, glands, organs, and hormones into more coherent communication, you accumulate the power needed to repair the short circuit so that energy can move at the speed of spirit, causing a more complete emotional shift into new awareness.

Underneath a lot of overwhelm are hidden resistances that need to be uncovered. Resistance can be a feeling like you can't move or a refusal to look at something, a burning sensation or blockage in the area of the heart, or like something is *stuck* in your feeling world. Psychologist Carl Jung looked at resistances as a shadow blocking the light of one's real self. He coined the term "shadow self" to mean what's repressed or hidden. After many years of working with people Jung concluded, "Your vision will become clear only when you look into your heart. Who looks outside, dreams. Who looks inside, awakens."

The mind's tendency is to hold onto and "chew" over resistant feelings, trying to figure them out. When you can't seem to release a resistance, you need to bring in more power from your spirit to move it out. Assign stubborn resistances to Heart Soak (see Tools in Action, Chapter 7). Ask your heart to help you "Take the Significance Out" of the resistance as you soak it in the heart. Keep reminding yourself that it's not so much issues that create resistance, but the *significance* you assign to issues.

June's overwhelming situation seemed to justify holding onto significance, but it was only in taking out the significance that her spirit could provide her with new intelligence and resolution. In a three-week period her mother died, her family needed six thousand dollars they didn't have, and her son and only grandchild moved to their own place after 13 months of living with her, which prompted her husband to angrily remove every evidence of their existence from their home. A few days later June was recalled to her job after a four-month layoff, which had brought her to financial ruin, and she faced a four-month backlog, proving to her that whether her job got done or not was insignificant to the company. All of the above left her with an immense feeling of pent-up pressure that wouldn't subside.

June wrote, "I read about 'Taking the Significance Out.' What a concept! Now, after one fully focused Cut-Thru just doing that, the pressure is gone. I was able to depersonalize what I've been going through and now see what to do. I am on track again. Not clearly knowing what to do was 80 percent of my problem." June saw that she had over-personalized everything and strayed from her core values, "reacting to everything instead of making conscious heart choices."

Overwhelm like June's is tough, but there is a way to pull in your spirit and Cut-Thru even when the world seems to be caving in around you. Emotional management from the heart is a practical method of manifesting more of your spirit in ordinary, daily life.

There's a planetary shift going on and many are going through rocky times. All the tools for managing overwhelm are not just for when things are already on tilt. They are especially for prevention and building resilience. Millions use diet or exercise for physical fitness and to prevent health problems. Emotional fitness and prevention is equally important; and in today's world, it's especially important. You want to move in a flow where your spirit is close to your heart and intuition can readily guide you.

With heart integrity and practice, it is possible for anyone, even in our chaotic society, to regulate their emotional energy and manage overwhelm. Through the heart, we can find a new flow no matter what comes up. The choice is ours.

Chapter 9

ELIMINATING ANXIETY

We gain strength and courage, and confidence by each experience in which we really stop to look fear in the face . . . We must do that which we think we cannot.

—Eleanor Roosevelt

"For a long time, my first experience of the day was a tension in my gut," says Matt. "Learn to relax more," his doctor advised. Matt had finally decided to talk to his doctor after what seemed like years of waking up feeling like he never went to bed. "As soon as I opened my eyes, I would feel the accumulation of concerns about the coming day or difficult people to deal with. Often the discomfort would be because of some uncomfortable conversation I needed to have with someone. No matter how well the day went, the anxious feeling would never completely go away." Matt is typical of many who suffer from anxiety.

A lot of people, like Matt, never thought of their ongoing anxiety as a *habit*. Just like a lot of people still don't associate emotions with stress—they don't make the connection that it's *their emotions causing their stress*. Everyone's tired and wonders why. We used to say, "that person over there acts old and tired," but now we are that person. Our modern life style has entrained us to constant activity and constant emotional

155

reactivity. We're all in it together. People of all walks of life and all ages are anxious and tired. Continuous emotional reactivity keeps the body flooded with stress hormones, and this is one of the most common reasons we lose energy.

An anxiety habit often starts by worrying about the future. We care, but then we overcare about something. We rehearse worst-case scenarios of what might happen—how someone will talk to us, respond or treat us. Worry can start with just one thought followed by a feeling, then another thought, then another feeling—until we are caught in an anxiety loop. We can end up in downright anger about what *might* happen. Real or not, when we get anxious and unhappy the tendency is to look for something to blame. Then blame further compounds anxiety because it stifles any hope for solutions.

Being anxious about how we'll "come out" in situations and projecting either pie-in-the sky or worst case outcomes sets people up for ongoing fatigue and destroys their happiness. Many walk around with storage bins of these projections coloring their lives. We knew an accomplished publisher who could edit everyone else's stories but couldn't edit her own projections. "I walk to the train station on my way to work," she says, "and have angry conversations in my head, rehearsing how I am going to defend myself with people I have upcoming phone appointments with that day. It's crazy, but I always assume the worse. I'm often exhausted by 11 A.M."

The mind likes to search for and examine all the angles it can find related to worst-case scenarios and other anxiety-provoking issues. This is a very private, internal process where we drain our energy and then drain it some more. Fear, insecurities, comparisons, and self-image bombers make up most people's anxiety arsenal. Some anxiety habits are so familiar they simply go unnoticed. We can be living for so long with a fear of being rejected, snubbed, left out, a failure, unaccomplished, or unable to communicate, that we adapt to it. We get so used to anxious or apprehensive feelings that it just wouldn't feel natural to be without them. Anxieties that have become ingrained are just there. Invisible to us, they rule our lives, and we never even notice we've handed over our power to them.

If fear were like a pat of butter, anxiety would be like spreading it with a knife, taking those fearful thoughts and emotions and working them over, day and night, week after week. This type of anxiety is a self-defeating habit because it isn't based on fact and doesn't resolve anything. Our repetition of it isn't perfecting a useful skill; it's dulling our feeling world while draining energy.

Here's a simple illustration of what an anxiety habit can sound like in your head:

> Let's say you were invited on a family camping trip and feel like you have to go, although you really don't want to. Immediately you start to negatively project into the future, triggering anxious feelings. What if it rains? What if you get poison oak? What if your sister-in-law takes over the cooking the whole weekend and makes you miserable? What if someone asks you a question about some touchy issue? Does this sound familiar?

Most of us can parallel this illustration with similar situations in our own lives. Whatever your personal worst-case scenario might be, you can project it into the future and then fear it as if it were a done deal.

Projecting fear slams the door on the heart. Clarity and intuition *cannot* get in. While fear is designed to warn us of real danger, the few times it does are offset by the thousands of times it doesn't. Most fears are byproducts of projecting insecurity and anxiety onto simple, everyday issues. These accumulate into the anxiety habit.

Experts now have a name for ongoing anxiety and worry that occurs for a minimum of six months. It's called Generalized Anxiety Disorder (GAD) and has joined panic, obsessive-compulsive disorder, phobia, and post-traumatic stress disorder as the fifth full-blown anxiety disorder common to millions. While GAD starts with repetitive unmanaged thoughts and emotions, it soon turns into a physical experience—muscle tension and fatigue, insomnia, irritability, pounding heart, and an inability to really relax.

Each of these five types of anxiety disorder has a gradient between very mild to a pathological medical condition where sufferers should see a doctor who specializes in the disorder. These conditions can be triggered by a number of factors: genetic, traumatic stress, environmental conditions, and repetition of stressful thoughts and emotional responses over the years. Having anxiety is nothing to feel badly about. You simply haven't known how to effectively deal with it. But now you *can* and must to improve your life.

Underlying anxiety often propels addictive behaviors to alcohol, food, sex, drugs, money, clothes, shopping, etc. Addictions are a front that gives temporary relief from obsessive thoughts and feelings. The real addiction is to the worrisome thoughts and feelings themselves. Underneath an addictive behavior is usually a vanity, a lack of self-worth and lack of self-security. So we look outside ourselves to feel better or feel safer. Then after indulging an addiction, we feel more powerless and out of control, which further reinforces the anxiety. Anxiety habits make many people shun intimacy or become over-attached and seek a great deal of reassurance from partners or children. It's a vicious, hopeless cycle until we break through.

Jane Phillimore, author of an excellent article on anxiety published in October 2001, shared her own and others' stories pertaining to Generalized Anxiety Disorder.

As she says, "Like many GADs, I worry that I'm making myself ill by worrying. I worry I'm becoming so tired that I soon won't be able to think, that I'll lose control and go crazy. Yet I still can't stop worrying." She described how for many, something as simple as your child or partner being thirty minutes late coming home can trigger anxiety that they have been run over by a bus. There is a story about a businessman who said his mind was very active "running about like hitting a tennis racket again and again. You start to ask yourself, am I doing it all right, you question your own ability, question yourself as a human being, and when you're like that, it's vicious."[1]

A Native American grandfather was talking to his grandson one day. The grandfather said, "I feel as if I have two wolves fighting in my heart. One wolf is the vengeful, angry, violent one. The other is the loving, compassionate one." The grandson asked him, "Which wolf will win the fight in your heart, grandfather?" The grandfather answered, "The one I feed."[2]

Like any addiction, repeated yielding to an anxiety only reinforces it. Feeding it creates or increases biochemical imbalances in the brain and neural misfiring. Thoughts keep looping and ignite fear feelings that have no basis in reality. Many feelings of panic are false signals. Heart arrhythmia is a medical condition that can trigger the brain to cause panic attacks. Once the irregular heart rhythms are medically treated, the panic goes away.[3]

You won't be able to eliminate intrusive thoughts or anxious feelings overnight. Stressed neural patterning takes time to reprogram. You can't just press delete like you do with a computer program. The Cut-Thru and Heart Lock-In Technique and Tools in Action add the coherent power of the heart needed to help change your brain chemistry and rewire your neural circuits to release anxiety.

Philosophies, religions, therapists, coaches, and a myriad of books teach people about overcoming fear. But for all the attention to the subject, fear is still one of the last things that most are actually able to let go of. Positive thinking won't do it. You can't just rationalize or affirm your fears away, because *feeling* and belief call the shots. If you don't deeply feel and believe what you're affirming, the fear will keep recurring and even engender other out of control reactions like anger, rage, violence, and revenge. That's why, even after all the well-intentioned advice and attempts, many still feel helpless about ever really getting rid of their fears.

To kick an anxiety or fear habit you have to start by *stopping* the emotional investment in what might happen and begin to replace fear with new perspectives. When things make you anxious or irrational, use the Cut-Thru Technique to identify the overcare, over-identity, or over-attachment feeding it. See if perhaps some of the anxiety is coming from your susceptibility to other people's worries and fears. Have you caught an emotional virus from those around you at home, at your children's school or at work? In turbulent times, many experience extra anxiety and fear. This is normal. But you don't have to over-identify with it. That can drive you into behaviors that in calmer times you might not do. Overcoming emotional chaos is not about numbing fears or denying real threats. It's managing your emotional investment in fear feelings and projections.

Each step of the Cut-Thru Technique is important in this process. Acknowledge when you are experiencing worry, anxiety, or fear. As soon as your heart vulnerably admits the fear, you start to diminish its power. Become aware of and label the feelings as best you can—worry, anxiety, or fear. "Notice and Ease" into the heart. Use "Attitudinal Breathing" to bring in power to shift and refocus in a more positive attitude. "Assume Objectivity" to depersonalize the experience, as if you were flying over in a helicopter looking at someone else's problem. Realize that when obsessive thoughts and anxiety feelings take you over, they are not you—not your real self.

This brings in more of your spirit to help you identify with your true self. While you are looking at yourself as someone else, have compassion for the irrational thoughts or feelings. Increased compassion takes out more over-identity. Each time you Cut-Thru to your higher intelligence you increase your power to say "no" to intrusive thoughts and feelings and mean it. It's your own higher intelligence—your heart intelligence—that cuts thru and changes your perspective and your belief.

Learn to rest in neutral in your rational, mature heart. "Hold to Neutral," when anxiety feelings, thoughts, worries, or fears come back. Don't cave into them—just tell yourself "I Can't Afford This." Soak any unresolved thoughts and feelings in the compassion of the heart and keep taking the significance (emotional investment) out of them. Sincerely ask your heart intelligence what to do next and write it down. Keeping a journal of your successes and insights will help you reinforce them.

Appreciate any progress, even if it's incremental, and appreciate it sincerely. If you still feel stuck, try writing a letter to yourself describing what you're feeling. Then do the Cut-Thru Technique and write yourself answers after each step. This will help you see the situation in a new way and help unglue the feeling.

Samantha taught younger children for 20 years, but when she began to teach junior high, anxiety and fear overtook her. Samantha had to confront her overcares about being an effective teacher and her vanity about wanting the kids' approval. She found herself awakening early in the morning with anxiety attacks. "I felt a sense of dread and resistance and didn't want to face the day ahead. It was hard to shut off the negative thoughts about it. I would worry and blame myself for my shortcomings, or anxiously think about how I could do things better."

Samantha started to use all six steps of the Cut-Thru Technique before going to bed and wrote down her insights. She used "Attitudinal Breathing" in the morning while getting dressed. By the time Samantha sat down for her morning coffee, she would usually feel a shift. "Sometimes it would be to a more calm, centered place. At other times a warm feeling of love and hope would flood into my heart. Many times I would just feel a sense of deep peace. These would replace my vanity concerns about whether they approved of me or not. No matter how agitated I felt upon rising, by sincerely doing the heart and solar plexus breathing of love, the sense of anxiety and dread would ease, and I'd feel ready to face the day by the time my students arrived." She now reminds herself to do "Attitudinal Breathing" during the day to maintain her sense of security and balance. Says Samantha, "I have learned much about how to approach, talk to, and guide this age group. I can feel their warmth toward me as I drop my fear projections and feel deeper care for them."

If we could see how much energy we lose in subconscious anxieties, we would appreciate the importance of addressing them. Like a slowly draining battery, subconscious emotional chaos leaks energy out of our emotional reserves. The longer we let this go on, the harder it is to recover. Eventually subconscious anxiety can lead to chronic exhaustion or panic attacks that seem to come out of nowhere.

Many of us *are* aware of our anxieties and are weary and tired of them. But we may not be *sincerely* tired of them yet—the kind of tired where our heart intelligence makes a statement that we must do something about them and then we act on it. Even if we haven't reached that point yet, we can break through emotional inertia just by looking at how much energy is lost daily to insecurities and anxieties. If we're honest with ourselves, the tally might make us get seriously tired of them quickly.

Here's the raw psychology: Let's say you're anxious that you're just not going to make it at your job. Well, what if you *don't?* What if you get fired and humiliated in front of everybody, or you just blow up and leave? Certainly it would take energy to find a new job, but it's not job-hunting that eats up all your energy. It's the fear projections about what might happen that are already eating up your energy, probably more than whatever the outcome would be!

Cut-Thru practice will help you understand that *all* emotions, whether anger and anxiety or care and appreciation, are accounted for in the human system. Accounted for means they come under the laws of physics and the law of cause and effect. Each of us is personally accountable for the effects of our emotions and attitudes. While *we're not to be blamed* for our emotions, we are responsible for them. Emotions have consequences, regardless of whether or not we like them, understand them, or can control them. Negative emotional energies stack in the human system and translate into electrical and chemical imbalances, immune system dysfunction, and a host of mental, emotional, and physical ailments, if not brought back into balance.

Realistically speaking, the majority of us have a lot more control over our emotional energy than we give ourselves credit for. We just have to know what to do. For example, let's say you suffer from a fear many people have—anxiety about giving a talk in front of a large group. It can help to picture a positive audience or look for a friendly face in the crowd. It's much more effective, however, to take a few minutes before the talk to shift the feeling of anxiety toward a feeling of deeper love for the audience or compassion and appreciation for yourself giving the talk. Since your discomfort about the situation was fueled by emotions, it's just more efficient to manage your emotions directly.

Often when we try to get over a fear, we focus on the object of the fear, in this case the audience, rather than on the *feeling* of the fear. To transform the feeling, we have to focus on the fear of humiliation or rejection and address the emotional vanity behind that. By learning to shift to a more positive feeling of love and appreciation of the audience, we get to see the fear in a new light.

For some, fear is a lifelong experience. Yet Cut-Thru can be applied successfully to longstanding fears. Even when fear has been branded into our neural circuits due to a traumatic shock, with enough coherent heart power we can take out the emotional imprint and reprogram those circuits. Such is the power of the heart.

In Cutting-Thru anxieties and fears, start with the smaller ones first. As you release these, it will increase your self-assurance to take on the bigger ones. Ask your heart to help. You have to "negotiate" anxieties and fears out of your system through dialogue between your mind and heart. The six steps of the Cut-Thru Technique serve as important negotiators. You can start your Cut-Thru practice by asking your heart to give you an animated review of the day-to-day anxieties you have about yourself, people, and situations. Target them and they will jump out. Then ask your heart intelligence to show you a better way to deal with each one. It will, as you proceed through the steps. Keep a journal and write down what your heart intelligence says to do. Have patience as you act on what your heart says. Don't beat yourself up if the anxiety comes back or you're afraid to act on what your heart says. Take it one step at a time, but keep moving forward.

Ask your heart to help you become aware when you mechanically start making negative projections regarding yourself, people, or issues. Remember how negative projections become anxiety generators. This you don't want. Tell yourself there's enough mounting anxiety in the world environment without your contributing to its formidable momentum. "Take the Significance Out" of fear projections, even if it's a little, to release the steam. By "steam" we mean emotional investment. It's the steam in a negative projection that generates most of the anxiety. From the heart, visualize shutting off the valve of any emotional investment you have in holding onto an anxious feeling or fear projection. This will help quell the anxiety and save you tremendous amounts of energy. If you can't totally release the anxiety, you will still have more energy to adapt and make peace with the situation. Whatever comes up, make an inner agreement to deal with life's situations day-to-day, moment-to-moment. Even in making that pact with yourself, some part of you will relax, and that helps take the significance out. Have patience. You may not stop all the mental processing, but with each increment of progress the energy saved will accumulate and the practice will get easier.

Scott, a special projects manager for a multinational corporation, used the Tools in Action to address his anxiety while his division went through downsizing. "Anxiety was at an all-time high, and morale at an all-time low. It had been very difficult for me to maintain my perspective and poise because I was angry at the situation. Through consistently practicing 'Attitude Breathing', along with 'Take the Significance Out' and 'Hold to Neutral', I was able to neutralize my anxiety almost completely, which astonished even me. I found myself going through the workday with a sense of buoyancy and clarity, and able to make decisions with a much greater sense of self-confidence. My co-workers have noticed and commented on it. I am much less affected by the chaos and despondency shared by my colleagues."

When overcare, worry, anxiety, or fear is intense and you need more relief, use the Tool in Action "Heart Soak." Make an integrity pact with yourself that you will assign the troubled feelings and thoughts to soak in a soft heart and not invest more mental energy in them. Visualize the compassion of your heart as liquid gold and soaking as alchemy that transforms the stuck feelings. Gold represents powerful liquid love, like rays of warmth from sunshine. Try to breathe through your heart while soaking until you feel better. Be gentle with yourself. Heart Soaking can bring some pleasant surprises. What if a fear about someone that you have carried around for years can be replaced by a more current perception that this person has truly changed? Or that it no longer makes you anxious if he hasn't changed?

It's important to shift to a positive caring attitude and action after you've used a Tool in Action. This helps sustain the coherence you've gained. Ask yourself, "What would be the most caring *attitude* I could have right now?" Take on that attitude. Then ask yourself, "What would be the most caring *action* I could take right now?" Do it. Radiate the attitude of care, whether or not you can actually feel it. If you find a pleasant feeling, hold onto it and radiate that feeling to help anchor it more in your system. You'll be surprised at how much relief and energy this can bring to you. It will help you learn to distinguish between real care as an energy that's efficient and overcare that feeds worry and drain. It also helps release you from vanity reactions. Care oils your system, allowing your brain to come into more harmonious coherent function. Overcare only adds to the incoherence and disarray.

As you keep practicing Cut-Thru and the Tools in Action, you'll start taking chunks of energy out of old anxiety habits. Their intensity will diminish as you gain more confidence and self-control. You'll become more aware of when you're draining energy and stop it sooner. Don't look at the tools as quick fixes, for that can lead to idealistic expectations. If you over-expect from a tool, you are likely to forget the part that *you* have to play to make it work. You have to practice, but even practice won't help much if it's not sincere and from the heart. Use the tools for maintaining lower stress levels while you are working through anxiety, fear or any painful issues that may take awhile to ease. The distance between you and your goals shortens as progress along the way is genuinely appreciated. Appreciation has been clinically proven to be effective in healing emotional pain, recouping lost energy, and restoring happiness.

Don't feel bad if you fall back on your efforts, feel good because you are even making efforts. That's proper. As you proceed, learn to make peace with what isn't yet peaceful. Don't let performance anxiety sap your energy. Cutting-Thru anxiety isn't about trying to get rid of all fears all at once but about eliminating them in stages—with love.

One of the last things to go before you can completely release anxiety, and one of the hardest to let go of because it's stored at a cellular level, is dread. Over-identity with anxiety taken to the extreme leads to dread. After we've invested enough significance in an anxiety or fear, we cause a feeling or sensation of dread. We color what might happen, in the next moment or later with a gloomy sense of apprehension. Whether it's about communications at work or at home, job assignments, performance reviews, or clearing out the blackberry bushes behind the house, there are always plenty of things ahead we could anticipate with dread.

You can almost feel the iron knot of dread in the pit of your stomach as you either drag yourself toward something that feels bigger than you, or you stall to avoid it. If you wait until the project or communication is done before you allow yourself to release the uneasiness, you will probably be exhausted by the time you're done.

"Oh, I've really tried"; "It's hard"; "It doesn't (ever) seem to work, but I'll keep trying"; "Well, I know I better go for it, 'cause if I don't, things will just get worse"—these are the typical results of meek attempts to overcome dread. A more constructive way to deal with a dread is to approach it as an *attitude* you need to change. Take a moment to focus in the heart, and make your most sincere effort to replace a feeling of dread with excitement. This may sound radical, but even if you get only halfway there, you've freed up a lot of energy. If you get all the way there, you've discovered an empowering freedom and continuous resource of energy. Or try this: in the midst of your reluctance, do something caring that benefits yourself or others. Shifting to an attitude or feeling of care even for a few minutes brings in renewed energy and can also shift your perception and attitude about the issue you were dreading.

Aimee lived with a sense of dread much of the time. "It's not that I'm great at dealing with challenges. But for some reason, I seem to attract them. When a difficult challenge arises I immediately feel fear, self-doubt, and *dread!* This makes me so tired I barely have enough energy to face the project and then haul myself through it," she lamented.

Recently Aimee faced one of those challenging situations. "But this time, as the automatic feeling of dread started, I decided to use the situation as an opportunity for growth, and try the Heart Soak. I took the time to find a feeling of soft heart and soak there, which immediately relaxed the knot in my stomach. I then focused on appreciating the chance to change, asking my heart to help me transform dread into opportunity. A subtle excitement flooded my system, and the dread melted away. This made me realize that with some practice I could get rid of my long relationship with dread and just move on through whatever challenges life brings. It was a hopeful moment."

Sometimes the sense of dread can be overwhelming, especially if you anticipate a big and uncertain change in your future. Stella, who had been using the Cut-Thru tools, tells us how she handled the dread when Darian, her fiancé, was diagnosed with an incurable illness. "Somehow, being in a situation like this makes you really appreciate how the heart can save you a lot of pain and confusion. I had to deal with the dread. Every time a thought would come up that had an emotional charge of fear or anxiety, I would anchor back to the heart with Attitudinal Breathing. I focused on taking the significance out of the situation as best I could and was able to get calm."

Stella found that practicing these tools throughout the process of receiving the diagnosis and getting educated about the illness kept her emotions in balance, which helped her make needed decisions more rationally. "I felt like I gave Darian great support and was doing the best I could do for him by staying steady in the heart, poised for anything. I knew it would be harder for him if he had to deal with my anxiety and dread on top of his own response."

As the months progressed, Stella realized that one of the biggest energy drains when caring for a person with an incurable illness is overcare and a sense of guilt that you can't do anything to help. "Staying in the heart and taking out the significance helped me live in the now, and made it so much easier to get used to this illness in our lives," says Stella.

Darian talked about his own experience. "I've always been inclined to be the one who takes care of others, and sometimes this got me into meddling, trying to fix other people's situations for them. Well, eight months ago I got a wake-up call that forced me to find balance with all that when I was diagnosed with multiple sclerosis." As the doctor delivered the news, Darian found all his worst fears coming up: "How will I take care of my family, how will I keep my job, how will I stay active, what will people think of me?" He dreaded going home from the hospital. "My projections of what would happen ran rampant. I was scared."

Driving home from the hospital, Darian practiced the Cut-Thru Technique. "It was only after breathing through the heart in *Step 2* that I remembered that the doctor said that getting MS at my age (47) could possibly be not as bad as if I'd gotten it earlier in life. As I 'Assumed Objectivity' of the situation in *Step 3*, I realized I could be in a lot worse shape. When I applied *Step 4*, 'Rest in Neutral', I realized I was overreacting, and my mature heart told me, 'There's no cure, so just do the best you can.' I then took my situation and soaked my feelings about it. For the first time I could feel sincere compassion for myself without feeling sorry for myself." Darian's dread started to dissolve. "As I took the significance out, an insight came to me: If I took care of myself more, I'd be able to take care of others better and my sincerity would increase. I could keep growing and have meaningful relationships. Over the months since then, I sense that the overcaring and meddling I used to do has been transforming into deeper and more sincere connections with people. I value the moments that we have together, rather than try to fix them for the future."

Valuing the moments, or living in the now, is about having more of our *real self* show up in each moment. Since most anxieties, fears or dreads are predicated on what happened in the past or on projections about the future, gathering our energies to be fully present in the now—which is the only time domain we have control over—gives us power.

Realize that *now*, in this moment of time, you are creating. You are creating your next moment based on what you are feeling and thinking. You can build power to live more fully in the present moment and let go of beliefs that being anxious about the past or dreading the future will somehow protect you. Instead, you can create a future free of anxiety habits and full of renewed vitality as you develop the ability to navigate your feeling world to feel better in the now.

Chapter 10

RELIEVING FATIGUE

*The heart is the perfection of the whole organism.
Therefore the principles of the power of perception
and the soul's ability to nourish itself
must lie in the heart.*

— ARISTOTLE

How well we manage our emotions, and especially anxieties, will determine to a large extent how much vitality or fatigue we experience overall. Fatigue is a big deal these days. The energy drain from chaotic emotions is a factor in fatigue that is often overlooked. We tend to think fatigue sets in because of all the things we have to do or by getting to bed too late at night. At times when we have plenty of energy, we may feel as if we are on a roll, everything moving in a smooth flow, and we carry a certain presence. But then come those days where we experience the subtle *fritterings* of anxious inner dialogue, mental pouts, and emotional insecurities eating up our vital energy. Most of us don't notice or understand the impact that these mental and emotional energy expenditures do have on physical vitality.

Every night we sleep to rest the mind and body from the previous day's concerns and recoup the energy we've spent. Many skimp on sleep because of the stimulation of so many things to do or the pressures of too many things they feel they must do. Sleeplessness, as a clinical problem, has become an acute disorder in the Western world. But even without the kind of restless sleep that sends one running to the doctor for sleeping pills, many aren't getting the rest and renewal their bodies need. They sleep fitfully due to overcares and over-identities. Everyday concerns drain their energy, and they drag themselves through each day wondering why life feels so hard.

The greatest cause of low vitality and fatigue is emotional or mental unrest. And the highest form of rest is the internal coherence created by emotional management. Without it, we need to sleep just to rest from our negative thoughts and feelings. The irony is that sleep gives us just enough energy so that we can do the same thing over again the next day—drain our energy in overcaring, over-personalizing, feeling anxious, getting angry, or blaming.

If you are experiencing crippling fatigue, especially if it accompanies other unexplainable symptoms, like memory impairment or muscle pain, it's important to consult a physician. Clinical illnesses, such as chronic fatigue and immune dysfunction syndrome (CFIDS), are qualitatively different from the kind of fatigue and exhaustion that show up as a result of how we respond to the wear and tear of everyday life. But even clinical illnesses can be made worse by a lack of emotional management.

The bioelectrical system of each human being has tides of energy flowing through it (physical, emotional, mental, and spiritual) during the course of a week or a month. As your heart awareness increases, you'll be able to discern when your physical rhythms are low and you need to slow down a bit; when your emotions are more sensitive and you need to be gentler with yourself; and when your mind needs a rest from activity before you can think clearly again. You will also be able to tell the difference between tiredness caused by low ebb in the tides and the kind of fatigue you feel, even at high tide, because your mental or emotional energy is getting drained through lack of self-management.

Tiredness should be a natural state, like after a long day's work, a strenuous physical workout, or an illness. When you're recovering from flu, people naturally say "take it easy for a while." Maybe after a full day's work and an upcoming meeting that night, a half-hour nap might be the best thing you could do to recharge your batteries.

When we listen to our heart's intuition and rhythms, we maximize our energy output by building in recharge times in between active times. People used to do this naturally when life was less hectic. We need to consult our heart even more when the pace is fast. Heart intelligence can take the burrs and spurs out of your feeling world during the day. This is energy saved, which then furthers emotional rest and presence. Your energy by day will be more vital and your sleep at night more rewarding and peaceful.

Vitality is renewed, as we are able to sustain "presence." When presence dims, the body is saying stop, do something different to recharge. The mind tends to want to push on, find some distracting stimulation, or look for something or someone to complain about instead of looking within to what attitude or perception might be causing the *brownout*.

One of the greatest contributors to low vitality and fatigue is *blame*. Blaming a boss who made you work late or your "impossible, overloaded life" will drain you. Blaming yourself for your shortcomings will drain you. Fatigue from emotional energy drain results in diminished presence during the workday. You're only half there.

If we use a flashlight and it starts to go dim, the first thing we do is shake it to try to get the electrical connection back. If that doesn't work, we open it up and check the batteries. When our personal presence dims because our batteries are run down, we don't tend to address the electrical connection inside or think about how to recharge the batteries. Instead we tend to get cranky and look for someone or something to take it out on. Young children do that, but so do adults. Human beings don't tend to respect their system's energy needs the way we respect the simple mechanical operations of a flashlight. Blame only perpetuates drain.

Once we let fatigue-driven blame get to a certain point of intensity, it flings open the door to other draining attitudes, such as feeling sorry for ourselves or wallowing in a pitiful state. After our ability to be present drops below a certain point, only an energy jump-start will build us back up to a basic operating level, where we feel everything's all right. But even then we haven't made it to feeling buoyant or full of vitality.

Car batteries diminish more rapidly when there's a breakdown in the generator or alternator. If you understood that your heart was your generator, and that it was bringing in *spirit* to keep your internal batteries continuously recharged, you would want to attend to it more regularly. Living more in the heart of each moment, consciously being in touch with your heart awareness, keeps your heart rhythm generator humming and your batteries charged.

When we're fatigued, we long for peace and quiet. Most feel that peace and quiet is something we have to go somewhere else to get. Yet whenever we listen to our heart intelligence, we are creating inner compartments of stored peace and quiet. We can accumulate peace and quiet inside through listening to the heart and making attitude adjustments as we go. That's self-management through heart intelligence. The buoyancy that comes from accumulated peace and quiet transformative energy and presence and brings in clear intuitive understanding of how to do things differently. It takes presence to track subtle intuitions from the heart.

Presence means being mentally, emotionally, and physically present by staying in the heart of the moment. We often put so much energy and focus on how we "present" ourselves—the way we appear, what we wear, what we say, what car we drive—that we don't realize how much anxiety and energy drain we create by doing that. If we put a fraction of that energy into how we *present ourselves to ourselves* on the mental and emotional levels, we would see what we are doing to ourselves.

By stopping our mental and emotional drains and building up heart buoyancy, we can see what drags us into a drained kind of tiredness and become aware enough to stop it the next time. Then we can enjoy the *peaceful tiredness* we knew as children, a state that recoups energy more easily. This isn't the tiredness that comes from overcare, over-attachment, or over-identity with all the stuff on your plate you have to deal with, or who did what to whom. It's the tiredness that will allow you to truly enjoy a good night's rest.

To eliminate fatigue and increase your vitality, use the Heart Lock-In Technique and go about your activities at a slower pace. It's natural to have rhythmic modulations of not feeling good or feeling down at times. The best thing to do then is to find the soft heart—a balancing and regenerative place to be. Keeping your energies in a soft heart can help recoup mental, emotional and physical presence. Assign your thoughts, feelings, and energies to soak in the soft heart while you do casual work for a while. At times, physical exercise or a brisk walk in fresh air can bring the change of pace needed for recharge and balance.

Start to observe the modulations in your energy throughout the day. Check in and ask yourself periodically, "Am I gaining or draining?" Note the times, circumstances, and emotional responses that give you energy gains and more presence. Make the same kind of notes when you notice energy drains and start to fade. If there are certain times of the day, like four o'clock in the afternoon, when you notice that drain tends to start, plan a break or some other restorative activity at that time. Take a ten-minute walk, do a Heart Lock-In, eat a nourishing snack, or talk to someone to improve your attitude and recharge your batteries.

If you suffer from chronically low vitality or fatigue, keep a piece of paper by your side and write down your energy gains and drains for a few days or a week. See what rhythms or patterns emerge, and ask your heart intelligence what adjustments to make in attitude, diet, exercise, etc. Making adjustments won't be easy if you anxiously compare yourself with others: "Well they always seem to be bubbling along. Maybe they don't have as much on their plate as I do" or "I have to keep going and keep up or I'll look bad." These attitudes devitalize and drain more. They increase the down time and remove the chance of finding the regenerative soft heart place.

It takes sincere respect for yourself, to depersonalize whatever's going on and rest in the soft heart to recoup energy. Take the significance out of things. It may be as simple as reminding yourself that you are tired and may not be seeing clearly. Sincerely rest in neutral. If you ease into the soft heart and move in slower motion for a bit, you will find fatigue delicately recharged with new presence, and eventually your vital energy and heart buoyancy will return. Once your energy and presence renew, ask your heart intelligence to alert you if your mind triggers on something and starts to drain again. Then you will be able to stop it before the drain runs.

Kate describes how this worked to reduce her ongoing fatigue: "Using these tools has been most powerful for me in dealing with low energy and fatigue and then getting sick. For weeks I felt fatigued, and sleep wouldn't cure it.

All my life I've been a go-getter, pushing on through projects and the last person to drop, so this was unusual for me. I asked my spirit in advance to show me when to go to soft heart before speaking or reacting to people's comments or actions. When I wasn't aligned with the heart, everything made me irritable. I had some great days and a few gray moments."

Then Kate came down with the flu. "I don't get sick or miss work often, but here I was. The first day, I had to surrender and just lie in bed and sleep." Kate found that surrendering to what her body needed, to the soft heart, allowed her to find "a very peaceful state that allowed me a feeling of regeneration that I had not felt before. I decided to look at the sick time as a vacation. I couldn't *feel* the flu unless my head would wonder *why* I was sick. I found if I wondered why I was sick, my fever would rise and my head would start to hint of a headache! So I asked myself why would I choose to think 'sick' over feeling like I was on vacation?"

Kate spent the next three days realizing that she couldn't push her recovery but just needed to ease and stay in a soft, relaxed heart. "Once I was back on my feet, the feeling of my experience remained. In my day-to-day relationships—personal and work—I knew that I had to treat all like I did the flu. I moved slower, respecting my energies, maintaining the regeneration of my 'sick-vacation' time."

A week after going back to work, Kate noticed several concerns coming up in writing down her energy gains and drains:

- "I wake up and wonder how long my energy is going to last. Will I get behind at work and feel overloaded?"

- "Will I dread meetings, certain people who drag out conversations?"

- "Will I offer to do things I shouldn't, which will use up some of my precious energy and cause me to poop out earlier in the day?"

Kate made a commitment to address each of her concerns and to do the following over and over:

- "Stay aware of my feelings. Keep all tension released in my physical body. Use heart and solar plexus breathing to relax my shoulders, arms, neck, and face muscles many, many times during the day."

- "Emotionally and mentally rise above every situation and conversation in a helicopter, looking down on it as if I'm a third party. I hear more clearly and feel more intelligent."

- "Nothing is important enough for me to assign it significance if it makes me feel tense. Nothing."

Kate reflects, "Getting sick slowed me down and gave me the opportunity to see how I had been causing my low energy and my fatigue. I know I don't need to push anything and can ease into things, speak my truth sincerely and with care, listen to my heart and spirit, do it, and actualize it in that moment."

Other people noticed the changes in her. "Feedback from people around me is that I look rested, have a presence and calmness about me, and everything is okay. I feel more grown-up inside in a very quiet way, yet quite powerful."

Fatigue is a huge issue in today's world. Your sincere efforts to maintain heart awareness will help you to stay conscious of your energy levels and to make needed adjustments to sustain your vitality. When presence is low, the heart can tell you to do one thing, but you go the other way because you're not present enough to hear it or pay attention to it. Maintaining presence means you are more able to hear the heart's intuitions in the moment and act on them. Then you won't slip too far into overwhelm, anxiety, fear, dread, or blame, all of which create fatigue.

In the end, building presence is what gives us the power to Cut-Thru and eventually eliminate anxiety and fatigue. It's where we connect with the power of our spirit and where we have the most choice and control over our body's biochemistry. As you use the techniques and tools to eliminate anxiety and fatigue, you will recharge your energy batteries as you go. Situations that throw you off balance when your energy is low, causing you to feel more hurt or anxious or to blame others won't have the same impact. You'll stay in flow longer, and flow is regenerative in itself, because it is the most efficient use of energy.

Learn to focus periodically in your heart during each day, becoming more present to yourself and to others. Gather your mental, emotional, and physical energies in your heart and relax them there. Put down your pen, stop fidgeting or multi-tasking, and be present. It will take only a minute or two. Ask your heart to get your batteries in line—physical, mental, emotional, and spiritual. *Be in the now*—in this moment. This will allow your heart intelligence to guide you to what adjustments, if any, you need to make in attitude or activity to rebuild your energy. Then the flashlight that is you will shift into a brighter beam—your highest potential in each moment. Use it and it will work.

Chapter 11

LIFTING DEPRESSION

*Is there anything men take more pains about
than to render themselves unhappy?*

— BENJAMIN FRANKLIN

Everyone feels temporary depressive symptoms from time
to time. But indicators of more serious depression include
persistent sadness, anxiety, hopelessness, or empty moods.
They can result in problems with sleep, eating disorders,
irritability, poor concentration, and inappropriate feelings
of guilt, thoughts of death, or suicide. The fact is, there are
a great many walking depressed people. Many don't know
they are depressed because they're so used to feeling that
way. They think depression is something more extreme
than what they have.

Tammy became a single parent in the early 1970s,
when her boys were aged two and four. She says, "Nothing
could have surprised me more than to realize that for the
next 18 years or so, I was to be the sole support and source
of both discipline and care for two lively human beings.
The problem was that, though I loved them without reser-
vation, I was depressed and I finally had to admit that I'd
been that way most of my life. I operated outwardly at a

very high level of responsibility and outgoing energy, but inside I felt desolate."

Tammy tried every form of therapy and medication she could find, but nothing helped. When Tammy learned to regulate her emotions with the Cut-Thru tools, she was finally released from the depression that had plagued her. "I finally got out of those insidious, gloomy thought-feeling loops that had run my internal life. I found out what it means to really love being alive, and my capacity to love others— even my wonderful sons—increased many times over."

We hear a lot about depression, but what exactly is it? The dictionary describes it as feeling pressed down, sad, gloomy, low in spirits, dispirited. It is a condition of general emotional dejection and withdrawal; sadness greater and more prolonged than that warranted by any objective reason and resulting in a low state of functional activity.

Depression is now the leading cause of disability worldwide.[1] Rates of depression have been doubling every ten years, and depressed people have a much greater risk for other illnesses, including cognitive decline, cancer, and heart disease. Those with anxiety are also at risk because ongoing anxiety often bottoms out in depression. If that's not enough to depress us, a long-term study of 1,200 male medical students at Johns Hopkins School of Medicine found that those experiencing depression today are twice as likely to develop heart disease 15 years later.[2]

The link between depression and heart disease is no coincidence. Depression starts with prolonged *dis-ease* of the feeling heart. Of course biological factors contribute to depression. But depression is usually caused by an accumulation of unresolved emotional issues that have tilted our biochemistry into a state of temporary or chronic imbalance. Unreleased minor and major issues that loom within our cellular unconscious create an emotional funk in our feeling world. Sometimes the funk is subtle, at other times obvious. As these feelings modulate within our emotional nature, they hinder our capacity to feel connected to our true self. This, in turn, makes it harder for us to connect with others or experience quality and resonance in communication.

People are different and therefore experience different types of depression. For some, periods of depression last a few hours or a few days. For others, depression can last weeks, months, or years Temporary or long-term depression usually takes us into a lonely place of self-absorption. Tammy, the mother we just read about, maintained a high state of functioning along with chronic sadness and emotional dejection, which is why it took her years to realize she was actually depressed.

The new psychology must address how people can become genuinely happier regardless of external events. And genuine happiness involves the heart. Happiness is a natural, resilient state once we free the heart from the burdens of over-identity, overcare, and over-attachment.

Tammy's sons quickly noticed the difference as she freed herself from her over-identities and over-attachments toward them. Her older son said to her, "Mom, I always loved you, but now I like you!" He could see who she was without the dark screen of depression hiding her real self. Tammy happily confided to us, "Both of my sons told me they felt so relieved that I was released from depression because they could now go on with their lives and not have to worry about me anymore." Tammy added, "That was the ultimate gift for me as a parent because, after all, I devoted many years trying to prepare them to live freely, happily, and with fulfillment in the lives they would create for themselves. The last thing young men need is strings of anxiety or guilt about their mother! I feel there is great hope for parents to become really free to love and care for their children and themselves—the way we always wanted to. These years since my depression lifted have been the finest of my life."

It's our chronic over-identity that starts the downward spiral into funk. We get over-identified with funk and trap ourselves in emotional density. We swim around in it but can't get out. The negative emotions automatically seep back in even when we're thinking about things that should make us happy. That's because of all the identity we've invested in them. They take us further down the spiral where a depressed mood leads to narrowed, pessimistic thinking, which in turns feeds our investment in the depressed mood, until mood and thinking keep influencing one another in an endless feedback loop. The feedback loop intensifies in ever-worsening moods then ends up in dark depression. No wonder depression is exhausting!

With the world as it is today, more people need help with depression than ever. It's so easy to succumb to a downward negative emotional spiral, especially when those around you are in a funk too. But the automatic feedback loop between emotion and thought can work in our *favor* too, and that's where there's *real* hope. If we can generate a positive emotion, even just a little, and use the Cut-Thru Technique and Tools in Action, we can *reverse the polarity* of the feedback. We can start an upward spiraling momentum leading to appreciable increases in well-being.[3, 4]

The capacity to *easily* generate positive emotions remains a largely untapped human strength, but that's only because we haven't developed it. Intentional positive emotion not only counteracts negative emotions but broadens our habitual modes of thinking, builds our resilience, and delivers that highly sought after quality: contentment.[5]

Contentment is not passivity but a healthy physiological state that expands our self-view and worldview. Positive psychology researchers believe that positive emotions loosen the tourniquet that negative emotions exert on the mind and body by dismantling the narrowed psychological perspectives and unbalanced biochemical reactions caused by chronic negative emotion. Our research at the Institute of HeartMath has found that by returning a person's heart rhythms to more coherent functioning, positive emotions create physiological changes for perceiving a wider array of possibilities. They also open our intuitive connection with our *core self*.

To take the new psychology to the street and lift depression, we have to understand the feeling world of depression. We use the term *funk* because it's distinctly appropriate. Thousands every day feel funky or dulled out but don't know why because nothing seems to be wrong. This is bewildering because when we feel the funk inside, we can't always trace it back to its source. We question what happened and why. It can leave us wondering why our spirits can be so low at a party or family gathering that we were originally excited about. We may be thinking, "This should be fun," while a cloud of funk settles in. We may find ourselves saying, "I should feel happier than I do—I had high sales at work this week, my physical examination showed that I was in the best of health, and my kid made the soccer team, yet I don't feel up to my usual self." What's baffling is that we can also have great days when funk doesn't seem to dip into the quality of our experience. We never know which kind of day it will be.

Funk is the result of incomplete communication on one side or another of a two-way communication circuit, either between our own mind and heart or between two people. The result is a short circuit that creates an internal sensation of darkness, dust, gunk, or density in our system. Some describe the feeling world as cobwebs in the brain or something that reminds them of grimy contacts on a battery. A major problem with accumulated funk that has stacked up over time is that it exerts its influence randomly when we least expect it and least want it. Funk stored in the unconscious can ride around inside, popping to the surface sometimes as mental funk, sometimes as emotional, sometimes as physical aches and pains.

Even when things seem bleak or there's a storm swirling inside, you can learn how to go to a place of a deeper knowing where the storm doesn't have to consume you anymore. You can ask your heart intelligence to help you eliminate the inertia that is often created by funk. Through use of Cut-Thru, you can effectively realign with your heart power, which then gives you more capacity to release and blow out the funk. The coherent energy that bathes your cells from Cut-Thru practice brings in more of your spirit to help regenerate your cells and lift your perspective. It gives new hope that you can take out the funk.

There is a good reason why depression means "low in spirit" or "dispirited." The entry of your spirit is slowed down by cumulative emotional and cellular funk. When funky feelings are not addressed, you get a buildup of emotional plaque, which blocks the flow of spirit throughout your system. After a while your spirit retreats, and that's when you can't seem to feel like yourself anymore or feel down in the dumps.

The route to depression follows several stages of spirit retreat. These stages can progress over short or long periods of time. In the early phases, we kind of notice a sense of funk. This signals us that our spirit is not making contact as it normally would. It's blocked by accumulated mental and emotional funk. Our spirit or higher intelligence cannot provide intuitive impressions or inspiration in our thoughts and feelings. Lacking access to our spirit, we tend to feel a sense of compression inside. Some feel compression around the heart area. Others feel "the weight of the world on their shoulders" or feel disoriented. If the feeling of compression persists, it will manifest eventually in biological imbalances such as electrical nervous system or hormonal imbalances. If not treated, we slide into a full-blown temporary or long-term depression.

PHASES OF DEPRESSION

- Accumulated mental and emotional funk.

- Lack of spirit impression.

- Compression—usually from built up anger, anxiety, despair, exhausted mental and emotional accumulators.

- Biological imbalances—electrical nervous system, hormonal.

- Temporary or long-term depression.

Lifting depression requires a download of spirit. The quickest way is to invite more of your spirit back in by increasing your heart coherence. Cut-Thru is specifically designed to do this and bring more spirit into heart, mind, and body. If you've been depressed for a while, you can start to identify where some funk has stacked inside, either from no communication, unresolved hurt, blame, or resentment. Using the Cut-Thru steps to release some of the overcares will immediately begin to rebuild and *renourish* your system.

One of the most important things to release is fault-finding or blame toward yourself or another. Blame keeps spirit in retreat. To bring in more of your spirit, you need to take full responsibility for yourself and realize that you have the power to release judgment, resentment, or hostility. You do it for your own health and well-being if for no other reason.

Our spirit or higher self decides when and how stored funk pops out in order to help us address it. If we can connect with our spirit, our heart intelligence can help us consciously address it. That's what it's designed to do—to help us make that bridge connection between our spirit and humanness so we can be our real self—our total self. Funky feelings are often unpredictable because funk shifts around according to directions given by our spirit, but usually affects weaker areas where we are most susceptible. When stored funk does make its appearance, as in a sudden nervous breakdown, many feel as if God or some unseen force is punishing them for no good reason. This attitude tends to make matters worse; it adds funk on funk. It's important to understand that funk is not punishment from any source. That it's your internal feedback system signaling you that in some area, your mind and emotions have been out of sync with your deeper heart for too long. You can bring more spirit into your system to help you address the funk and take it out. You can draw on your religious or spiritual background or simply the coherent power of the heart.

You move funk out more quickly by sending love to it. Yes, love. Don't judge, repress, or resist it. Depersonalize whatever funky experiences you go through. You have not been selected for some special (bad) treatment; most everyone is experiencing some funk from past experiences. Know that your spirit has asked for the funk to come up in order to move it out of your system. Appreciate your intuition for revealing any issues underlying the funk, but also realize that you don't have to get entangled in them.

The Heart Lock-In Technique will show you how to send or radiate love. Don't be discouraged, have the courage to love. Through radiating coherent heart energy (love) to funky feelings, you start to transmute the accumulated incoherence, and this dislodges the funk, making your Cut-Thru practice easier. Send love or compassion to whatever comes up, find your deeper heart coherence, then continue on.

The Cut-Thru steps will guide you in understanding your underlying causes of funk. Different steps can work better for different people. Meghan describes how *Steps 1 and 2* helped her through a period of depression regarding work. "About a year ago, new responsibilities were added to my job. The new part of the job involved many, many tedious tasks. Prior to my new assignment, I really loved my job. It often seemed more like play than work. But the new responsibilities were the kind I had always avoided since I never felt that I was good at keeping up with lots of different things at once. After a few weeks, I wasn't having much fun anymore and felt compressed. I was deeply worried that I would forget something important."

Not long after, the thing Meghan feared most actually happened. "I forgot an important piece of information, which created a major inconvenience and an awkward situation for two of my colleagues." Megan suffered a severe blow to her vanity. "I immediately went into intense gloom and depression," she says. Meghan found the Cut-Thru Technique. "After an hour or more of trying to go to my heart, but mostly replaying my mental tapes on how I could have done things differently, I finally took a time-out to *really* go through the Cut-Thru steps," she says.

Meghan reports that she had to use only the first two steps. "I was definitely aware of how I was feeling in the moment, and I didn't want to feel that way ever again. I began breathing love in through my heart and out through my solar plexus, asking my heart to help erase the *yuk* I was feeling. Within 30 minutes, I was peaceful again. However, my intuition came in and told me that even though I felt better about this particular incident, I would need to put forth some sincere effort to erase my tendency to depression permanently. I harbored a deep approval vanity insecurity, and if I didn't clear that out, there would be other situations that would create this type of situation again."

Meghan set about sincerely to get rid of the vanity. "At lunchtime each day I would take as much time as possible to breathe love to my cells, asking my heart to help melt the density and insecurity from my cells. Doing this felt 'like sunshine melting ice.' Practicing the Heart Lock-In Technique gave her new feelings of security, not dependent on what others might think of her. "I would do a Heart Lock-In each morning and each night before going to sleep, again breathing love to those insecure cells. I continued this practice every day for a month or two."

Her consistent effort paid off. "I was tenaciously going for it, and I have to say, I have never experienced the insecure panicky and depressive feelings again. I look forward to each day. I have my can-do attitude back. I am sure there are some more insecure cells hiding within me, so I do preventative maintenance. I still ask my heart regularly to erase the density in my cells, and I take some time to appreciate the success I have earned."

Like Meghan, you can learn to ask your heart to help. Talk to your heart like a close buddy—a buddy you can be vulnerable with, who doesn't judge and can't wait to help. You have to be sincere and open to inner guidance to get past your presets and address the funk. Old mental and emotional habit patterns will try to get in the way of moving the funk out of your system. They can act like the tail of a dragon. You've had new inspiration and released some funk, but as you turn the corner in feeling better, the tail of the draconian pattern snaps back and whips you. Here's what can happen and what to do.

Beware of whining. Your heart gives you clarity on which way to go and you start out with the best intentions, but then there's a part of you that decides to whine or moan and groan about having to do that. Sometimes that part can feel like an emotional or stubborn child inside.

If you find yourself beginning to whine, spend extra time with *Step 3*, rest in neutral, in your rational, mature heart and apply business heart. Remember, business heart is an aspect of heart intelligence that "means business." Tell yourself, "I Can't Afford This anymore," then keep easing the whiny thoughts and feelings out through your heart. Recall all the energy that you already have spent going round and round chasing your tail on the same old thing. Breathe through the heart and solar plexus to anchor your "I mean business" attitude into your cells. If the whine comes back, keep going back to your rational, mature heart, telling yourself, "Enough, I don't need this anymore. I absolutely cannot afford it."

The second thing to be on the lookout for is "cellular pout." Pouting is deeper than whining about any one thing. In Chapter 2, we talked about self-pity as a pout, like the tantrums little children throw when they don't get what they want. If you've had extended occasions of falling into self-pity or throwing inner tantrums when life didn't go your way, this can imprint an underlying pout into your cellular memory. It's cellular because the subconscious emotional processing can seem like it belongs to another person living inside you. You may think you've let go of your self-pity, but your cells can retain pout long after you think you're done with it. This leads to strong emotional mood swings at times, either too ebullient or too pitiful.

Unconscious, cumulative cellular pout is one of the chief contributors to today's epidemic of depression. A pout can seem so innocent. Why not complain and pout inside?

Everybody does. And who would know? But pout accumulates until it casts a pall on our worldview. Even when we *know* we are pouting and want to stop, the weight of accumulation makes it hard to do anything about it. Then we start pouting about that, and this makes it even worse. Some people take on feeling pitiful or pathetic as part of their identity. Cellular pout runs a subtle but continuous energy drain in their bodies, affecting them down to the hormonal level. If we want to feel better permanently, then we have to address how we are spending our energy. We have to learn how to "out the pout!"

Cut-Thru practice will reveal the preset cellular patterns that have trapped you in pout. It will guide you to the heart vulnerability needed to bring in more spirit for emotional healing. This releases the trapped judgments, the unseen over-identities and overcares, and the pout. Life can still seem tough, but it can be tougher if you don't Cut-Thru.

When self-pity and pout are your problem, spend time with *Step 1* to become more aware of how you feel inside about anything. Then ease the feelings into the heart. Practice "Opening the Heart" and become heart vulnerable to yourself without sinking into self-pity. Don't worry if you feel like you're trying to pry open a clam. Just keep practicing and your heart intelligence will help you. Spend time with *Step 2*, breathing higher heart feelings like love, appreciation, care, or compassion through the heart and solar plexus to bring your heart rhythms into greater coherence. Then radiate that coherence to your cells. When you're finished with your Cut-Thru practice session, use the Tool in Action "Be In the Now" and move on with what's next in your life even if there is some residual pouting feeling. Assign what's left to soak in the heart and move on. As you keep doing this, you *will* free your cells from the pout.

Another thing to watch out for when clearing out cellular pout is a quiet or loud feeling of "It's not fair." Memories of what's not been fair are one of the major components of pout and they will erupt to the surface to be cleared out. Don't get caught in their net. It's only human to try to use our ideas of what was fair or unfair as a way to substantiate what we think we know. In most cases, we're substantiating our hurt ego vanity and not open to seeing another perspective. We've set ourselves up as judge and jury, decided that what happened was not right or fair, and sentenced *ourselves* to prison without knowing it. Whether we feel that others, God, or life treated us unfairly, the effect on our body is the same. While thinking that we are blaming something outside ourselves, we put our mind and cells on the receiving end of the sentence.

So if we are going to gain our freedom and happiness, we have to release feelings of "it's unfair" or "my situation is so different" that underlie pout and funk. What we need is to reach a new state of neutral so that we can unlock the prison door. In many situations, we will never achieve the larger understanding we crave until we can go to neutral. In neutral, we can ask ourselves, "What if there is another purpose for this than I'm seeing?" and be open to receiving new information.

When your feelings are screaming or whispering, "it's not fair," spend more time with *Step 3*. Assume objectivity as if it were someone else's problem so that you can find a solid neutral. Increase compassion to depersonalize the issue and see from a larger perspective. As you take out over-identity, you'll see things in a new light.

Laura's story describes why letting go of "fair or unfair" comparisons is so important in lifting depression. "I'd experienced a lot of depression as a young woman but learned ways to keep the black hole at bay. That bleak, unyielding feeling state was a thing of the past for me, and I forgot what it felt like. Then, at age 48, my partner of many years surprised me with the news that he was leaving me, taking many of our joint possessions, including our car, and relocating across the country. He said it wasn't personal, that he needed a change and had to go."

Laura was devastated. They had lived very modestly, and now she was faced not only with the loss of the relationship, but with severely diminished finances. "It may not have seemed personal to him," Laura said wryly, "but it felt very personal to me! I felt a powerful sense of injustice at the loss and felt blame and anger at being left, being close to broke, and suddenly aware that I was now middle-aged and single on top of it all. It wasn't fair, pure and simple. I got lampooned by life or that's how it seemed—and here I was, a good person who clearly didn't deserve it."

After her partner left, Laura had to move out of the home they had been leasing, so she took a room in the home of a family she knew, which placed her within walking distance to work. "At first, the emotional shock of the change kept me busy adjusting to the new lifestyle, but after a while I realized that I was depressed and it was getting worse. It's hard to describe, but my depression felt like a seeping drip that rots the area around the leak but isn't noticed until you open the cupboard under the dripping faucet to look for something long forgotten." About this time Laura learned Cut-Thru and found that it helped to shift her out of depression into peace and into deeper compassion— for herself and others. "To do this has been enormously empowering," she adds.

Laura lists the tools that worked best for her:

- Sincerity in Appreciating: *I made it a habit to be aware of a negative feeling state and to stop and ask myself, "What do I appreciate, in this moment, right now?" There was always something to appreciate when I asked my heart, and often I was surprised to see what it was. Diligence with this tool made a serious dent in releasing my depression and getting me to a new state of neutral.*

- Take the Significance Out: *I've come to love this tool when I'm feeling anxiety about the future as one that can instantly allow a new perspective to come in. I came to view my new living situation as a new lease on life, a transition and a new beginning. I knew that's how I would help a friend try to see it, if it was her life.*

- Be in the Now: *This tool helped me stop lamenting about what I'd lost and stop the dread and blind alleys my fear projections showed me as my future, colored as they were by depression. When I'd wake myself up and "Be in the Now," in this moment, everything would shift and be all right. Then I'd find myself automatically circling around to appreciation again.*

The above may sound simplistic, but for anyone who's experienced depression, to know there is freedom from that state by incorporating simple techniques and tools into daily life is a miracle. It's a miracle that can help us "walking wounded" become healthy and whole again and able to go on to develop our full potential with a peaceful heart and with care to give the world around us.

To lift depression, a structured Cut-Thru practice program will provide the quickest results. Study and practice the six steps of the Cut-Thru Technique in 15-minute or longer sessions five times a week. Ask your heart to help you address the stored funk at the cellular level. Your cells can put up resistance for a while. Your subconscious vanity identities may fear the funk will be hard to move out, or fear that you'll be "nothing" without the *unfairs* or pitiful pouts. The cellular feeling world often seems to have a mind of its own which is why *enlodged* funk can remain so potent. Just keep cutting through. Use the Tools in Action. Your heart knows what needs to be addressed.

Use the Heart Lock-In Technique at least several times a week to help sustain the coherence you are building with Cut-Thru. For maximum effect, use it with music that helps lift your spirit playing softly in the background. When you practice Heart Lock-In, simply stay in the heart and gently radiate a feeling of love. Sending love to funk in Heart Lock-In is a passport to accelerated recovery. Sending love during Heart Lock-Ins will help you lock into your heart's power. It will also improve your nervous system balance and immune response. [6, 7] Make a commitment to regular practice and harness the power of coherence to regain your peace. If issues needing forgiveness or self-forgiveness arise, use the Heart Lock-In to send forgiveness and use Heart Soak to release your hurt and resentment.

Taking the "big deal" out of whatever cards you've been dealt and releasing the vanity of "my stuff is so much worse than others" invites your spirit to deal more kindly and pleasantly with the stuff that's left. The answers to many unsolved mysteries of people's lives are to be found right underneath the depression.

The more regularly you adhere to a structured practice program, the more power you will accumulate to clear out the cellular residue. You are not going to be able to "out all pout" overnight. But you will gain a lot of free energy and new fun by seeing how fast it can start to work. This gives you passion and can-do heart power to keep going.

You can gauge the degree of heart power you're building by observing the distance between "hear" and "do." That's the time between when you hear your heart intelligence and when you *act* on it. Transmuting the funk that's stored in the cells changes the vibratory rhythm of your cellular structure, bringing it into sync with your deeper heart, empowering you to more quickly put into practice what your heart intelligence says. Do that and you will find your happiness.

Chapter 12

CREATING SECURITY IN RELATIONSHIPS

What is uttered from the heart alone,
will win the hearts of others to your own.

— GOETHE

Have you ever had a close friend and then one day noticed the warmth or ease just wasn't there any longer? Did you ask yourself, "What did I do?" or "What's the matter with him?" How we respond to those questions will determine the course and level of that friendship. We can either care enough to find out what's really going on, or we can assume the worst, get angry, and close off. That's when your inner dialogue starts resounding with, "What's his problem!" This is the birth of a preset and probably the end of a friendship, unless we take care.

Emotional management is the caretaker of love. Care is the ingredient that keeps friendships alive, despite separation, distance, or time. Care gives latitude to another and gets you past the projections, dislikes and annoyances. Quite simply, caring sustains love.

Many people stay angry with a former friend for years, sometimes forever. At best, they'll feign indifference, like, "Well, the heck with her—if she wants to be that way, that's fine with me," or "He's changed for the worse and I don't want anything more to do with him." We can stay mad or distant forever if we choose, but consider the cost of resentment on physical health, in addition to the loss of a friendship.

"I was in a relationship with a man," writes Carol, "that had been going sour for the last eight months. I finally decided I didn't want to see him anymore." Carol's mind told her they were finished, but her feelings were confused. She decided to use Cut-Thru. Surprisingly, her heart kept telling her to try to renew the relationship. Carol reports, "I couldn't get past the fact that I really love him. My heart kept telling me to change myself, not him. I have done just that, and it is working. He loves me very much, and I love him, but I had to be willing to try this relationship with a clean slate."

In the early stages of intimate relationships, the hormones and brain chemicals of love produce a natural high. The easy, intense connection, wide-open feelings of surrender and synchronicity, and the rich textures of feeling totally alive can take us far beyond our everyday emotional experiences. We say we're "crazy about him," "madly in love," "I've never felt this way before," or "this is amazing." As great as this is, when we're on top of the world is exactly when it's smart to be emotionally managed.

Emotional balance isn't just for stressful feelings; it's needed just as much when we feel exuberant. Over-identity with excitement or emotionalism can pull us out of balance like a rubber band and snap us right into stress. Sustaining the joy and novelty of a relationship requires going deeper into the heart. Otherwise, the initial high can get lost in a "happy head" and we lose contact with our deeper heart and emotional balance. The high starts to fade and hormonal patterns start to change due to overcare and over-attachment. Maintaining the depth of heart connection and sincerity that first touched us takes heart intelligence.

Without heartfelt compatibility and emotional balance, intimate relationships become laced with unspoken overcare expectations and attachments that drain the juice right out of the love. A typical sequence is that first you enjoy being together and doing caring things for each other. As you care for every detail in this heightened emotional state, insecurities that haven't been addressed can take you into overcare and dependency attachments. Then if your lover behaves differently from the way you think she would if she really loved you, you feel hurt or even betrayed. It takes emotional balance to build heart security so you don't lose your own center in relationships. If your partner is practicing emotional management as well, you have a much better chance for a growing and fun relationship. You can catch yourself at any stage and begin to release the overcares to regain the original care with Cut-Thru. This takes assuming responsibility for yourself, as Carol found out.

Our first and foremost relationship is the one with ourself. Building a secure relationship with our own heart allows us to create and enjoy meaningful relationships with others. When our heart is not secure, we can easily lose emotional balance and clear perspective.

There's a difference between surrendering to the heart for the sake of love and placing the responsibility for your happiness in the hands of your romantic partner. When you're in love, you have to listen carefully to your quiet heart signals and not let personal desires ride over them. Surrendering that responsibility to another means that if she or he doesn't fulfill your desires, you might close your heart to what could have been a great relationship. Let's say you were sailing a boat, and one day a perfect wind came along and filled your sails. You're marveling at how in sync you are with the wind, dancing across the water with it, and you think, "I can just release the tiller and surrender to the wind and it will still care for me." Soon you are flapping in the wind, and your romantic illusions are dashed on the rocks. With emotional balance, surrendering instead to your heart signals, you would have still danced with the wind and held onto the tiller.

Surrendering to the heart doesn't mean that the other person will do everything the way you want. Lasting intimate love is nurtured by the vulnerability of sharing your hearts, with care, appreciation, respect, honesty, and compassion, not by depending on the confirming actions or responses of the other person.

We tend to delude ourselves when we fall in love, since new sexual passion can blind us to a deeper heart discrimination about the compatibility for relationship. It's hard to see past the big blue eyes, gorgeous body, or drop-dead smile. Your radar screen is jammed, and your thoughts and emotions continuously reinforce your desire! Without emotional management, your appreciation of your lover can become inflated by your ego vanity desire, idealizing his or her qualities. When the responsibilities of real life and the humanness of both of you burst the bubble of romantic illusion, the relationship can become a fertile ground for judgment, hurt, and blame.

When you're contemplating an intimate relationship, use the Heart Lock-In and Cut-Thru Techniques to understand your motives and desires. Be honest with yourself as you listen to your subtle thoughts and heart signals. The Cut-Thru steps will help you assume objectivity and a helicopter view that can dispel self-delusions and give you a more secure foundation from which to proceed or not. Learning to love and respect ourselves at a deeper level is the first step in relationship building. Learning emotional management skills is needed for relationships to flourish and last.

When we've reflected on the richest moments in our

lives, as well as the most painful ones, they usually involved relationships with other people. We've found that success in building and sustaining friendships requires that we lead with the heart and manage our attitudes and emotions along the way. This demands the courage to be heart vulnerable and overcome fears that if we address a glitch we'll lose something. We learned the hard way that if we didn't address the glitches we would lose the very thing we feared most. It takes strength to realize that the qualities that nurture long-term friendships are qualities of the heart: courage, care, respect, authenticity in communication, appreciation, compassion, and forgiveness. It takes self-security to actualize these qualities. They're not soft skills as many may think and therefore excuse themselves from developing. It's the lack of these qualities that injure relationships and it's skill at developing these that repair friendship. Whether it's the tender vulnerability of intimate love, the mature appreciation of marriage, or the compassion of friendship, the sincerity and quality of our heartfelt feelings are what deepen our relationships.

The changing roles of men and women in society require that both genders become more adaptable and sensitive to each other if we are to all get along. Heart vulnerability is an essential tool in relationships. As we have seen, being heart vulnerable is not the same as being emotionally weak. It means being open to what you are feeling and perceiving, then honestly questioning that to gain more clarity.

Heart vulnerability builds strength in relationships. We don't know anything that adds more value to conversation. It's being authentic, in touch with your real heart that guides you as you speak and listen. Authentic communication nurtures understanding and loyalty in relationships.

Listening authentically from the heart conveys support. Often, men or women don't know how to say what they feel, or they balk out of fear of what the consequences of sharing their feelings might be. You build the capacity to be authentic as you develop heart strength and self-security.

Here's something to consider that can really help in communication. Next time you want to have a heart-to-heart talk, start by going deeper in your heart and sincerely appreciating the other person. Doing a Heart Lock-In before having the talk and sending that appreciation to the other person really can make a difference.

Positive experiences of communication, no matter how subtle, build more confidence and courage to keep trying. It's this sincerity and heart connection that sustains or renews friendships despite challenges, separation, or time.

Have you ever said to yourself, "I'm doing my part, but if only she were more like this or that, then things would be better?" Maybe you saw a movie and wished you had a friendship more like the one in the film or longed for your partner to have the same attractive or passionate qualities as the movie character.

If you notice something about a friend or mate that you wish would change, try improving the relationship by radiating a sincere attitude or feeling of love to him.

Remember that our heart rhythm pattern changes with different emotional states. Frustration produces an incoherent pattern, while appreciation creates a coherent one. That electromagnetic information is transmitted through one's body and radiates outside the body to others. We really are picking up one another's frequency or "wavelength."

In fact, researchers have discovered that when we touch someone or are in close proximity, a measurable exchange of electromagnetic energy—from our heart to their brain—takes place.[1] The charts below show what this looks like. Two people in the lab at the Institute of HeartMath were holding hands. The heart's electrical signal (ECG) in

Person B is clearly reflected in the brain waves (EEG) of Person A. Our laboratory and others have also measured this when the subjects were not touching but were within a few feet of each other.[2]

THE ELECTRICITY OF TOUCH
HEARTBEAT SIGNAL AVERAGED WAVEFORMS

No Contact

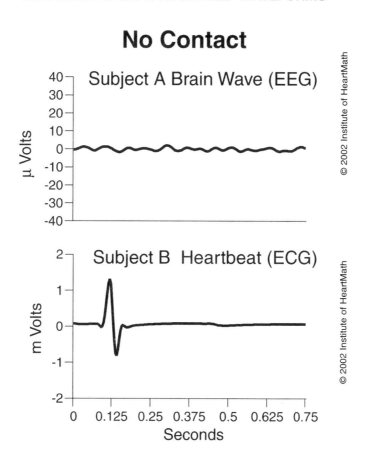

THE ELECTRICITY OF TOUCH:
HEARTBEAT SIGNAL AVERAGED WAVEFORMS

Holding Hands

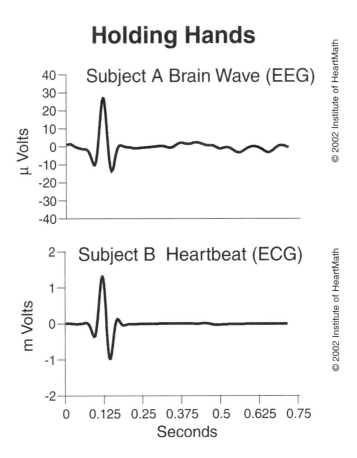

Research suggests that the electromagnetic signals generated by our hearts affect not only ourselves but also the people around us. These graphs show that when two people touch, there is a transfer of electrical energy generated by one person's heart, which can be detected in the other person's brain waves. Note the registration of Subject B's heartbeat signal (ECG) in Subject A's brain waves (EEG) when the two are holding hands.

If anyone we touch or stand close to can pick up our heart's electromagnetic signal and we theirs, we are, in effect, broadcasting and receiving one another's emotional states all the time. Most of this exchange occurs below the radar of consciousness, but it can influence how we feel and communicate. This has tremendous societal implications. Scientific instruments are only able to measure the heart's signal eight to ten feet away from the body, but many feel that the heart's energetic effect reaches much farther than today's instruments can measure.

By putting out more love, appreciation and heart coherence to others, we energetically help to facilitate positive change. When you do a Heart Lock-In and radiate love to someone, do it to clean up your world and find more understanding, no matter what the other person does. This is a high level of maturity and integrity—it's love for love's sake. No love is ever wasted. Sending love may or may not create the change you'd like to see, but it may energize or reveal a more important type of change needed.

When we identify qualities that we dislike in ourselves or in another, we often unmask a deeper issue that we need to address in order to become whole. Your intuitive awareness may be identifying aspects of love that need fine-tuning in you, but you need to put the energy into actualizing these insights.

Jenna, a workshop participant, shared her discovery. "I have always related to men from the learned behavior of observing the way my mother was with men when I was growing up. She would try to help the men in her life see what they were missing in themselves and help them grow." The practice seemed like a good one, so she adopted it in her own relationships with men. "Somehow it wasn't working. I felt this intense overcare, over-responsibility to help them change and see what they were missing—usually different aspects of warmth and caring. Typically the men would shrink away and close off."

Jenna decided to look deeper at this pattern, and in doing so she discovered something more important. "I saw that I wanted my partner to change, not because I really cared about him, but because I wanted him to become someone that I felt would fulfill me more. It was really motivated from self-centeredness, not from deep care." Jenna says she is learning "that the fulfillment that I want comes from my own heart." Trying to get it from someone else is "not only not fair, but not possible."

Jenna is married now, and she practices sending love and appreciation to her husband "as often as I can remember, especially in those moments when I really don't want to. I'm finding that putting out love is helping to create the kind of relationship that I've always wanted. My husband and I are both growing so quickly that it's beyond under-standing. The fun part is that the new care we have for each other feels like one of life's gifts instead of something that I need."

Everyone wants to be able to trust their relationships. We want to trust those we're close to, but the funny thing about trust is that even a small breach can cause separation between relatives, friends, or business partners that often lasts for years—or forever.

Trust is loaded when we put others in a box made of our expectations. It sets us up for disappointment and hurt. Here's what we mean. Joe has to be somewhere important, but Becky needs the car. She tells Joe she'll pick him up at 4 P.M., in time for his appointment. "Can I trust you?" asks Joe. As soon as those words are out of his mouth, Becky gets a funny feeling. She's trustworthy of course, but she feels uncomfortable having her trust questioned and now feels pressured. Her mind darts to what if she's a few minutes late because of traffic? "Can I trust you?" causes uncomfortable feelings because of the pressure of the expectancy.

Many try to get a little security by putting others on the spot about trust. People join new businesses, churches, or groups saying, "Glad I found you, because I can trust you." This sounds sweet and congenial, but it's motivated by an underlying insecurity. Trust is really an inside job. As we build trust in our own heart discrimination and choices, we become secure in ourselves. Then we can enjoy people without being so desperate about trusting them.

When we put a trust tag on someone, it actually takes longer to find our own security, especially if it becomes clear that the person or group can't or won't live up to our trust. Until we get more inwardly secure, life has a way of setting up trust disappointment traps over and over again. If this keeps happening to you, try not to get defensive toward life but build security and trust inside yourself regardless of what others do. See if the following applies to you.

Before you decide to invest your trust in people, it's usually okay with you if they're *human*. But after you trust them, they have to be perfect and dance to the tune of what you expect or you'll get hurt and have to close off your heart. That's an underlying theme in a lot of marriages— where marriage means you trust the other to live up to your expectations. Nearly half of all marriages end in divorce, and breach of trust is the major stated cause. Even when marriage involves clear agreements or commitments that one party breaks, there's usually something else going on that's deeper than breach of trust.

Families and loved ones would often have longer and healthier relationships if they didn't squeeze one another into so many promises and obligations based on trust as a projection of their own insecurities. At this very moment, while you are reading this, there are probably a million people scattered all over the world in tears right now, because they had trusted someone then found out they couldn't.

Parents stay dismayed and hurt because they thought they could trust their children. Often children are not developmentally ready for the trust expectations their parents put on them. Teens and young adults need to be given a certain amount of flexibility for discovery. Parents make the most progress trying to guide children if they understand and respect their need to explore and take risks. They'll remain closer to teens if they don't throw, "I thought I could trust you" in their face at the first indiscretion. That message of blame only engenders separation and resentment—not good for emotional health in any family.

Even adults in their early twenties are often not mature enough for parents to place hardcore trust on them in all areas. They aren't seasoned in the ways of life and therefore will not be able to honor a rigid trust. So parents fly to pieces, not just because their 20-year-old dented a fender, but because they trusted he would take care of the car. There are other ways to deal with disappointment besides feeling wounded or destroyed over the trust issue.

More times than not, when we demand trust externally, we're trying to get security about things that we finally have to deal with inside ourselves. The emotional maturing process involves building trustworthiness first within ourselves, then extending that to others. Most want to skip right over the building blocks into, "I hope I can trust you," or "Just trust me." These are co-dependency compensations, revealing what isn't yet solid inside ourselves. "Just trust me" tends to raise a subconscious warning flag that questions, "Why is he saying that?" We may go ahead and surrender our responsibility to him anyway because we want to trust someone totally. Dependency is attractive when we're not secure in ourselves. In romantic relationships especially, this is usually a setup for failure.

If you are one who tells others to trust you, make sure you want to deal with the responsibility if they do. If something goes awry and they feel you've let them down, you're going to have their heat and resentment on your back much longer than if you hadn't set up the expectation of trust. A safer approach is to tell people you're going to give your friendship your best shot, then do the best you can.

It's healthy to agree to build mutual trust in relationships, but when disappointment occurs, it's not healthy to accuse each other of broken trust. Companies tell employees and customers that they want to build a trusting relationship. Employees or customers often interpret this as the company taking care of them instead of as "building" mutual trust. As soon as something disappointing happens, they assume a transgression of trust and the blame begins. A lot move from one company to another looking for trust when what they're really looking for is security. They may as well pack it up if they're hoping for a trusting relationship with everybody and every company. As you build trust in your own heart intelligence, you won't have to even hope for that. You'll be able to roll with the punches of others' miscues, immaturity, or thoughtlessness instead of resenting someone your whole life because they made a bad call and offended you.

Learning to trust your own heart gives you more latitude and compassion for others when needed. It builds the maturity to have emotional flexibility so you don't drain your energies just because someone offended your trust. You'll find you are fairer with others when you remain in the heart; you will tend less to over-blame or label someone untrustworthy if they bruise your ego or produce disappointments in your world.

Naturally, if someone has *intentionally* broken your trust, healing can take much longer. But we can never fit inner peace in the same room with blame and resentment. There's no way out except heart vulnerability, authentic communication, and forgiveness. Forgiveness doesn't mean you have to be a doormat, setting yourself up for the same experience again. Forgiveness is an act of inner strength because it clears the emotional aftereffects that get stored and will cause drain and depletion of your system if you don't forgive. Trust in your own heart to put the pieces back together and give you healing and peace.

Further along in a relationship, emotional presets can start to prompt friends or partners to feel wounded by the other's words or actions. Here's an example. Let's say you were looking forward to spending some intimate time with your mate, and you made special preparations, only to find him indifferent to the idea. Instantly, you feel hurt. Maybe this is the fourth or fifth time you tried to pull off some intimate time, but it just didn't happen. You've started to develop some judgments about your mate, and as these incidents repeat themselves, the judgments stack up.

Not knowing how to clean up the judgment and hurt, you might "numb them out." But they will come up when you least expect them. Your unmanaged mind and numbed emotions will turn the next minor miscommunication into a major stumbling block. Even if you patch things up, you may just be covering them up. Letting this go on will cause your relationship to lose its shine or dry up into cardboard.

If this is your situation, use Cut-Thru to find out what to do next and to gain the courage to do it. Your heart intuition can guide you on how to initiate the heart vulnerable communication and appreciation needed to unearth hidden agendas, help clear them up, and get your relationship back on track. Practicing *Step 1* especially and using the *Step 1*

Tools in Action will bring more awareness of real feelings underlying the numbness. Once you identify these, *Steps 2–6* will give you increased coherence and clearer perspectives needed to move forward. Having the courage to identify subtle anxieties or vanities so you are honest with yourself is half the battle in freeing up what's been frozen. Having the courage to communicate them from the deep heart is the other half needed for release and progress.

It's easy to justify being numb to our own or to our partner's feeling world when we get self-absorbed in work, career ambitions, children, or projects. We can even perceive our partner's feelings as an interruption, so we brush them aside to get back to our main interest. Over-identifying with work, children's needs, and projects are triggers for blame and fault-finding. Using Cut-Thru on relationship triggers can help give you deeper clarity on what you need to do to honor your commitment to the relationship and keep it rewarding and thriving, or to part ways if you find it's truly not workable. If you want to improve or save a relationship, first be prepared for your heart intelligence to show you what attitudes or behaviors you need to change, rather than trying to change your partner. Then be aware of the mind's resistance to making any change and its justifications for not doing what the heart says. Usually it's a fear of upsetting your comfort zone, even if it's numb comfort.

Let's say your intuition tells you about an attitude to change in yourself, but your mind comes in defiantly saying, "I already know that," so you never take action on your insight. That stubborn defiance blocks you from taking action that could get you out of numb love and enrich the relationship.

Most of us probably don't regard ourselves as defiant, but it's worth another look. Defiant thoughts and feelings can be subtle. To break the defiance habit, practice the

Heart Lock-In Technique and find a feeling of sincere care. Radiate that feeling of care to yourself and your partner, with the intention of being able to stay with an insight and put it into action or making peace with a situation if you can't change it. Be prepared to address subtler feelings and thoughts of insecurity that can arise as you do this. "Notice and Ease" them out through the heart and go back to sincere care. Do this several times and you will start to see results. Even a small effort with sincerity can unlock and deepen your experience of love.

A mature marriage is a valuable accomplishment. But the stresses of today's world can overload marriages to the point where separation seems easier than challenging the assumptions that are driving the relationship apart. In addition to the pain of the partners, a failed marriage too often results in confusion and long-term pain for children who get caught in the middle. For the sake of our families, perhaps we should include in the marriage vows, "Until death do us part, we promise to apply emotional management tools and sincerely try to stay in our hearts." This might sound outrageous, but we offer it as a fun gesture of hope for the challenge of marriage. Here's an example:

Rose wrote from Australia that she's been coaching her husband in the tools—a sensitive undertaking. "The situation we had in our home life was pretty awful," she says. "It was so bad I thought the only way I could cope was to walk away from it and take my two youngest children with me." Not one to give up easily, Rose had been talking to her husband for a long time about the need to get some bottom lines sorted out in their home life. But he often took her comments as criticism, and when he did agree they could never figure out what to do to change. "What turned things around was when I explained to him about the HeartMath studies on energy efficiency and that through heart intelligence you can see how to be more energy efficient. He liked that and because I have changed so much, he is now really keen to try the tools to work things out. I know that if we can get this strong foundation established in our lives I may be able to eventually do some of the things I've always dreamed of."

Rose continued, "HeartMath has helped me to hang on to my heart hopes without letting my head set up all sorts of 'must be met' expectations. I'm open to whatever the heart has planned and I know whatever it is will benefit all, not just my ego." Rose feels they are walking into a different future together. "I had searched and searched for answers. I read lots of books and tried different things. A lot of things helped me to better understand my situation but nothing ever gave me the power to really change things. That was until I discovered these tools."

What most people don't realize is that the conflicts we have with those we love don't have to be extreme to take their toll not only on a marriage but on physical health. Even the day-to-day negative interchanges that many couples take for granted significantly elevate heart rate and blood pressure and increase stress hormone levels. Even after a quarrel that seems trivial, immune systems may be suppressed for as long as 24 hours.[3]

Outward behaviors associated with negative physiological changes include criticizing, denying responsibility, making excuses, interrupting, and trying to coerce the other into accepting one's own point of view. Interactions characterized by hostility, criticism, sarcasm, and blame, because they demean the other partner, are the most damaging. Even more striking, according to researchers, is that these effects occur in couples that say they are highly satisfied in their marriages, lead healthy lifestyles, and are in optimal physical health. It doesn't make a difference whether the couples are newlyweds or have been married for over 40 years; similar physiological responses are observed.

On the other hand, to the extent that marriage fosters a deep heart connection, it can significantly benefit health and may even help protect against serious disease. Researchers studied ten thousand married men with no prior history of angina (chest pain). The men were tested for a whole gamut of heart disease risk factors, including age, blood pressure and cholesterol levels, diabetes, and electrocardiogram abnormalities. Their anxiety levels and family and psychosocial histories were also evaluated. Remarkably, the researchers found *the factor that most predicted the development of angina over the subsequent five years was the men's response to one simple question, "Does your wife show you her love?"* Those who answered "yes" were significantly less likely to develop angina, even when they had high levels of the other risk factors.[4]

In numerous studies across cultures, age groups, and social strata, it's been found that people who lack close and meaningful relationships have a significantly higher risk of mortality, are more susceptible to both infectious and chronic disease, and have reduced survival rates after a heart attack. An article summarizing the findings concluded: "Social relationships, or the relative lack thereof, constitute a major risk factor for health—rivaling the effects of well-established health risk factors such as cigarette smoking, blood pressure, blood lipids, obesity, and physical activity."[5] Conversely, studies have also shown that emotional support (but not dependency) benefits the cardiovascular, hormonal, and immune systems; and there's evidence that emotional support can lower blood pressure and cholesterol, and alter levels of important brain chemicals.[6, 7]

In 1998, 25 percent of American households consisted

of a single person. This was unprecedented. Of course, being single doesn't necessarily mean being lonely. For many, living alone can be the most emotionally healthy life choice. Being happily single is preferable to being in an unhealthy or abusive relationship or jumping in and out of relationships in order to avoid being alone. Loneliness is more a product of one's emotional state and social connectedness than household status. Loneliness comes from feeling cut off from others' hearts and this can occur even if we live in a house filled with people. The more lonely we feel, the more self-absorbed we become. Loneliness and separation left unchecked lead to distorted perspectives, depression, and despair.

When people feel lonely for extended periods of time, their physical health also suffers. A colleague, Jim Lynch, author of *The Broken Heart: The Medical Consequences of Loneliness*, says, "Almost every segment of our society seems to be deeply afflicted by one of the major diseases of our age—human loneliness. Loneliness is not only pushing our culture to the breaking point, but is also pushing our physical health to the breaking point, and indeed has in many cases already pushed the human heart beyond the breaking point."[8]

By keeping your heart open and loving, you can feel connected to others and gain needed social support whether you are in an intimate relationship or not. If you feel lonely, try doing a five to ten minute Heart Lock-In to get your heart energies really moving. Stay focused in your heart and radiate an attitude of appreciation to anything or anyone that you care about or love, then extend that love out to more people, nature, and life. Keep radiating heart energy and listen to your heart intuition on what you can do to express more of that love and care in your daily life. Practice this daily until you can lock onto positive heart feelings for longer periods and express them more frequently with others. This will help heal loneliness and lead you to more rewarding relationships if you are open to what your heart says.

When we lose love, it can feel like our heart is broken. The pain in the area of the heart is very real. When a relationship is ending or we feel rejected by someone we love, a broken heart is like a broken world. Most of us have experienced many little broken hearts since we were children, and some have had devastating emotional hurt. It seems like a rite of passage that life can set us up to open our heart and then take away that which we love. While it's normal to feel sorrow, hurt or regret, it is important for our healing and our growth to make an effort to reconnect with the heart and with others as quickly as possible and not close off. Then we don't have to work as hard to reopen our heart again later.

When you're trying to mend a broken heart, it's easy to blame the other person for being unfair. But blame keeps retearing the fabric of the heart. If you're at the point of tears, let a few tears come—you sincerely hurt. You may find that your mind seeks comfort by asking why—"why didn't he love me," "what did we do wrong as a family," or "what could I have done differently?" While the intention to understand is healthy, this inner dialogue, if pursued while emotionally upset and incoherent, will only reinforce hurt feelings and hopelessness. You are trying to understand from the mind, but it will only dig a deeper hole of despair.

When we are disappointed in love, it is not our real heart that is broken, but our mental and emotional expectations. The mind's presets about how life is supposed to work or what "might have been" are shattered. The stress and incoherence are so strong they create an electrical short-circuit that we feel as a deep pain or a hurt heart. If we shut down the hurt in the heart in self-protection, the pain grows numb. Unfortunately, so does our intuition. Repressing hurt may shut down the pain, but it shuts down the heart as well. It is common to turn to self-pity, anger or resentment to compensate for this loss of love.

To release hurt and resentment, it is necessary to open the heart again. We can't gain access to the compassion and intuition needed to let go and move on until we do. If the heart remains closed, the stress can accumulate into depression. It's important to remember that the mind and a shut down heart can never find the intuition of the deeper heart. The mind is designed to think linearly, calculate and remember the familiar, but it is not designed to understand feelings without the heart. Once we shift to the domain of the deeper heart beneath the pain, we begin to regain emotional balance. This brings new understanding and hope. We perceive how to begin picking up the pieces and move forward with life. Over time, practicing the Cut-Thru Technique and Tools in Action will give you the heart intelligence to bring coherence and peace back into your world. The sooner you begin this process after a heartbreak, the less hurt, blame, and incoherence you will assign and store in your cells and the sooner you will be free again.

In the Appendix you will find an adaptation of the Cut-Thru Technique that people have successfully used to help mend broken hearts. While you may get insights, understanding, or some emotional release at first, a deep or long-standing hurt usually requires repeating the steps several times over a period of days, weeks or longer. Often the heart's mending comes in incremental stages of release and understanding. There is usually a vanity behind the hurt that needs to be revealed. Your spirit or higher self directs this process as well as the length of time it will take.

After using this technique, Jessica wrote about how she

had healed from a breakup. "Even though things had been strained, I did not want to break up. Since he worked near me and we shared a lot of the same friends, I kept seeing him, making the situation worse. I was hurt and resentful, but most of all I began to feel very insecure about whether I was lovable. In the past, I would have blamed him and felt afraid of the future and quickly slid into low self-esteem." Jessica realized that going that route had not worked for her before, so she decided to deal with the situation in a new way.

"I went deep in my heart to appreciate myself as a worthwhile person who could create better ways of dealing with things. Whenever a feeling of future dread would emerge, I focused on staying in the moment. I sent myself a lot of soft heart and appreciated the supportive family and friends I had. If I began to feel overwhelmed by my feelings, I used the tools to deal with them one at a time. Most important, I dealt with feelings of blame toward him or toward myself ('What could I have done differently?') by taking them to neutral in my heart."

Jessica's heart practice paid off. "By being consistent, I got over the breakup faster than I would have thought. It's now nine months later, and while I never thought this was possible, we are back to being good friends with the support and care we originally had, but without the blame and resentment." She was also in for a surprise: "I am happy being single. I have been passing up opportunities for romance because I want to first spend time getting a better relationship with myself. This way, I will have more of my own security to bring to any future relationship."

Take a broken heart to heart, and use it to reconnect with life. The heart has the strength it takes to show you how to renew and use a broken heart to become more of your real self. It also has the strength to love and allow another person to go his or her own way. Appreciate the depth of your experience and what you have learned. Appreciate the other person for having been part of your learning. Life often seems designed to teach us that lasting fulfillment never comes from another. Security and the fulfillment of love come from within our heart, and we have to unfold that in ourselves.

Chapter 13

EMOTIONAL MANAGEMENT IN THE WORKPLACE:
UNLOCKING CREATIVITY, INNOVATION, AND SATISFACTION

*Perpetual devotion to what a man calls his business
is only to be sustained by
perpetual neglect of many other things.*

— ROBERT LOUIS STEVENSON

Most of us spend the largest portion of our waking hours at work. Our workplaces can provide our greatest tests for managing our emotions and many are breeding grounds of emotional viruses. Overcare, over-identity, and over-attachment thrive and feed ego vanities, blame, and resentment. Pressed to perform and pressed for time, we feel internal pressure and resistances as we move through our workday. Things are changing so fast; each day can feel like a wild roller coaster ride. We work longer hours, but there's always more to do. Anxiety can be high and morale low. Few feel like they're working to their full creative potential. Employers blame employees and employees blame management. An emotional virus is the net effect and includes the contagion of defeatism and *us vs. them* behavior. The virus eats away at commitment and teamwork, blocks creativity and innovation, increases costs, and diminishes profits. Yet emotions aren't yet acknowledged as important in most companies.

Does this sound like your workplace? If it does, you can take some comfort in the fact that you're not alone. Nearly 75 percent of people in the U.S. *often* dream about doing something different from their current job.[1] Many feel like they are near the breaking point. We have to look at the situation, be heart vulnerable and admit it, before we can do something about it. As you read, track the language of your feeling world when triggers come up. Use the tools. Listen to your heart intelligence and make notes.

Millions wake up in the morning dreading the day. They put on their dread clothes and they add dread to every little thing that comes up. Their mind chatter starts with dread about their appearance, how someone will respond to them, whether they'll know anyone at the business luncheon. These dread projections are on top of a general heaviness they feel from missed opportunities and unfinished dreams that have been left to gather moss.

The unprecedented speed of change in the workplace and the onslaught of technology are part of the problem. The average office worker gets about 196 messages between voice mail, e-mail, and memos, every single day. People feel like they don't have the time to step back and process or reflect on the work they're doing. Many walk into meetings, launch into conversation, flip open their laptops, hook up to the phone line, and shoot out e-mails *all at the same time*. They can multi-task and get more done than ever before, then try to move faster to get the rest done.

What happens as we speed up is that emotional reactivity speeds up too. We can multi-task faster, but we can't balance our emotions very fast. Not many of us can easily drop an angry reaction, shift out of a depressed mood, or stop a spell of anxiety from burning a hole in our work quality and enjoyment. As a result, we can experience a constant overwhelm or a quiet desperation, unable to create our lives the way we want or find satisfaction in our jobs. Of course not everyone feels this way. There are some individuals who have said "enough" and have been able to create a different type of work experience. There are forward-thinking workplaces where employers recognize and are trying to address the emotional issues. But most don't connect the dots between an emotionally toxic work environment and business results.[2]

Years ago, the pace of work was much more leisurely. We had fewer interruptions. Maybe the phone would ring once or twice or someone would knock on our door. We had less technology. Remember when there was no e-mail, there were no fax machines, no pagers, no cell phones or beepers; when we didn't have the Internet. It was not that long ago. It was 1980. Today, the pace of information hurtling into our workspace often requires us to shift our focus 20 times an hour or much more. Many of these shifts in attention demand nimble mental gymnastics. We can be focusing on a financial report, be interrupted by an employee problem, then by an urgent e-mail from the boss requiring an immediate response, then by our beeping pager and our child on the phone asking to be picked up from soccer, all within a few minutes.

When we shift focus or concepts that often, it puts a strain on our heart, brain and body, which hasn't had time to sync up. Then if even one or two concept shifts are accompanied by a negative emotion of irritation or frustration, our body goes into a stress response, releasing cortisol and other stress hormones. When everything has to be done now, and we find ourselves having to shift focus constantly, our reaction times get skewed, so we can easily spill water on the computer keyboard, delete the wrong e-mail, and get too abrupt with people. We drain our emotional energy reserves, fall prey to anger and resentment, and have little energy left for satisfaction or what we value in our lives.

Then came September 11, 2001, and the world stopped. We went into a global freeze-frame—workplaces slowed down, people started reevaluating their lives. The reverberations are still going on. Some called it 911—an emergency distress call that has awakened us to our over-identities and over-attachments. Our ego vanities don't have the same hold over us. The lure of materialism doesn't have the same glitter. Family and helping others are suddenly important. We don't want to go back to the way we were and we don't know what going forward really means.

These problems haven't gone away since September 11. It's just that many are unwilling to operate under the same pressures. Managers, worried about profits and the economy, push people to go back to the way it was. Under the surface, anger is mounting. It's not just the few who "go postal" (current slang for blowing up, derived from angry postal workers who have gunned down former bosses and co-workers). In 1999, one employee out of six reported being so angered by a co-worker that he or she felt like hitting the person, but didn't. Some lose it while they wait for technicians to fix their computers. Network managers complain that employees smash monitors, break keyboards, or kick hard drives when faced with computer woes.[3]

Being successful at work in this day and age demands a lot of skills, but the most obvious skill lacking is how to manage basic human emotions. Few bosses know how to address emotional issues. Some managers are fine working with their own division but territorial and defensive when dealing with others. Some stifle creativity, promote destructive competition, omit essential information, leave people out of the loop, and never form a team. Some focus solely on technical issues and write off people problems as a waste of time. Some still naively think that constant stress keeps people productive. The funny thing is that many people are so adapted to an emotionally chaotic work environment they don't even recognize their stress.

Stress can become an unseen addiction like any other. Many become stress junkies and experts now say that stress may have a greater impact on rising health care costs than physical factors like obesity, smoking, and high blood pressure. First time heart attack patients often show few, if any, of the traditional risk factors associated with heart disease. Instead, it is reported that the most common characteristic shared by these patients is job dissatisfaction and negative attitude.[4] Workers reporting high levels of stress cost our health care systems almost 50 percent more than their less stressed colleagues.[5] They call in sick or take unscheduled absences because they are stressed out, exhausted or have personal needs they want to attend to.

Some people see the handwriting on the wall. Daryl R. Conner, author of *Managing at the Speed of Change*, says, "The future will generate even more ambiguity and chaos than we face today. Learning how to raise our individual and collective resilience is not just a good idea—it is imperative."[6]

Most of us live and breathe our organization's climate at least eight hours of every workday. The emotional demands of the workplace aren't going to just disappear. Ignoring an emotional virus or denying its effect won't make it go away. It spreads beyond the office building to our homes and schools and communities. It spreads through the Internet and will spread even faster as we become more connected through high-speed communication networks. It will spread from the bottom line on company spreadsheets to their stock price on Wall Street. But so can its antidote—heart intelligence and emotional balance—spread in the same way.

On a personal and societal level, emotional management in our workplaces is not an option if we are to survive or thrive. We can take individual responsibility, whatever our job title or position. There are isolated pockets of executive groups, work teams, and individuals quietly realizing that they can start to make a difference by changing their own *internal* climate. People need tools to address their own emotions and the undercurrents going on around them. As they raise the bar on their own emotional management, their quality of experience in the workplace improves and is sustained.[7, 8]

Some companies are offering emotional awareness training programs. HeartMath tools have made an impressive difference in assisting workers to better manage stress and deliver higher levels of performance that are maintained over time. Dr. Chris Roythorne, corporate medical director for BP (British Petroleum), one of the world's largest corporations, says, "Like many organizations, the organization I work for is performance driven—it's data driven—and people like to see the proof that something works. HeartMath gives you that proof."

Emotional balance, not high stress, is what brings us the clarity and intelligence we need to perform at our best. Everyone has a different stress threshold performance curve. When we are energized and stress is a creative challenge, our performance increases. When we hit our stress threshold, where we can't maintain emotional balance or sustain a positive feeling, our performance capability drops off sharply. Early stages of performance deterioration tend to go unnoticed. We push on. Pressures or expectations imposed by ourselves or by the job keep us going, even though our performance is dipping. Too much pressure for too long leads to breakdown. We all live somewhere on this curve.[9]

THE STRESS/PERFORMANCE CURVE

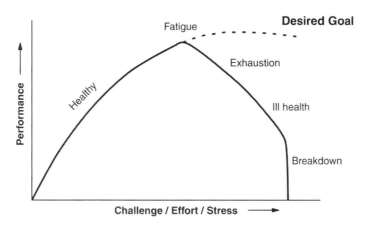

Adapted from: Nixon P. in *Mind-Body Medicine,* 1997

The stress-performance curve illustrates the relationship between performance, stress, and health. The curve shows that performance increases with increasing challenge or effort—up to a point. After this, any increase in stress actually reduces performance, which can often cause us to miss our desired goal. When we continue to press on without effectively managing our stress, it can lead to fatigue, physical and emotional depletion, ill health, and ultimately breakdown.

There's a difference between stretching past our comfort zone of work pace in order to meet an important deadline, and pushing ourselves *past* the line constantly. Continued high performance or peak performance can be achieved only if we remain ahead of the stress curve. Positive attitudes are actually what drives success in business.[10, 11] The Harvard Business School found that employee attitudes drive financial results, not the other way around.[12] Some companies are waking up to this and offering employees flex time to tend to personal or family needs, psychological counseling, corporate gyms, even massage therapy to reduce stress. Some are encouraging employees to take paid time off to volunteer at local charities or schools. Nevertheless, many employees say that while these benefits help, they don't remedy the culture of stress and negativity that keeps everyone on edge. Furthermore, they don't always have time to go to the gym to manage their emotions and the relaxing effects of a massage soon wear off. They need solutions they can use at their desks or in the moment of high stress.

So what can you do? The first step in managing your emotions in the workplace is to be present enough to recognize stressful feelings that arise in you. You have to notice the stress in order to do something about it. Use *Step 1* of Cut-Thru periodically during the day. Simply pause to be aware of how you feel about the issue at hand. If there is stress or tension, use the Tool in Action "Notice and Ease" to release it and be more fully present. This will help you regain emotional balance without losing energy. If you find yourself multi-tasking or having to shift your focus a lot, pause to use the Tools in Action—"Open the Heart" and "Be in the Now"—to increase your presence. Then use "Attitudinal Breathing" to synchronize your system so you stay grounded as you go.

Each of the Cut-Thru steps and Tools in Action can be applied to different workplace situations. Experiment and see which act quickest for you and in which situations. You may find that in tense negotiations, you'll want to use *Step 2*, "Breathe Love and Appreciation" or "Breathe Balance" to increase your heart coherence. Then you might move to *Step 3*, "Assume Objectivity" about the feeling or issue— as if it were someone else's problem, for more clarity in negotiating.

In those endless, boring meetings you can't do anything about, try *Step 4*, "Rest in Neutral"—in your rational, mature heart, to help you stay poised and sustain your energy. Then from neutral you can add *Step 5*, "Soak and Relax" any disturbed or perplexing feelings in the compassion of the heart, dissolving the significance a little at a time.

Probably the handiest Tool in Action to recalibrate your emotions throughout the workday is "Take the Significance Out." Jason, a manager, tells how this tool helps him cut through corporate density and malaise.

"As a manager, dissolving significance has meant having the maturity to help others stay neutral when their 'justified' reactions would otherwise have gotten the best of them." A few years ago Jason faced the job of integrating a new manager into his staff. "There were several times when I saw him overwhelmed by the complexity of his job. He needed to learn to motivate others without over-personalizing their lackluster responses. Concerns were creeping into my perceptions of him—is he going to be strong enough in leading others? Has he got too much overcare to be an effective manager?" Practicing "Take the Significance Out" showed Jason that these were premature concerns; something simpler was going on. His intuition showed him that the real issue was an understandable awkwardness of being new to the job and new to the company. Says Jason with satisfaction, "Helping us both reduce significance sped up the integration process tremendously. He is now one of the most effective, passionate, and caring members of our staff."

After you use Cut-Thru for a while on your own work issues, you're ready to use the tools to help clean up a toxic work environment. It's become the culture in many workplaces to stand around the water cooler, spend time at lunch or at social gatherings, or log onto the Internet to communicate a tirade of judging and "dissing" others. What often starts as gossip can turn into a blame game with each contributor adding more negativity. "Can you believe what she did today?" "I can't stand how he talks." And so it goes until it builds into a vendetta. If you participate in this culture-wide blame fest, you will increase the accumulation of negative energy both within you and in your environment, making it harder to restore equilibrium and peace. Even when you decide you're not going to contribute to it any longer, it's easy to get swept up in a momentum of negativity around you.

Accumulated workplace negativity creates an atmosphere of incoherence that has its own momentum. Once an environment acquires an atmosphere of anger, blame, or cynicism, it's hard to disengage from the seduction of it. Blame draws blame, and drain increases drain. It can cause people to become more deeply mired in the very problems they're trying to escape. The negativity becomes highly magnetic, spreading its devastation in a chain reaction that can infect work teams from customer service to the boardroom.

Ongoing faultfinding or venting without resolution keeps everyone out of balance, then daisy-chains into overwhelm or lashing out and finally drains into lackluster feelings and dread. A culture of overwhelm is one of the paramount consequences of faultfinding. We've talked about overcare and over-identity as key contributors to overwhelm, but one of the least understood factors is faultfinding. And faultfinding is highly contagious. Like a computer virus, it gets broadcast globally and threatens everyone locally. We often get signals from our intuition not to join in the berating of others. But, because of the intrigue, the mind stimulation of it, we can get pulled into the negative flow of the latest controversial upset. If we observe ourselves closely in these situations, we may notice an ambivalent feeling. We sort of want to say something else, something doesn't feel quite right, but it's easier to keep going into faultfinding or blame. To protect ourselves, there are several things we can do.

Use the Cut-Thru and Heart Lock-In Techniques together to detoxify negative emotional accumulation in yourself and in your environment. This will help you harness your emotional power to neutralize reactions and not get into all that. Practice creating a coherent "heart-field" environment within and around you by radiating a feeling of love, care, or appreciation wherever you are. An electromagnetic energy field radiates from each person's heart. This field is more or less coherent depending upon a person's emotional state.[13] Creating a coherent heart-field environment has many benefits. It helps to balance and protect you from negative energy, such as anger, judgments, or blame that others may be expressing. It makes it easier for you to not over-personalize a situation or get emotionally colored by what's going on. It also makes it easier for others to connect with their own hearts. Radiating love through your heart can actually help create an environment of increased coherence and heart resonance that can facilitate a roomful of people.

Goal Breathing is a powerful exercise to create a more coherent heart-field environment and one of the most effective things you can do for workplace (or household) harmony. Here's how you do it. Have a goal to facilitate more balanced and harmonious energy. Breathe that goal while radiating love through the heart and solar plexus area for a few minutes. It will help you become conscious of creating a heart-field environment in any situation you are in.

You can use Goal Breathing to rebuild a heart-field environment when a situation starts to deteriorate—to help restore harmony to your system and buffer you from the incoherence. Here's a picture. You're in a place where people are having a conflict. It's tough going, and the energy between them is hostile. Watch out for your own preconceived ideas about why one or the other party is not going to discuss the problem fairly or be in their heart. Instead of projecting more judgment or negativity into the situation, take that same energy and build a heart-field environment around them. Do Goal Breathing, to facilitate more balanced and harmonious energy. As you send them love, see the coherent energy from your heart as gold warmth surrounding the situation they're in. Radiate the warmth for a few moments. You can also do this before potentially challenging situations.

Ray describes using this tool. "I had to meet regularly with a work group that was quite contentious, and the meeting usually went overtime, ending at 6 or 7 P.M. Before the third meeting I decided to do Goal Breathing and send love to the room and the people around the meeting table. When someone was getting upset during the meeting, I would send love to that person. In fact, the meeting ran much smoother than the previous ones and actually ended on time at 5 P.M."

Ray also noticed something else. "During the whole meeting, I was using listening more deeply (it kicked in all by itself), and I could take notes verbatim in longhand. In the previous two meetings, I could hear what was being said, but with all the scattered, intense energy, when I tried to write I would lose my train of thought and not record everything. So this Goal Breathing really works!"

Remember that even one person's increased heart coherence can help bring more coherence into a relationship or an environment. Only by many individuals taking responsibility can we create a countercurrent of coherent energy to offset an emotional virus epidemic of negativity in the workplace or at large.

"Emotions are energy in motion," writes Lynn, in describing how she protects herself from others' emotional baggage. "Remembering this has given me new ways of handling negativity and a whole new way of being. When confronted by a negative person, I tell myself I can react the same old way or do something different. My first priority is managing my own emotions, then see what my heart directs me to do. I do a Cut-Thru, going to my heart and listening to what it says. Sometimes it tells me to send compassion and stay away. Other times, it guides me to talk to the person from a centered heart, and that helps him or her calm down. If I really get upset, my heart often says to write a letter to the person, put it aside, read it again, and revise it. Then I am able to release the problem. This seems to affect the other person too."

Creating a more coherent heart-field environment within you and around you to help change a culture of negativity is a high form of creativity and innovation. While organizations want their employees to be creative and innovative, not many understand the cultural change in the workplace this requires. In order to unlock creativity and innovation, emotional incoherence has to be addressed.

Negative emotional states keep people locked into limited thought tracks. Positive emotional states open the heart and generate the coherence needed to find an intuitive bandwidth that can track new and innovative ideas. A Harvard University forum asked a group of CEO's how often they used intuitive judgment to make their decisions. They estimated around 65 percent of their decisions were intuitive. And when asked why they used intuition instead of data analysis, the executives agreed, "If we wait for the data, someone else will have done the deal." Intuition gave them the creative edge to accomplish what they couldn't without it.

With positive emotional states being so essential in sustaining intuition and creativity, it would only make sense that leaders (and anyone who wants to advance in their career) study and harness the physiology of emotions. Research shows that when we have more positive feeling, we have greater cognitive flexibility and better negotiation outcomes. We retrieve more extensive and interconnected positive material from memory. This is not seeing the situation idealistically or through rose-colored glasses. We are less defensive and can better address any negative information. We are more open to different ideas. When a bargaining situation requires a problem-solving approach and we can take the other person's perspective, we perceive more diverse aspects of a situation, more positive possible outcomes and more different possible outcomes. *This is creativity and innovation in action.*[14]

Emotional chaos and negativity deafen us to intuition— yet one intuition can become the next patent or product improvement or process change needed. One intuitive insight can solve a human resource problem that has kept an entire work team or workplace embroiled in chaos.

George, a very capable executive, describes how he came to understand this. "I'd learned the Cut-Thru Technique but hadn't used it much, not until I was backed into a corner," says George. "When chaos finally hit, it hit in a big way. There was just no time to accomplish what had to be done, and there were consequences that affected people's lives if our problems didn't get solved." George sank into despair, seeing no way out. "I thought, what the heck, why not try Cut-Thru." He tried what he remembered of the technique while sitting at his desk. He began breathing appreciation through the solar plexus. "This sort of helped but it didn't release the overwhelming intensity I was experiencing or the big knot in my stomach. Then I realized I'd forgotten the heart. So I shifted my attention up to the heart area and just breathed appreciation through the center of my chest. After a minute or two of doing this, I started to feel like a very gentle breeze was passing right through my chest. But the knot was still there. I then focused my attention back to the solar plexus. This time it worked. I felt the knot dissolving. I was able to actually feel the rhythms in my solar plexus come into sync with my heart."

Before long George's despair was gone. "After just a bit longer, the sense of appreciation I was breathing became real, not just a concept. First of all, I appreciated not feeling that heaviness and intensity anymore. I appreciated the neutral state I had reached regarding the unsolved problems in what was really a very short period of time. Then the other Cut-Thru steps just came to me automatically. I was able to actually assume objectivity and look at my situation as if it were someone else's problem. I saw it was just not as big of a deal as I'd been making it. Several very practical solutions that would benefit both our customers and our employees became intuitively clear in the space of a few minutes. Just knowing what to do was a huge relief."

George found that implementing his solutions went very smoothly. "That experience is now indelibly printed in my memory. Chaos can still happen, but it never gets to that same intense level. I'm quicker to Cut-Thru and the more I use it, the less time it takes me to balance and get intuitive clarity about what to do."

Daryl, another executive says, "Intuition is essential for executives. We have to make fast decisions and if they're not right the buck stops with you. Cut-Thru supplies intuition in real time when it's most needed, even in difficult situations. It supplies creative insight which gives you foresight, so you no longer have to live with the regret of hindsight." Darryl discovered that the better he got at managing and balancing his emotions, the easier it was to stay connected with his intuition. "I'm more able to track intuition, more able to see and feel others potentials—and I make choices from there. It's as though there are parallel universes of potential outcomes, and depending upon our perceptions and choices we activate different potentials. Intuitive decision-making unlocks creativity needed for a more optimal future."

When most people think of creativity, it's usually in reference to music, art, poetry, ideas or inventions. These aspects of creativity, though important, are still secondary. Positive emotions—love, appreciation, nonjudgment, deeper care, compassion, and forgiveness—are primary. These are higher manifestations of creativity. They open us to readily accessible inspiration and innovation. One of the most effective creative maneuvers that anyone can do during a workday is to bridge the gap between mind and heart through sincerely loving more. Increasing our ability to love also brings in higher and more pure aspects of our spirit. Then as we merge with these higher aspects of our spirit, we receive more intuitive clarity from spirit and our intuitions become more powerfully effective. We create an energetic field environment that makes it easier for others to connect to an intuitive flow and unlock their creativity as well.

Leadership generally shapes both the stated and unstated values that drive a workplace or work team culture. Leaders can say one thing about business alignment, but their actions set the pace and tone that others follow. Whether or not the leadership of your company manifests alignment between its stated mission, values and actions, you can create that alignment within yourself through managing your emotions and emerge as a skilled leader of yourself, your department or your team. It doesn't take a lot of effort to make a difference. We tell people, from line workers to presidents, "Try a little love or appreciation and see what happens." Take out the overcare and over-personalization and try it. As basketball coach Phil Jackson says in his book, *Sacred Hoops*, "Love is the force that ignites the spirit and binds teams together." Many people can be on the same team, yet feel very disconnected from each other. This blocks effective teamwork.

The idea of love and its appropriate expressions in the workplace can make people queasy, and that's where the research studies and tools can make the difference. It takes the "touchy-feely" out of love and appreciation. But the care still has to be sincere. Some leaders give appreciation lip service or create recognition programs that are merely window dressing, as the underlying culture is still one of mudslinging and backbiting. Kevin Cashman, author of *How to Be a Real Leader*, laments how appreciation has become a lost skill in business. "In the business world, confrontation, criticism, and even hate are more socially acceptable than expressions of appreciation. That's too bad, because appreciation is a truly value-creating activity. It energizes people, and makes them want to exceed their goals and perceived limits." [15]

Don't think that appreciation is gratuitous fluff. It's one of the fastest acting things you can do to shift your mood or the mood of your environment. Use the Tools in Action "Sincerity in Asking" and "Sincerity in Appreciating." Appreciating anything can also unlock intuitive clarity on other issues and can time shift a terrible or so-so day into a dynamic and effective one. "Sincerity in Appreciating" is one of the easiest ways to transform relationship dynamics between co-workers.

As you practice "Sincerity in Appreciating," your co-worker may not turn from a "frog into Prince Charming" but you will gain more clarity on his or her positive qualities and enhance your work relationship. Presets will only muddy clarity and communication. Workplace relationship quagmires can drain you emotionally more than having too much on your plate or feeling pressured by deadlines.

Workplace relationship dynamics inhibit performance probably more than any other factor. Use the Cut-Thru Technique on workplace relationships that are the most challenging for you. Start with the people who are most critical to the smooth functioning of your work—whether a supervisor, colleagues on your team, or direct reports— then move to clients, vendors, or others. If you see that you are habitually reacting to one of these people and that it's inhibiting your performance or satisfaction in some area, make it a priority to use the tools with the goal of removing the emotional obstacle from your own perception, not changing the other person. This is one of the quickest ways to gain insight past what you expected and possibly magnetize more cooperation from others.

Mary unlocked a whole world after she applied Cut-Thru to one difficult work relationship. She'd joined a new department and felt from the start that Don, one of her superiors, was not going to be easy to work with. "I felt like I was invisible to him," Mary says. "He seemed to give other people credit for my ideas and when I proposed something to him directly, it seemed to take months for it to 'get on his radar.' I had a hard time respecting his leadership." To counteract what she perceived as his negative attitude toward her, she developed what she called "guerilla tactics" to get things done, and inside accumulated a private list of his inadequacies. "I even stooped to share my frustrations with my colleagues," Mary confesses. "It was obvious to me that he was limited, sexist, and unable to appreciate the special gifts that I brought to the department."

Of course she didn't reveal any of this to Don. "At key meetings I tried to stay on my best behavior, acknowledged strategies he proposed, tried to be friendly and contribute.

But I always felt disappointed; we just didn't connect." After a year of struggling with her reactions to Don, Mary considered leaving the department. While exploring other options, she began to feel that her relationship with Don needed to be resolved, and she decided to try to make this happen. "Some instinct told me that this was unfinished business."

About this time, Mary learned the Cut-Thru Technique. After just a few practices, she began to see that her relationship with Don was similar to relationships with other male authority figures. "I realized that I was also intimidated by policemen if I got a ticket, by other male senior managers in the company, and that this pattern of intimidation and rebelliousness was connected with not embracing my own power."

She continued her practice of Cut-Thru and found that she was shifting her focus in the relationship. Instead of trying to change Don, she was focusing on addressing her emotional attitudes. She began to see a change happening in her perceptions of Don. Talking with an old friend one day about Don, she realized that he reminded her of her father. Mary says, "Like Don, my dad was charismatic and visionary, but his inattention to the everyday events and challenges of my life left me unprotected from some very traumatic experiences as a teenager." Mary adored her dad but now realized for the first time "just how much I had felt let down by him." The grief released. "I cried and forgave him. Afterward I felt about a hundred pounds lighter, emotionally." She discovered, then, that she had been projecting those feelings about her father onto Don.

"At the next department meeting that Don attended I found that the old emotional charge I usually felt in his presence was completely absent. I found myself admiring his work, his ideas, and his growth." She felt as though she was seeing him clearly for the first time. "At an appropriate moment, I shared some of the story about my insights with him, telling him that I wanted him to know that I had cared about the relationship enough to sort it out. I thanked him for his patience with me. He was really touched. And he shared a bit about his own life and challenges with me."

A door was open. "All that time that I'd felt invisible, I had been unable to see him clearly. A few months later I got a call about a raise and a big bonus that he'd approved for me. I was thrilled. I felt deeply acknowledged for my work and contribution." The bigger bonus, though, was in Mary's heart. "There's a saying about 'difficult people,' those who challenge our equilibrium," says Mary. "Bless those who challenge us, for they remind us of doors we've shut and doors we've yet to open."

To increase your quality of life in your job or to find a more rewarding occupation, practice listening to your heart. As you release your overcares, over-identities, and over-attachments, you will gain the personal control of your life that you want, and this will help open doors that can further career fulfillment.

Wherever you are in your career, whatever type of job you have, ask your heart periodically, "Is my care stress-producing or stress-reducing? Where it's stress producing, ask yourself, "What do I need to do to find balance?" Then listen to what your heart intelligence has to say. By taking care of yourself, you'll have more to give yourself and others. Finding the flow through the heart again is what makes it all worthwhile.

Workplaces will be less stressful when core values of real love, appreciation, balanced care and respect accompany the bottom line. These are practical strategies for mission and business alignment. Have compassion for yourself and others. Overcoming emotional chaos to increase performance and innovation will be the knowledge capital of the future. Reduced stress, accompanied by heightened intuition, creativity, and job satisfaction, means less turnover, higher-quality products and services and more profit. Managing emotions in the workplace to create a viable and healthy future simply makes good business sense.

Chapter 14

THE GLOBAL OPPORTUNITY

To put the world right in order,
we must first put the nation in order;
to put the nation in order, we must first put
the family in order; to put the family in order,
we must first cultivate our personal life;
we must first set our hearts right.

— CONFUCIUS

Accessing the coherent power of the heart is important as we face global threats that impact us personally and collectively. How we address the cumulative anxiety that follows in the wake of chaos becomes increasingly critical in a world that's instantly connected through TV, satellite, cell phones, and Internet. With each televised catastrophe, there are emotional shocks and aftershocks that generate a wave of incoherence throughout the planet. Add to this any stressful change in one's health, family, or work life, and it's no wonder that feeling emotionally fragile or edgy has turned into an epidemic.

One of our purposes at HeartMath has been to develop simple, scientifically tested tools for managing individual and societal fear projections and reactions. We bring the heart to bear on some of the most pressing issues of our time. We address hard questions, such as, how do you respond to hatred and blame generated by religious or ethnic conflicts and terrorism? If you were a child who lost your parents and your home due to war in Africa, Kosovo, Palestine, Afghanistan, Sri Lanka, East Timor, or other areas, how do you forgive being hated and displaced just because you are of another religion or ethnicity? As you grow up, what do you do with the pain, grief, and bitterness? If you are a parent whose child was gunned down by another child, what do you do with the anguish and knowledge that this tragedy could have been prevented? Or if you are a police officer overwhelmed by all the real and suspected threats that come to you every day, and realize that you may not have responded appropriately to one, how do you handle your guilt and the social blame?

To answer these difficult questions, we have to understand the feeling world of human beings. People's deep feelings of hurt, anger, and resentment need to be addressed in order to repair the emotional damage and restore hope. Through honoring feelings, we open our own hearts to the deeper care required in finding viable answers.

Unfortunately, it often takes tragedy to finally open the heart of a person, family, or community. Natural disasters like floods and earthquakes bring together people of different races, ethnicities, and socioeconomic levels to cooperate for the good of the whole for a while. Catastrophe throws people into their hearts, and some experience deep bonding with people they wouldn't have even talked to before. While working together, they let go of judgments, connect in the heart, and show more care and allowance.

The challenge is to sustain this care. The emotional after effects of crisis remain long after the world has gone back to business as usual. Only sustained care can bring the kind of sensitivities and understanding that begin to resolve hurt and pain, restore trust and allow us to move forward as better people. It's deeper care that motivates a *passion to understand and feel* what others feel, then compassion and reconciliation have a chance. It's deeper care that motivates a courageous, strong yet wise business heart that can stop emotional histories from repeating themselves.

Deeper care makes insight easier. It activates the coherent power of the heart needed for intelligent solutions to appear, which are not accessible in an atmosphere of incoherence. Deeper care organizes emotion and helps us "Hold to Neutral," giving us a solid chance to avoid acting until balance is restored. Cultivating deeper care starts with each of us, and extends to our families, workplaces, schools, and nations. One of the key premises of HeartMath tools is that you *can* bring in more care from your spirit to create the constructive changes you want to see. You can bring more spirit into humanness, so spirit can infuse human nature.

BRINGING MORE SPIRIT INTO HUMANNESS

Almost every recorded culture and religion has referenced spirit as a source of power, love, and intelligence. But the different ways that people and religions have interpreted "spirit" have spawned over-identities, overcares, and over-attachments to their interpretations, leading to separation, ongoing conflicts, and war. If, today, you ask a dozen people walking down the street what connecting with spirit means to them, you are likely to get a variety of answers. Some will say it's becoming their real self or higher self. Others will tell you it's making contact with their personal source, Christ, Buddha, Allah, the part of God that's in them, universal intelligence, or the power of love.

Scientists today are also divided about the existence of "spirit." Most agree with Albert Einstein's statement that, "Everyone who is seriously involved in the pursuit of science becomes convinced that a Spirit is manifest in the laws of the universe—a Spirit vastly superior to that of man, and one in the face of which, we, with our modest powers, must feel humble."

From our experience, spirit is indeed a powerful source of love and higher intelligence. Each person has a connection to a universal spirit that is non-physical, yet connected to everything. Because it is everywhere, spirit connects with humanness through all aspects of our system, heart, mind, emotions and cells. But it's *through the heart* that we find the main trunk line for our individual connection to spirit, our higher self. This is because more spirit comes in through love, and the heart is designed to receive and generate love to the wholeness of oneself and others. That's why you can manifest more of your true spirit through increasing your love through deeper care and compassion. As you send love and compassion to yourself and others, you draw more spirit into your humanness, resulting in more intuition, fulfill-ment, and sense of purpose.

Humanity as a whole is more ready to understand the love and intelligence of spirit than ever before. Science is revealing that love is not just a religious concept or an emo-tion, but a coherent force needed to facilitate harmony and healing. Technology is enabling us to research the effects of love on physiology, perceptions, and behaviors. As we learn how love works, we can learn how to love more.

Regardless of people's religious beliefs or non-beliefs, unmanaged emotions and ego vanities create incoherence that blocks their experience of love. Until the emotions are regulated and fine-tuned, whatever spiritual insights people have cannot be fully translated through their nervous system and integrated into their attitudes and behaviors. *Therefore, understanding and regulating the emotional nature is the next frontier for spiritual or psychological advance.* Bringing your mental, emotional, and physical systems into increased coherence creates *alignment* with the heart and opens you to a new bandwidth of intelligence and love. Without organized emotion, there can be no such alignment and spirit cannot enter unimpeded. It's just math.

Emotional management from the heart is a practical method of manifesting more spirit in ordinary daily life, whereby spirit becomes demystified and spirit and humanness merge. Prayer, meditation, better foods, and therapies of all kinds are helpful add-ons, but can lead us only to the point where we have to take responsibility for our own emotional management. You can't meditate your emotions away and you can't pray or affirm them away. It's important to respect all religious or spiritual practices and realize they can assist, but can't replace, the individual interactive work with self that is needed to complete the missing connections. There is a code that has to be decoded that lies within the heart. Each person has to address emotional management to crack that code in order to access his or her higher power and intelligence with continuity.

When we start any new practice, we always hope for immediate results. We also may worry that we won't do it correctly, that it won't work for us, or that it's not as effective as it was said to be. It's important to ease into a new process rather than try to take it by storm. Easing into a process means approaching change with *heart ease* instead of mental effort. Heart ease power rather than mental willpower can reduce resistances and keep you motivated. The art of easing helps you connect with the power of your spirit and accomplish what you couldn't before. Even *assuming* an attitude of ease helps connect you to your heart and to the flow of spirit.

Usually, what's lurking behind our most uncomfortable resistances is our ego vanity. That's nothing to feel bad about. Vanity is one of the last hiding places of separation between people and their real self. Ask your heart to identify the hidden vanity when you feel an emotional resistance that won't go away. Once you identify the vanity and admit it to yourself with heart vulnerability, your spirit often gives you an emotional release.

One of the upsides of the current momentum of global change is that positive emotional changes can happen more quickly. If you've had an insight about something that you need to change, it's easier to act on when so much is changing around you. Start with one thing that your heart is saying, then manage your emotions to listen to and follow your heart.

As we practice tools for emotional management, they turn into tools for spiritual management—allowing more spirit to come into the human system. Emotions become the carrier wave for the spirit of love. One of the main purposes of emotion in nature's design is to provide a means of expression for qualities of spirit, like love, kindness, care, compassion, forgiveness, joy, and appreciation. But because heart intelligence isn't developed in most people, the mind and ego vanities more often direct emotional energy to express insecurities, frustration, worry, hurt, and anger.

It's the amount of spirit regulated into your humanness that determines how much joy and fun you feel and experience. During periods of accelerated change, the spirit at times puts more "squeeze" on the humanness to pop through major attitudinal hindrances. Sincerity is the generator that powers all the techniques and tools and brings insight faster. Once you've practiced for a while, your heart signals will become stronger and clearer, and your intuition more automatically accessible. The more incoherence you release from the vault of your cells, the more you free your spirit to manifest in your life. You reactivate hormonal flows that tend to diminish with age, regaining much of the mental and emotional flexibility that you had as a young child. You move through life's challenges with more flex and ease.

Flex is love in a usable form. It rounds off the corners and edges of events in life. It helps you be more adaptable in your mental and emotional responses to change and gives you increased resilience. Flexibility and adaptability don't happen just by reacting fast. They result from mental and emotional balance, having care for self and others, and not being attached to specific outcomes.

As you increase your flexibility, your spirit can permeate your mental, emotional, and physical nature, down to the cellular level, and unfold a new *blueprint* for fulfillment in your life. Many of us have become so accustomed to living with incoherent feelings and resistances (fear, worry, guilt, resentment, etc.), that we have built our identity around those moods and attitudes. This blocks our ability to find real fulfillment. Issues left unattended can cause one's spirit to squelch the release of personal joy, even if everything else seems to be going well. Joy is not determined by external achievements, or achievers would all live in bliss. Neither is it determined by how many things you have, or the rich and middle-class would automatically be happier than the poor. The difference between happy and have is one of the hardest lessons to learn in life. You can have plenty and not be happy at all. Yes, it helps to have some things—but not as much as it helps to have heart security and joy if you're without things. Money and success can't assure happiness in relationships, neither with yourself or others. That's where core heart feelings come in.

If love were an apple pie, then joy would be one of its larger slices. Joy is a gift from spirit that increases to the degree that one's mind and emotions align with one's heart integrity. It decreases to the degree that this alignment is breached. The human system ages as joy retreats and regenerates as joy is increased. Mind stubbornness in yielding to intuitive heart feelings causes spirit to turn joy off, just like closing the water valve on a faucet. Mind resistance isn't the only dampener of joy in the complex human system, but it's especially one of the first places to look when joy starts to become a low-key experience. Often a matured realignment with what your heart really knows can re-open the valve to your spirit. This frees up the joy that was withheld due to a self-imposed attitudinal block between you and your authentic self.

People will learn in the future that they can, while in a joyful or positive emotional state, build up their emotional energy reserves to slow aging and improve health, just as they build their physical energy reserves through physical exercise. Often, when we feel good emotionally, we have a sense that we don't need to do anything but enjoy the feeling. But there is something we can do that has a big payoff—more than you might know. When times are good and you're feeling positive, do an exercise of breathing joy from the heart. Breathing joy builds a spiritual reservoir that comes in handy when emotional disturbances arise. It's like putting money in the bank or investing in an insurance policy. Breathing an attitude of joy sets up a frequency of buoyancy in your emotional energy bank account with numerous benefits. It helps to heal old emotional disturbance patterns that are stored in the cells. It helps you maintain closer intuitive contact with your spirit. And it helps to create a positive energy environment that makes it easier for those around you to find intuitive clarity.

Breathe in joy the same way you breathe love and appreciation in Attitudinal Breathing. You're not looking for an exhilarating joy but more of a quiet joy. Breathing quiet joy is an especially good exercise to do for extended time periods, like when you're taking a walk or jogging, or driving on a trip from town to town. You may want to alternate breathing joy with breathing love, appreciation, or balance to build up your emotional accumulators and offset energy drains. Each of these positive attitudes has a different energetic frequency, but they are all part of love.

Breathing joy is especially effective for giving you more emotional capacity so you don't have as strong negative reactions to standard trigger patterns, like office issues, personal insecurities, or problems with a relationship. These are the three areas where people quietly drain the most energy. The triggers are so automatic that most don't have enough emotional power to change them. So they keep cycling through the same drains but can't quite put a finger on where their depletion is coming from. Even if they make progress through a month, there's still a sense of something missing, or a feeling that they got too drained in the process of making progress. *Why* usually remains a mystery, but most blame it on worry, anxiety, or some other aftereffect. When we cycle through emotional drains enough, they can outplay in physical ailments and feeling older than we should, and most have experienced this at times.

Exercises that build higher frequency emotional energy are what give you the power and consciousness to start to arrest subtle triggers of overcare, over-identity and over-attachment, and to take more significance out of a reaction on initial contact. Catching reactions on initial contact will boost your energy savings tremendously. It will raise your emotional set-point or threshold of over-reaction. But you have to have enough high frequency emotional energy built up to be able to shift an attitude fast enough to stop payment on its drain. Remember, it's not the issues that drain people so much; it's the amount of repetitive thought and emotional download they assign to the significance of issues and disturbances. Again, you can conserve energy and accumulate extra energy by consciously breathing higher attitudes and feelings of joy, love, appreciation, and forgiveness while jogging or exercising. This will be understood as *energy economy* in the new psychology. Using exercises to increase your emotional energy reserves will make a lot of difference in healing old patterns in the mental, emotional and physical self.

By breathing the higher energy of joy along with your practice of the other techniques and tools, you can build up your spiritual reservoir enough to be able to catch automatic reactions, then have enough emotional reserve power to change them faster. This saves you more and more from being a victim of your own *mechanicality*. It's like objectively viewing a split screen. The higher screen is the larger helicopter view that allows you to see emotional histories and mechanical reactions in the lower screen with less over-personalization, then use a tool to take them out.

Spiritual maturity is reflected in our ability to stop energy drains and regain a sense of joy amidst life's changes. Sustaining joy accelerates a shift into a new bandwidth of intuitive intelligence and energy where we consciously co-create with life instead of being its victim. Joy empowers our love so we can recreate our lives to our fulfillment. Love fulfilled sees where we could have gone the way of love before, if only we'd known how, and how insecurities limited many of our choices. Love fulfilled perceives new meaning and higher reasons behind many of the mysteries of why things happened as they did. Living from the heart is business—the business of caring for self and others. Understanding this will take us past the age of information into the age of intuitive living.

THE NEW INTUITIVE BANDWIDTH

We've talked a lot about intuition throughout this book, so now, from a new perspective of how spirit merges with humanness, let's take a deeper look at intuition. Intuition is commonly defined as direct perception of truth, fact, etc., independent of any reasoning process, yet few can explain how this works. For most of us, intuition sounds intriguing, but the mystique placed around it makes many think that it's only available to the gifted.

At one level, people use intuition casually all the time—finding the right place to live, trying to predict the stock market, knowing it will rain on a company picnic, knowing when someone's thinking about you, knowing if it's going to be a boy or a girl, or having a hunch you will succeed or fail. More dramatic instances of intuition include predictions of the future, psychic readings that help police find criminals, and so forth. These are all aspects of intuition, but since most people can't call up these skills at will, they tend to view intuition as something to envy or suspect in others, not strive for in themselves.

The types of intuition mentioned above may be intriguing, but they are just isolated strands of intuitive ability. They are not the most important function of intuition. *The core function of intuition is applying the voice or feelings of the heart in your moment-to-moment relationship with self, others, and life.* We all have this fundamental capacity for in-the-moment intuitive connection with the feelings of the heart.

The next bandwidth of intelligence for the planet is the intuitive bandwidth. Here we are using bandwidth to mean an added dimension of consciousness or intelligence. That's the planetary or global shift unfolding. This sounds spiritually exotic until you realize that learning intuition at its most effective level starts with using it to manage your mind and emotions from the heart.

The intuitive bandwidth increases in range as you practice following your heart with sincerity. The first priority of intuition is to guide you in getting along better with yourself and others. This fundamental guidance in dealing with attitudes and emotions is intuition in its most effective form. Having hunches, guessing the right number, and so forth, are only add-ons.

Usually, if we pay attention, we can distinguish a feeling inside that prompts the appropriate reaction in our relations with family members, co-workers, and friends. A sustained avoidance of acting on these heart promptings squelches the release of spirit in our interactions. Emotional energy can be the carrier wave for intuition, love, and joy. But until we learn to manage our emotional energy, we won't know the difference between intuition and over-identity, overcare, and over-attachment to something.

Increasing your bandwidth of intuitive intelligence requires that, no matter what comes up in life, your reactions contain a high proportion of emotional balance. This enables you to access new levels of potential within yourself, to move your life more in the direction your deeper heart wants. It takes building and harnessing your emotional energy to manifest that true creativity.

Accessing intuition and creativity does not have to be a random event, as many suppose. Intuition is a steady operative frequency or bandwidth that you tune to, as you would a radio station. Increasing your power to love will give you access to this frequency. Attuning to the intuition bandwidth through love powers up coherence between your mental, emotional, and physical natures, then alignment with your heart of hearts. This is why, as people learn to operate from heart intelligence, they have more creative capacity for self-healing. Mind and emotions aligned with the heart invoke the higher power of spirit, which is what brings healing. Other people do not heal you; although some have the gift of helping you connect more with your own spirit. You can pray to God for healing, but you can also learn to love more, and then God often gently helps you learn how to heal yourself through your spirit.

Intuition is a hotline to recommendations from God. Act on those recommendations, and your spirit can't wait to download more goods. Once you create coherence, and build a solid connection between heart and mind through practice, you can count on higher ratios of peace and fulfillment. In other words you will feel more joy. Bringing more spirit into humanness isn't about walking around being perfect, but about enjoying your progress with less resistance. As you get used to operating in the new intuitive bandwidth, you'll wonder how you ever got by without it.

GLOBAL COHERENCE

Achieving social coherence among people of different religious, cultural or political belief systems will necessitate a universal guiding principle, scientifically based, that all can agree upon. Such a universal principle can shape and validate collective values and behaviors for the good of the whole while honoring different religions. Coherence (or love) is such a scientifically (and physiologically) based, universal principle. As Mother Theresa said, "The greatest science in the world, in heaven and on earth, is love."

A new world based on the guiding principle of coherence has to start with learning how to recalibrate back to coherence within oneself, then within our families, schools, organizations, churches, and groups. Studies of urban social groups have shown that a balance of loving bonds and social control tends to predict group stability and survival. The balance of love and control for the good of the whole helps dissipate emotional tensions, interpersonal conflicts, and other stressors. Based on these studies, social scientist Dr. Raymond Bradley and neuroscientist Dr. Karl Pribram developed a general theory of social communication. They predict that a successful social organization, whether a one-on-one relationship, a family, a group, or an organization, first and foremost involves collaboration—individuals working together in relation to a common function or goal. Their findings show that for people to work collaboratively, managing emotions is critical. Negative emotions, like fear or hate, block cooperation and result in dissipation of energy and social incoherence; separation or chaos ensue. What's required is what they call "adult love"—passion and commitment which come from a combination of positive affect (love, care, appreciation, kindness) and self-regulation (self-control or power). When positive affect (love) and self-regulation (power) are linked in balance, then social coherence, maturity, and stability are the likely result.[1]

Religious unity is based on principles of love and *communion*—bonding with one's spirit and with others from the heart. This was the intent of great religious founders. Religions provide supportive atmospheres for communion, whether in places of worship, homes, or workplaces. But religious dogma and bigotry have generated some of the most horrific atrocities. Once we take away religious separatism and vanities, then all can commune together from the heart. The potential for coherence belongs to everyone.

Today's religions can help foster coherence as they practice real love and release separatism. The world doesn't need a new religion, but a reference point from where we all learn to love more. Spirit is supposed to be brought to the street so that inner heart direction on how to love and care more can increase. Inner heart direction increases as we practice emotional management. So emotional self-management is the bottom line that needs to be addressed.

HeartMath Techniques and tools for overcoming emotional chaos are designed to move people into that stream of love as they get in touch with their own hearts. Spiritual leaders from both Western and non-Western traditions have found them useful and non-threatening or competitive with their religious beliefs and practices.

CREATING SUPPORTIVE ENVIRONMENTS

In many workplaces, employees are seeking those of like mind, even a few, to create lunch or after-work support groups for discussion and bonding. These support groups, forums, affinity groups, hubs (they have a variety of names), are made up of two or more friends meeting to talk about finding their own balance in the thick of it all. They're not about forming a new clique within an organization. They're just friends and associates getting together for mutual support to benefit the entire organization.

Thousands of support groups of many types meet regularly in homes, coffee shops, churches, and clinics throughout the world. By practicing compassion and making the managing of one's emotions in the midst of challenge a priority for discussion, they can help one another renew. They can leave the support group meeting with more coherence to help offset the self-pitying and blaming culture they may have at work or at home. If instead they add to one another's feelings of anger, victimization and emotional drain, their sense of self-worth diminishes, as does their capacity to solve the problems back at their homes and workplaces.

There are times when venting blame and anger can provide a temporary discharge, like releasing a valve on a pressure cooker; however, in most cases venting keeps recharging the emotional negativity inside. Any time one person manages their emotions and deflects a momentum of negativity, all benefit. As more people meet with the intention of helping each other recalibrate in the heart, they create a *heart-field environment* that sets up a momentum toward coherence and helps offset the counter-momentum of emotional chaos around them. Heart-field environments can be created in person, on the phone or over the Internet, as core heart feelings can be conveyed through any networked connection. The desire for emotional balance can be just as infectious as being randomly victimized by emotion. Support group bonding and coherence pave the way for greater hope and breakthroughs in addressing any problem.

"I'm slowing down and going to the heart at home with my wife, and it's helping my marriage a lot," says Charles. "Learning how to go to the heart has taken big chunks out of my destructive thoughts and emotions," adds Celeste. "My inner dialogue with myself has changed—I have more awareness of angry, negative, destructive things I'm going through and the ability to do something about that," says Barbara, "it saves energy." David offers, "Things don't bother me as much anymore. I don't feel like I'm better than anyone else; I just value myself more, and I'm not intimidated by anyone any longer."

These people, from different cities, are talking with one another on a telephone conference call about their practice of the tools. Each one is describing how they feel stronger, happier, and more able to handle the ups and downs of everyday life. They are learning the power of the heart—the power of love. Support groups of people practicing tools for overcoming emotional chaos together (which we call "heart hubs") stimulate bonding and coherence in each individual member. They draw more spirit and heart into their midst and help each other recoup and prevent emotional energy drains. A heart hub serves as an inoculation against an emotional virus. Practicing with others strengthens the heart-field environment to accelerate you more quickly into a higher bandwidth of intuitive intelligence. If you decide to start a small hub studying these tools together in your home or workplace, you may be surprised to find how many want to participate. Yet effectiveness is not about numbers. It's about a few building their individual and social coherence and strength. Learning to connect with your heart in social situations will provide you with appropriate intuitive guidance and empowerment so you don't contribute to your own emotional drain or that of the collective environment. More people become interested as a few model new authentic behaviors.

A hub is not a new religion; it's people and their own hearts getting together. Alan says, "Our hub is just three people, but it's a time together for appreciation and remembering to just ease into our heart. It helps me keep looking at life in a new way. We remind one another of the tools and share which ones we use and how they work for us. It's not about any religion, as we each have a different religion, just communion with the spirit and hearts of each one."

It's time to realize that we all need to go deeper in the heart and connect more with the hearts of others to renew hope. There are no quick fixes for global problems until the emotional infrastructures change. It's heart time.

CREATING YOUR FUTURE

Creating is what we each do, in every moment, as we mechanically react or consciously choose our responses to situations. You might say that life is a moving hologram or video that we are constantly helping to create with others and with nature. It's in your responses to the video of life—mentally, emotionally, and in your actions—that your highest creative potentials are unleashed. The sincere, consistent effort of getting in touch with your deeper heart builds a network of connection between your spirit and humanness. Building that bridge is the first level of higher creativity.

True creativity comes from inspired contact with your spirit, unveiling hopeful new perceptions with feelings of joy and excitement. It allows you to track life with your heart, not just your mind. As you track from your heart, you unfold more creative capacities for business, the arts, science, parenting, relationships—anything you put your heart into. True creativity, quite simply, starts with balancing your emotions and activating the power of the heart. Through practicing emotional management from the heart, you tap into the highest form of creativity possible—*recreating your perceptions of reality*. But practice is the act of bridging sky to street (heaven to earth—or philosophy to actualization).

A GLOBAL MISSION

Helping adults and children change emotional patterns and unlock their higher blueprint for fulfillment is one of HeartMath's chief intents.* Fulfillment is individual; the blueprint of each person is unique. When you achieve your own custom designed fulfillment, then it doesn't matter what others have that you don't. It makes feelings like envy archaic. As heart intelligence increases in humanity, eventually emotions like anger, jealousy, hate, and anxiety will have served their purpose in evolution and, like a vestigial tail, will become extinct.

Philosopher and scientist Teilhard De Chardin said, "Some day, after we have mastered the winds, the waves, the tides, and gravity, we will harness for God the energies of love; and then for the second time in the history of the world man will have discovered fire!" As you intentionally practice loving more, the fire of coherence acts as an incubator that brings to birth the image of God (highest pattern) blueprinted in your soul. You experience a new kind of joy and higher gifts from your spirit—be they gifts of healing your own emotional wounds or helping pioneer a new attitude of coherence and equilibrium to the earth and its people.

Each person's highest blueprint is more than individual. It's global, for in the heart we are all interconnected. And it will take an interconnected effort to create a new mode of relating to self and others based on developing one's inner strength and deeper care, and not relying on political leaders or others to do it for us.

Those who heart-empower will generate a new unified heart-field environment that will bring in more spirit to assist the collective whole. As pioneers achieve this, it sets a baseline grid for a new era of peace and cooperation that many are still waiting for someone else to create. As more spirit flows into mass consciousness, new intuitive guidance on issues becomes more accessible. It helps people more easily find the magic of their own heart to guide them toward what's best for the whole.

While the onslaught of new technologies is contributing to the global stress momentum, technology is also focusing attention on the interconnectedness between people and the need for collaboration. The authors of a popular book on the Internet, *The ClueTrain Manifesto* observe a deep underlying hunger pervading Internet communications—a longing for meaning and for meaningful connections to other people. This longing, they say, "isn't mere wistful nostalgia, not just some unreconstructed adolescent dream. It is living evidence of heart, of what makes us most human."[2]

The power of the Internet to connect people, either in anger, pornography, terrorism, or in heart intelligent creativity and collaboration, demands new strategies. Once groups of people understand how to access the new intuition bandwidth through heart coherence, there will be new inner and outer technologies that serve the good of the whole. These coming new technologies of the heart are what we call *Intui-technologies* based on the unfolding of heart feelings and illumination of the mind's higher capacities. *Intui-technologies* will inspire a new mode of intuitive living and connectedness between people. The mind alone cannot achieve that potential. Without activating core heart feelings, the mind short-circuits. A new era of planetary love is required.

While the global mission of people connecting with their core heart and spirit begins with each individual, it will take enlightened leadership in business, health care, politics, and educational systems before coherence can be established worldwide. This can also be facilitated by the tremendous influence of the media and entertainment industries. Through movies, TV, and software, these industries can convey powerful stories and messages about emotional management and the heart. When leaders in these industries become conscious players in a global mission to bring in more heart intelligence, they will accelerate the planetary awakening of the spirit of cooperative care. This will help reduce the emotional chaos and disruption of global change.

Emotional management in the collective whole will be the hallmark indicator that more spirit dwells in human consciousness. It won't take a lot of conscious players to launch this. It can start with hubs of leaders who have the power to put strategies into action in their areas of influence. That's the opportunity of the millennium—people listening to their heart and creating the practical steps and technologies for others to do so.

It's no coincidence that more business leaders are talking about the importance of managing with heart. They will become motivated to implement coherence-building strategies to stay innovative and profitable. Children will need a youth corps to help orchestrate coherence through the Internet, through video games, and through their schools. Software technologies will be created to help adults and children increase heart coherence, develop intuition, live from compassion, and become their real selves.[3] Techno kids learning heart coherence will help motivate adults to do the same and discover *Intui-Technologies* to bridge the digital and economic divide between the haves and have nots.

It's all about love. Love is a big word, and humanity has only scratched the surface of understanding its intelligent potentials. It's been said, "Love conquers all," but love is much more than a platitude. To really change our old mechanical and historical ways of responding to each other and to life, we need to understand that love has to be demonstrated through active care.

Using a tool to manage your emotions—that's mature love in action. Adding love where you have judgments or presets, understanding that people may be doing the best they can from where they're coming from, is love in action. It's time for all of us to respect love as a higher intelligence and use it to help diminish human separation, if we want to have personal and global peace. Christ was obviously ahead of the times in understanding the need for love as a mode of interactive living.

Learning to step love down into practical applications of care is humanity's next learning curve. We have developed rigorous academic standards for learning in every other area. It's time to apply those standards to learning about love.

People love romance, love children and love pets, and that's great. But we have to love one another as human beings—with passion and commitment—if we're going to resolve the problems of humanity and the stresses of modern life. It's easier to love children because they haven't been around long enough to give us as many reasons to judge them, resent them, or not forgive them when the need arises. It's time for us, as adults, to treat one another with the same flexibility, tolerance, and resilience we have with children— giving latitude and going deeper in the heart to understand each other. This is the foundation for interactive coherence that can result in the global change that everyone's hoping for.

Our mission is to scientifically prove that love is not just a sweet intent, but a foundation for a whole new physiology, psychology, and way of living. At HeartMath we are engaged in proving at every level, from the biological to the spiritual, that love is the missing "X" factor that will solve the age-old question of how to release emotional and social incoherence.

It's an illusion that the mind will correct the current environment of stress, powered by self-centeredness, ambition and addiction to stimulation. As we've said many times, the mind can't effectively address these issues without consulting the intelligence and the intuition of the heart. Through intentionally practicing mature care, people can bring in more spirit, resulting in a deeper bonding with one another and with God or whatever they call their personal *Source*.

Love is the answer, but remember, it takes applying a little elbow grease to learn how to love more to release unprofitable attitudes and old mind-sets. The techniques and tools given in this book are offered to help guide you systematically and help ease you through that effort. Increase your ability to honor the feelings of your heart, and then the mysteries of life will start to dissolve. Let living in the heart of the moment become your aim of aims. And in the future, if you hear someone ask, as people often do, "Can't we all get along?" You can tell them, "Yes, and it starts with increasing individual care." By becoming engineers of self-responsibility, we build hope and security for the whole.

---

*Doc Childre's Cut-Thru Techniques for children ages 2 to 18 are available from the Institute of HeartMath and can be downloaded from the Website, **www.heartmath.org.**

APPENDIX

CHAPTER 2

Releasing Overcare and Over-identity Worksheet

The following worksheet will help you identify overcares, over-identities, and over-attachments that drain your power, then show you where you need to Cut-Thru. Use the Cut-Thru Technique on each one to reclaim your power.

A PICTURE OF YOUR CARE

Sometimes the people, issues and things we care the most about can also be the source of our greatest stress. When we become *over-identified* with what we care about, it can lead to overcare. *There is often a very fine line between care and overcare,* but you can learn to distinguish them by how they make you feel. To start with, ask yourself, "Is my care stress-producing or stress-reducing?" If it's stress *producing*, then overcare is draining your power. If it's stress *reducing*, then your care is regenerative and adding to your power.

In the first column below, make a list of the people, issues, and things that you care most about in your life. In the second column, on a scale of 0 to 5, with 0 being the lowest and 5 being the extreme, how much overcare do you have around this item or issue. In the third column, describe your overcare thoughts, feelings and actions.

EXAMPLE:

I care about my elderly father.	_5_	_Yet, whatever I do for him never seems to be good enough!_

What I care about	Scale 0–5	Overcare thoughts, feelings, actions

Make a similar list of things about *yourself* that you care most about.

EXAMPLE:

I care about my weight.	4	I worry about my health and feel unattractive. I diet and exercise, but then I eat the wrong foods again and get too busy to go to the gym. I feel guilty all the time.

What I care about	Scale 0–5	Overcare thoughts, feelings, actions

See where sentiment, attachment, expectation, sympathy, or self-pity are involved in the overcares you listed.

_____

_____

_____

_____

_____

_____

_____

_____

_____

_____

_____

_____

_____

_____

Picking one overcare at a time, use the six Cut-Thru steps to bring yourself back into balance and connect with your heart intelligence, in order to transform overcare into balanced, true care. You may find that relinquishing overcare in even one area will unravel overcares in other areas at the same time. Make notes of your insights from using Cut-Thru.

The Steps of Cut-Thru

- **Step 1:** Be aware of *how you feel* about the issue at hand.

- **Step 2:** Focus in the heart and solar plexus: *Breathe love and appreciation* through this area for 30 seconds or more to help anchor your attention there.

- **Step 3:** *Assume objectivity* about the feeling or issue, as if it were someone else's problem.

- **Step 4:** *Rest in neutral* in your rational, mature heart.

- **Step 5:** *Soak and relax* any disturbed or perplexing feelings in the compassion of the heart. Dissolve the significance a little at a time. Remember it's not the problem that causes energy drain as much as the significance you assign to the problem.

- **Step 6:** After taking out as much significance as you can, *from your deep heart sincerely ask* for appropriate guidance or insight. If you don't get an answer, *find something to appreciate* for a while.

CHAPTER 3

Identify Emotional Vanity Worksheet

Check the areas where your motivation is strongly influenced by one or more of the following phrases. Write the phrase(s) or others from Chapter 3 that best describe your type of vanity in the space below and on the following page.

- *Approval Vanity:* *They'll like me better if I say/do this; What will they think of me if I choose this over that?; If I say/do this you might be mad at me; Am I good enough?; I'm not getting the recognition/attention I want;* (Performance vanity or performance anxiety).

- *Communication Vanity:* *If I let him know he hurt me, he might see it as a weakness to take advantage of me; If I truly express my needs, I might be rejected; If I just talk over her words I might get my point across* (Get What I Want). *They don't understand me; No one can understand; I'm different* (Needing to be Understood). *All I meant was . . . ; I was just trying to . . .* (Needing to Understand).

- *Desire Vanity:* *I'll choose this (instead of what I really want) because I'm sure I can get it. I won't choose that (what I really want) because it might not happen.* Got to have it—can't be happy or fulfilled without it, wanting to be somebody, worried your talents aren't being used, needing to be perfect, good getting in the way, resignation, regret/guilt.

———————————————————————————

———————————————————————————

———————————————————————————

———————————————————————————

———————————————————————————

———————————————————————————

———————————————————————————

Now use the Cut-Thru Technique in Chapter 4 to understand your vanity motivations and gain more insight. Make notes below:

———————————————————————————

———————————————————————————

———————————————————————————

———————————————————————————

———————————————————————————

———————————————————————————

———————————————————————————

———————————————————————————

———————————————————————————

To help free yourself from vanity, take frequent time-outs during the day and ask your heart, "What is the best attitude of care for myself and the whole that I could have right now?" Listen to your heart, and make a sincere heart effort to shift to that attitude. This will help clarify your motives and bring a deeper care that connects you more to your real self and to others. Then ask your heart, "What would be the most appropriate action of care to take right now?" Listen to whatever common sense direction your heart shows you, and act on it.

CHAPTER 5

Cut-Thru Worksheet

In practicing Cut-Thru, it can be helpful to write down the issue you are addressing, along with feelings and insights, as you go through the six steps. Some issues take more heart soak time to mature into new understanding and release. Remember that appreciation of anything often facilitates intuitive clarity on issues you were working on. Repeat the steps as needed.

PRACTICE CUT-THRU STEP 1

Issue:

_____

_____

_____

_____

_____

_____

Feelings about the Issue:

_____

_____

_____

_____

_____

_____

_____

PRACTICE CUT-THRU STEPS 2-3

What would you tell another person with this problem?

_____

_____

_____

_____

_____

_____

_____

_____

_____

_____

PRACTICE CUT-THRU STEP 4

What options do you see from a more neutral state?

_____

_____

_____

_____

_____

_____

_____

_____

_____

_____

_____

PRACTICE CUT-THRU STEP 5

On a scale of 1 to 10, how much significance have you invested in this issue?

_____

_____

_____

_____

_____

_____

_____

_____

_____

_____

PRACTICE CUT-THRU STEP 6

Cut-Thru Response (new insight: what did your heart intelligence offer?)

_____

_____

_____

_____

_____

_____

_____

_____

_____

_____

CHAPTER 7

"The 30 Minute Game"

Try this exercise to clear out morning funk. Use "Attitudinal Breathing" as soon as you wake up. Do it before you get out of bed, in the shower, getting dressed, driving to work, or anywhere to *defunk* in the morning. Start by shifting your attention to your heart and solar plexus, and take a few easy breaths. Think about something, anything, you love and enjoy that doesn't have negative emotional history attached to it that could pull you down. Then breathe appreciation for what you love and enjoy through the heart and solar plexus for 30 seconds or more. Really sense the love you feel for it. Mean business about doing this to shift your mood and anchor your energy. You can advance quickly in cleaning out old cellular stuff as you increase the time you do this exercise in the morning.

Work your way up to doing this morning tune-up for five, ten, then thirty minutes. Make it into a fun game and it will set a whole different tone for your day. If you can't feel any love or enjoyment, then put out the attitude you feel would be love or joy, even if it seems kind of dry or empty at first or if an emotional sluggishness or resistance weighs against it. Think about old-fashioned water pumps. Sometimes they had to be primed with a little water and cranked and cranked until the water flowed with ease. It can be the same with your heart. Don't stop before your pump gets primed. Just a little effort to prime the pump of your heart will bring your heart rhythms into coherence, and that can harmonize your entire day.

CHAPTER 12

Cut-Thru Exercise for Heart Break
(Healing from Heartache or a Broken Heart)

PHASE I:
Finding peace and compassion for yourself.

- **Step 1:** Take a moment to become aware of *how you feel*. Do you feel hurt, angry, confused, sad?

- **Step 2:** Focus in the heart and solar plexus: *Breathe love and appreciation* for 30 seconds or up to three minutes. Continue this step until you feel some bit of calm and the beginnings of a more even internal rhythm.

- **Step 3:** *Assume objectivity* about the feeling or issue—as if it were someone else's problem. This is a very important step for heartbreak. Here is where you can really start picking up the pieces. To assume objectivity, pretend you are watching another person feeling this, not you. Use a helicopter view, or imagine this person is sitting near you. You may notice that you feel more compassion and understanding of how he or she feels. Some find with this step, they want to hold and comfort this person. In the heart you can. Embrace that hurt part of yourself with care, as if you were your own mother, father, or best friend. Compassion can soothe the painful feelings, like dipping a burn into cool water.

- **Step 4:** This objectivity allows your feeling world to begin to ease toward neutral, to realize that there may be a bigger picture here, one that contains a spark of hope. *Rest in neutral*—in your rational, mature heart.

- **Step 5:** *Soak and relax* in the compassion of the heart, dissolving the hurt a little at a time.

If you have an overwhelming hurt, you may need to spend time with these last few steps over several days before you go on to Phase II. How long you take depends on you, but don't linger too long in Phase I.

PHASE II:
Release: Letting go and moving on.

Start again from *Step 1*, and be prepared to mean business. As you revisit *Step 4*, focus on a deeper neutral and on finding a new, more rational, mature heart. Then as you go through *Step 5*, don't just soak the hurt out, really soak the significance, too. Few things feel as significant as heartbreak, but remember, wounded vanity can be behind much of that significance. Ask your heart to identify the vanity. What is important to your recovery is your ability to keep your heart open and release the entrapments of what your mind is insisting should have happened instead.

Soak the feeling of "poor me" out of your system. Being a pitiful version of your former self doesn't serve you.

- *Step 6:* *From your deep heart sincerely ask* for appropriate guidance or insight. The understandings your heart can deliver are always valuable, but when you are "up against the wall" they are worth more than their weight in gold. Whether you experience insights or simply a glimmer that everything will be all right, write it down, honor and appreciate whatever you find, and make it a new reference point.

REFERENCES

CHAPTER 1
Emotions:
The Next Frontier

1. Kelleher KJ, McInerny TK, Gardner WP, Childs GE, Wasserman RC. Increasing identification of psychosocial problems: 1979-1996. *Pediatrics* 2000; 105:1313-1321.

CHAPTER 2
Overcare, Over-identity, and Over-attachment:
How to Overcome the Draining Cycle

1. Fredrickson B. Cultivating positive emotions to optimize health and well-being. *Prevention and Treatment* 2000; 3: Article 0001a. http://journals.apa.org/prevention/volume3/pre0030001a.html

CHAPTER 3
Understanding Emotional Vanity

1. Vaillant GE. *Aging Well: Surprising Guideposts to a Happier Life from the Landmark Harvard Study of Adult Development.* Boston: Little, Brown, and Company 2002.
2. Albert Einstein, quoted in Eves H. *Mathematical Circles Adieu: A Fourth Collection of Mathematical Stories and Anecdotes.* Boston: Prindle, Weber, and Schmidt, 1977.

CHAPTER 4
The Heart of the Matter

1. Guyton AC. *Textbook of Medical Physiology, Eighth Edition.* Philadelphia: W.B. Saunders Company, 1991.
2. Sapolsky R. *Stress, the Aging Brain and the Mechanisms of Neuron Death.* Cambridge, MA: MIT Press, 1992.
3. Shealy N. A review of dehydroepiandrosterone (DHEA). *Integrative Physiological and Behavioral Science* 1995; 30:308-313.
4. McCraty R, Barrios-Choplin B, Rozman D, Atkinson M, Watkins A. The impact of a new emotional self-management program on stress, emotions, heart rate variability, DHEA and cortisol. *Integrative Physiological and Behavioral Science* 1998; 33:151-170.
5. Eysenck HJ. Prediction of cancer and coronary heart disease mortality by means of a personality inventory: Results of a 15-year follow-up study. *Psychological Reports* 1993; 72:499-516.
6. Kawachi I, Sparrow D, Vokonas PS, Weiss ST. Symptoms of anxiety and risk of coronary heart disease. The Normative Aging Study. *Circulation* 1994; 90:2225-2229.
7. Seligman MEP, Csikszentmihalyi M. Positive psychology: An introduction. *American Psychologist* 2000; 55:5-14.
8. Fredrickson B. Cultivating positive emotions to optimize health and well-being. *Prevention and Treatment* 2000; 3: Article 0001a. http://journals.apa.org/prevention/volume3/pre0030001a.html
9. Fredrickson B. Positive Emotions. In: Snyder C, Lopez S, eds. *Handbook of Positive Psychology.* New York: Oxford University Press, In press.
10. Isen A. Positive affect. In: Dalgleish T, Power M, eds. *Handbook of Cognition and Emotion.* New York: John Wiley & Sons, 1999.
11. McCraty R, Atkinson M, Tomasino D. *Science of the Heart.* Boulder Creek, CA: HeartMath Research Center, Institute of HeartMath, Publication No. 01-001, 2001.

12. Childre D, Martin H. *The HeartMath Solution*. San Francisco: HarperSanFrancisco, 1999.

13. Watkins A, Childre D, eds. *Emotional Sovereignty*. Amsterdam: Harwood Academic Publishers, In press.

14. Armour J and Ardell J, eds. *Neurocardiology*. New York: Oxford University Press, 1994.

15. Sandman CA, Walker BB, Berka C. Influence of afferent cardiovascular feedback on behavior and the cortical evoked potential. In: Cacioppo JT, Petty RE, eds. *Perspectives in Cardiovascular Psychophysiology*. New York: The Guilford Press, 1982: 189-222.

16. Frysinger RC, Harper RM. Cardiac and respiratory correlations with unit discharge in epileptic human temporal lobe. *Epilepsia* 1990; 31:162-171.

17. McCraty R, Atkinson M. Psychophysiological coherence. In: Watkins A, Childre D, eds. *Emotional Sovereignty*. Amsterdam: Harwood Academic Publishers, In press.

18. Cantin M, Genest J. The heart as an endocrine gland. *Scientific American* 1986; 254:76-81.

19. Gutkowska J, Jankowski M, Mukaddam-Daher S, McCann SM. Oxytocin is a cardiovascular hormone. *Brazilian Journal of Medical and Biological Research* 2000; 33:625-633.

20. Tiller W, McCraty R, Atkinson M. Cardiac coherence: A new, noninvasive measure of autonomic nervous system order. *Alternative Therapies in Health and Medicine* 1996; 2:52-65.

21. McCraty R, Atkinson M, Tiller WA, Rein G and Watkins A. The effects of emotions on short term heart rate variability using power spectrum analysis. *American Journal of Cardiology* 1995; 76:1089-1093.

22. Michael Gershon, quoted in Blakeslee S. Complex and hidden brain in the gut makes stomachaches and butterflies. *New York Times*, January 23, 1996.

23. LeDoux J. *The Emotional Brain: The Mysterious Underpinnings of Emotional Life*. New York: Simon & Schuster, 1996.

CHAPTER 5
The Cut-Thru Technique

1. Pribram K , Melges F. Psychophysiological basis of emotion. In: Vinken P, Bruyn G, eds. *Handbook of Clinical Neurology.* Amsterdam: North-Holland Publishing Company, 1969: 316-341.
2. Goleman D. Brain may tag all perceptions with a value. *New York Times*, August 8, 1995.
3. McCraty R, Barrios-Choplin B, Rozman D, Atkinson M, Watkins A. The impact of a new emotional self-management program on stress, emotions, heart rate variability, DHEA and cortisol. *Integrative Physiological and Behavioral Science* 1998;33:151-170.
4. Childre D. *Speed of Balance: A Musical Adventure for Emotional and Mental Regeneration* [music]. Boulder Creek, CA: Planetary Publications, 1995.
5. McCraty R, Barrios-Choplin B, Atkinson M and Tomasino D. The effects of different music on mood, tension, and mental clarity. *Alternative Therapies in Health and Medicine* 1998; 4:75-84.

CHAPTER 6
The Heart Lock-In Technique

1. McCraty R, Atkinson M, Rein G, Watkins AD. Music enhances the effect of positive emotional states on salivary IgA. *Stress Medicine* 1996; 12:167-175.
2. McCraty R, Barrios-Choplin B, Atkinson M, Tomasino D. The effects of different music on mood, tension, and mental clarity. *Alternative Therapies in Health and Medicine* 1998; 4:75-84.
3. Katz J. *How Emotions Work.* Chicago: University of Chicago Press, 1999.

4. Luskin F. *The effects of forgiveness training on psychosocial factors in college-age adults.* Ph.D. Dissertation, Counseling Psychology, Stanford University, 1999.

CHAPTER 9
Eliminating Anxiety

1. Phillimore J. Generalised Anxiety Disorder. *The Observer*, October 14, 2001.
2. Excerpted from "The Grandfather Story" by Vicki Smith.
3. Lessmeier TJ, Gamperling D, Johnson-Liddon V, and others. Unrecognized paroxysmal supraventricular tachycardia. Potential for misdiagnosis as panic disorder. *Archives of Internal Medicine* 1997; 157:537-543.

CHAPTER 11
Lifting Depression

1. Murray CJL, Lopez AD, eds. *The Global Burden of Disease and Injury Series*, Volume 1. Cambridge, MA: Harvard University Press, 1996.
2. Ford DE, Mead LA, Chang PP, and others. Depression is a risk factor for coronary artery disease in men: The precursors study. *Archives of Internal Medicine* 1998; 158:1422-1426.
3. Fredrickson B, Joiner T. Positive emotions trigger upward spirals toward emotional well-being. *Psychological Science*; In press.
4. McCraty R, Tomasino D, Atkinson M. Research, clinical perspectives and case histories. In: Watkins A, Childre D, eds. *Emotional Sovereignty*. Amsterdam: Harwood Academic Publishers, In press.
5. Fredrickson B. Cultivating positive emotions to optimize health and well-being. *Prevention and Treatment* 2000;3:Article 0001a. http://journals.apa.org/prevention/volume3/pre0030001a.html

6. McCraty R, Atkinson M, Tiller WA, Rein G, Watkins A. The effects of emotions on short term heart rate variability using power spectrum analysis. *American Journal of Cardiology* 1995; 76:1089-1093.

7. McCraty R, Atkinson M, Rein G, Watkins AD. Music enhances the effect of positive emotional states on salivary IgA. *Stress Medicine* 1996; 12:167-175.

CHAPTER 12
Creating Security in Relationships

1. McCraty R, Atkinson M, Tomasino D, Tiller W. The electricity of touch: Detection and measurement of cardiac energy exchange between people. In: *Proceedings of the Fifth Appalachian Conference on Neurobehavioral Dynamics: Brain and Values*. Mahwah, NJ: Lawrence Erlbaum Associates, 1997.

2. Russek L, Schwartz G. Interpersonal heart-brain registration and the perception of parental love: A 42-year follow-up of the Harvard Mastery of Stress Study. *Subtle Energies* 1994; 5:195-208.

3. Kiecolt-Glaser JK, Glaser R, Cacioppo JT, Malarkey WB. Marital stress: Immunologic, neuroendocrine, and autonomic correlates. *Annals of the New York Academy of Sciences* 1998; 840:656-663.

4. Medalie JH, Goldbourt U. Angina pectoris among 10,000 men. II. Psychosocial and other risk factors as evidenced by a multivariate analysis of a five-year incidence study. *American Journal of Medicine* 1976; 60:910-921.

5. House JS, Landis KR, Umberson D. Social relationships and health. *Science* 1988; 241:540-545.

6. Uchino BN, Cacioppo JT, Kiecolt-Glaser JK. The relationship between social support and physiological processes: A review with emphasis on underlying mechanisms and implications for health. *Psychological Bulletin* 1996; 119:488-531.

7. Berkman LF. The role of social relations in health promotion. *Psychosomatic Medicine* 1995; 57:245-254.

8. Lynch J. *The Broken Heart: The Medical Consequences of Loneliness*. Baltimore: Bancroft Press, 1998.

CHAPTER 13
Emotional Management in the Workplace: Unlocking Creativity, Innovation, and Satisfaction

1. Galinsky E, Kim SS, Bond JT. *Feeling overworked: When work becomes too much*. New York: Families and Work Institute, 2001.

2. Childre D, Cryer B. *From Chaos to Coherence: The Power to Change Performance*. Boulder Creek, CA: Planetary, 2000.

3. Love AA. Poll: Co-workers want to lash out. *Business Week*, November 29, 1999.

4. National Safety Council. *Stress Management*. Boston: Jones and Bartlett Publishers, 1995.

5. Goetzel RZ, Anderson DR, Whitmer RW, and others. The relationship between modifiable health risks and health care expenditures. An analysis of the multi-employer HERO health risk and cost database. *Journal of Occupational and Environmental Medicine* 1998; 40:843-854.

6. Conner DR. *Managing at the Speed of Change: How Resilient Managers Succeed and Prosper Where Others Fail*. New York: Villard Books, 1993.

7. Barrios-Choplin B, McCraty R, Cryer B. An inner quality approach to reducing stress and improving physical and emotional wellbeing at work. *Stress Medicine* 1997;13:193-201.

8. Barrios-Choplin B, McCraty R, Atkinson M. *The effect of employee self-management training on personal and organizational quality*. Boulder Creek, CA: HeartMath Research Center, Institute of HeartMath, Publication No. 99-083, 1999.

9. Nixon P, King J. Ischemic heart disease: Homeostasis and the heart. In Watkins A., ed., *Mind-Body Medicine: A Clinician's Guide to Psychoneuroimmunology*. New York: Churchill Livingstone, 1997:41-73.

10. Staw B, Sutton R, Pelled L. Employee positive emotion and favorable outcomes at the workplace. *Organization Science* 1994;5:51-71.

11. Staw B, Barsade S. Affect and managerial performance: A test of the sadder-but-wiser vs. happier-and-smarter hypothesis. *Administrative Science Quarterly* 1993; 38:304-331.

12. Maister DH. Practice What You Preach!: *What Managers Must Do to Create a High Achievement Culture*. New York: Free Press, 2001.

13. McCraty R, Atkinson M, Tiller WA. New electrophysiological correlates associated with intentional heart focus. *Subtle Energies* 1995; 4:251-268.

14. Ashby FG, Isen AM, Turken AU. A neuropsychological theory of positive affect and its influence on cognition. *Psychological Review* 1999; 106:529-550.

15. Kevin Cashman, quoted in LaBarre P. How to be a real leader. *Fast Company* 1999; 24(May):62.

CHAPTER 14
The Global Opportunity

1. Pribram K, Bradley, R. The brain, the me, and the I. In: Ferrari M, Sternberg R, eds. *Self-Awareness: Its Nature and Development*. New York: The Guilford Press, 1998: 273-307.

2. Locke C, Levine R, Searls D, Weinberger D. *The Cluetrain Manifesto: The End of Business as Usual*. Cambridge, MA: Perseus Books, 2000.

3. Childre D, McCraty R. Exploring the physiology of spiritual experience: Heart-based tools to increase spiritual connectedness. *Caduceus*; 2002: In press. *Medicine* 1997; 157:537–543.

INDEX

LEARN MORE ABOUT THE HEARTMATH EXPERIENCE

HeartMath techniques help people manage mental and emotional responses to life through unlocking the common sense of their own heart intelligence. Explore and experience more with HeartMath's other books, music, learning programs and software.

OTHER BOOKS AND LEARNING PROGRAMS BY DOC CHILDRE:

The HeartMath Solution

From Chaos to Coherence: Advancing Emotional and Organizational

Intelligence through Inner Quality Management

From Chaos to Coherence (CD rom)

Freeze-Frame: One Minute Stress Management

Teaching Children to Love: 80 Games and Fun Activities for Raising Balanced Children in Unbalanced Times

The How to Book of Teen Self Discovery

The HeartMath Method (audio learning series)

Freeze-Frame Learning Program

MUSIC BY DOC CHILDRE:

Scientifically designed to enhance the use of the HeartMath techniques.

Heart Zones

Speed of Balance

Quiet Joy

FREEZE-FRAMER SOFTWARE

The Freeze-Framer is an interactive learning system with patented heart monitor. This software based program allows you to see and learn how to control your heart rhythms to assist you in increasing coherence, health and performance. Call for a free catalog of our complete product line at: (800) 450-9111. Write us at: HEARTMATH, 14700 West Park Avenue, Boulder Creek, CA, 95006. Or visit the HeartMath online store at: **www.heartmath.com/store/index.html**

HEARTMATH TRAINING PROGRAMS, SEMINARS, AND WORKSHOPS

HeartMath provides world class training programs for organizations and individuals. These highly effective programs have been shown to dramatically improve performance and health.

In a composite study of 1,000 employees in HeartMath client organizations around the world, these results were achieved after just one session of HeartMath training and were sustained after six months:

- 67% reduction in anger—58% reduction in anxiety.

- 52% reduction in exhaustion—4% reduction in depression.

HeartMath results affecting the bottom line are equally impressive for organizations of all sizes. After HeartMath training for 400 employees at Delnor Community Hospital this organization:

- Saved $800,000 in one year by reducing employee turnover.

- Boosted customer satisfaction from the seventy-third to the ninety-third percentile.

- Reduced Medicare Patient Length of Stay by 9%, representing $1.4 million annualized savings.

Learn More About the HeartMath Experience

HeartMath training is available through on-site programs for organizations and sponsored public workshops, seminars and conference presentations. For more information on training call (800) 450-9111 or visit our web site at **www.heartmath.com.**

RESEARCH AND EDUCATION

The Institute of HeartMath (IHM) is a non-profit research and education organization that's changing our understanding of emotions, intelligence, and the role of the heart.

The Institute of HeartMath offers a comprehensive range of tools, techniques, and learning programs for use in educational and classroom settings.

- Resiliency programs designed for teachers and principals seeking quantifiable improvements organizational culture.

- TestEdge programs for improving academic performance and test scores.

- The Emotional Security Tool Kit for Children and Teens to increase emotional maturity while teaching youth how to reduce anger, worry and anxiety. Includes Cut-Thru Techniques adapted for children ages 2–18, available for free at **www.heartmath.org.**

For details about the Institute of HeartMath research initiatives and education programs, as well as endowment inquiries, please contact: Katherine Floriano, Executive Director, at (831) 338-8500; katherine@heartmath.org; **www.heartmath.org.**

ABOUT DOC CHILDRE

DOC CHILDRE is a leading authority on optimizing human performance and personal effectiveness. In the early 1970s, Doc anticipated that emotional chaos would be increasing exponentially in people's lives. Over the next 30 years, he dedicated himself to researching the causes of stress and to finding user-friendly solutions that anyone could use to reverse its effects. In 1991 Doc founded the non-profit Institute of HeartMath (IHM) to research the effects of mental and emotional stress on the heart, brain and nervous system. IHM clinical research, published in peer-reviewed scientific journals, case studies with Fortune 500 companies, governmental and police organizations, hospitals, clinics and schools, using the HeartMath techniques and tools have resulted in the highly acclaimed, *HeartMath System.*

Doc chairs the scientific advisory board of the Institute of HeartMath, is Chairman of the training and consulting company, HeartMath, LLC, and Chairman and CEO of technology licensing firm Quantum Intech. He is the author of seven books and a consultant to business leaders, scientists, educators and the entertainment industry on Intui-Technology. In addition he created the *Freeze-Framer*, heart rhythm technology for coherence building, and composed two highly acclaimed music releases including *Heart Zones,* which spent 50 consecutive weeks on *Billboard* magazine's music chart.

ABOUT DEBORAH ROZMAN

DEBORAH ROZMAN, PH.D., is a psychologist and author with 30 years of experience as an educator and business executive. She studied attitude change theory at the University of Chicago, and developed innovative programs for parents and educators to enhance emotional awareness in children. She taught transpersonal psychology and conflict resolution, authored five books, founded and directed an innovative elementary school and teachers' training center, and served as Executive Vice President of a biotech company where she directed sponsored research projects with Harvard University.

Deborah has been working with Doc Childre since 1987 and in 1991 became Executive Director of the Institute of HeartMath, overseeing research and development of HeartMath books, publications and training programs. In 1998, she became Executive Vice President and Chief Strategy Officer of HeartMath, LLC, and today is Executive Vice President for Quantum Intech, Inc., overseeing strategic alliances and the expansion of HeartMath technologies worldwide. She continues to serve on the Institute of HeartMath's scientific advisory board. Dr. Rozman is a key spokesperson for the HeartMath system, giving media interviews and keynote addresses on heart intelligence and intui-technologies for executives, scientists, and health professionals throughout the world.

Notes

Notes

Notes

Notes

We hope this **JODERE GROUP** book has benefited you
in your quest for personal, intellectual,
and spiritual growth.

JODERE GROUP is passionate about bringing new
and exciting books such as *Overcoming Emotional Chaos* to
readers worldwide. Our company was created as
a unique publishing and multimedia avenue
for individuals whose mission it is to
positively impact the lives of others.
We recognize the strength of an original thought,
a kind word and a selfless act—and the power
of the individuals who possess them.
We are committed to providing the support,
passion, and creativity necessary for these individuals
to achieve their goals and dreams.

JODERE GROUP is comprised of a dedicated
and creative group of people who strive
to provide the highest quality of books,
audio programs, online services, and live events
to people who pursue life-long learning.
It is our personal and professional commitment
to embrace our authors, speakers, and readers
with helpfulness, respect, and enthusiasm.

For more information about
our products, authors, or live events,
please call (800) 569-1002
or visit us on the Web at
www.jodere.com

JODERE
GROUP